Fashioning the Asian Century

FASHION, MEDIA AND CULTURE: PERSPECTIVES ON GLOBAL LIFESTYLES

Series Editors: Mariella Lorusso, Stefano Marino, Federica Muzzarelli
CFC (Culture Fashion Communication) – International Research Centre, University of Bologna, Italy

This series brings together authors from different contexts, countries and disciplinary fields to explore fashion's intersection with mass culture, media and communication.

Series titles

Amanda Sikarskie (ed.), *Fashioning the Asian Century: Sustainability, Aesthetics, and Popular Culture in the New Millennium*
Mariella Lorusso, *The Decolonization of Fashion in Native North America: Language, Appropriation and Sustainability*

Fashioning the Asian Century

Sustainability, Aesthetics, and Popular Culture in the New Millennium

Edited by
Amanda Sikarskie

BLOOMSBURY VISUAL ARTS
LONDON • NEW YORK • OXFORD • NEW DELHI • SYDNEY

BLOOMSBURY VISUAL ARTS
Bloomsbury Publishing Plc, 50 Bedford Square, London, WC1B 3DP, UK
Bloomsbury Publishing Inc, 1385 Broadway, New York, NY 10018, USA
Bloomsbury Publishing Ireland, 29 Earlsfort Terrace, Dublin 2, D02 AY28, Ireland

BLOOMSBURY, BLOOMSBURY VISUAL ARTS and the Diana logo are trademarks of Bloomsbury Publishing Plc

First published in Great Britain 2026

Cover design: Adriana Brioso
Cover image: Photo by Minh Ngoc via Pexels.com

A catalogue record for this book is available from the British Library.

A catalog record for this book is available from the Library of Congress.

ISBN: PB: 978-1-350460-84-3
HB: 978-1-350460-85-0
ePDF: 978-1-350460-86-7
ePub: 978-1-350460-87-4

Typeset by RefineCatch Limited, Bungay, Suffolk
Printed and bound in India

For product safety related questions contact productsafety@bloomsbury.com.

On October 29, 2022, when I was writing what was to become my own chapter of this book, tragedy struck South Korea, as over 150 people, mostly in their teens and twenties, were crushed to death in a crowd surge during Halloween festivities adjacent the Hamilton Hotel in Itaewon, Seoul's trendiest bar and nightlife district. This book is dedicated to the memories of those whose lives were cut short that night.

Amanda Sikarskie
October 29, 2024

Contents

Figures

Tables

Contributors

Dr. Mukulika Dattagupta An alumnus of the Department of Comparative Literature,Jadavpur University, Mukulika Dattagupta is a recipient of the Fulbright-Nehru Doctoral Research Fellowship and has done her PhD on children's literature. Her research interests are in postcolonial studies, comparative Literature, children's literature and American literature.

Nandini Gopalarathinam is a fashion historian and archivist whose research explores the historical, cultural, and political dimensions of dress. She is an Adjunct Professor at the Fashion Institute of Technology and New York University, USA, where she teaches courses on fashion history, theory, and global textile cultures. Her current work reimagines luxury by examining global fashion systems through the lens of digital storytelling and contemporary production practices.

Dr. Jingru Sun is a Postdoctoral Fellow at the School of Journalism and Communication, Tsinghua University, China. She received her Ph.D. from Peking University. Her Ph.D. thesis explores the return of Chinese mythology to the screen in the twenty-first century. Her research interests include Chinese culture studies and East Asian film studies.

Dr. Rimi Nandy is an Assistant Professor in the Department of English and Cultural Studies at Christ University, Pune Lavasa Campus, India, with over ten years' teaching experience. Her research interests span digital humanities, narratology, new media studies, posthumanism, autobiography studies, and Japanese cultural studies. She is also a HASTAC scholar, working at the intersection of humanities and computer science.

Dr. Cringuta Irina Pelea is a Lecturer in Communication Sciences at Titu Maiorescu University, Romania, specializing in Japanese culture, intercultural communication, and social justice across media. She edited *Culture-Bound Syndromes in Popular Culture* (Routledge, 2023) and served on the editorial board for the *Routledge Handbook of Language and Mind Engineering* (2024). Her work appears in *Storytelling In Luxury Fashion Brands, Visual Cultures, and Technologies* (Routledge, 2020), the *Routledge Companion to Literature and Social Justice* (2023), the *Routledge Handbook of Endangered and Minority Languages* (2025), and *Future of Media in Asia* (Springer, 2025).

Dr. Babette Radclyffe-Thomas FRAS is a fashion academic, journalist, and consultant who specializes in the Chinese fashion and beauty industries. In 2023, she obtained her Ph.D. specializing in Chinese fashion media and is the only person in the world (to date) to have a Ph.D. in *Vogue China*.

Dr. Queen Sarkar is an Assistant Professor-II (English) at KIIT School of Economics & Commerce, and holds a Ph.D. from IIT Kharagpur, India. Her research encompasses plant humanities, cross-cultural communication, and cultural studies. She has received fully funded invitations to present her work at the University of Kentucky and University of Oregon, USA. Her multilingual poetry has gained international recognition.

Dr. Wang Shuhua, Associate Professor of Art Studies, currently works at Changzhou Textile and Fashion Institute of Technology in Jiangsu Province, China. She specializes in design education and anthropological research on apparel aesthetics and design. She has published multiple core journal papers, including "Research on the 'Digitalized' Expression and Transmission Mechanism of the Cultural Gene in Octagonal Pattern Design of Southwest Ethnic Minorities" in *Art & Design Research* (China).

Dr. Amanda Sikarskie is a Lecturer in the Comprehensive Studies Program at the University of Michigan, USA. She is a fashion scholar whose work explores the intersections of dress with popular culture and the digital. She is the author of *Digital Research Methods in Fashion and Textile Studies* (Bloomsbury Visual Arts, 2020) and co-editor of *Male Idols and Branding in Chinese Luxury* (Bloomsbury Visual Arts, 2023).

Preface

In the pursuit of Asian fashion in the twenty-first century, it is perhaps best to begin with a bit of history. This volume is organized into three sections—Sustainability, Media and Aesthetics, and Cultural Heritage and Popular Culture—told here through a very abridged history of Japanese dress over the past thousand years or so.

Sustainability and the Animate World

The Buddhist-inspired sensibility or understanding of beauty, especially as it evolved in Japan, emphasizes the transience of things, essentially, change. If we take "fashion" as meaning "a regular pattern of style change," then we can say that Heian elites were truly wearing fashion, and not just dress. But this regular pattern of change did not constitute wastefulness, as does today's fast fashion. Rather, this recognition of the transience of things coexisted with a culture of mending and reuse through techniques such as *boro* (for mending clothing and textiles, the topic of Wang Shuhua's chapter in this book) and *kintsugi*, the art of mending cracked and broken ceramics with gold. The belief in *tsukumogami*, that household objects can, over a long period of time, develop a spirit, also influenced the aversion to throwaway culture in traditional Japan.

Media and Aesthetics

Neophilia, the love of the new, has a major place in Japanese dress, dating back to the Heian period one thousand years ago (794–1185), as much as today. The Heian court in Japan, which, like Tang Dynasty China (618–907), exhibited rapid, successively changing styles that we can call fashion,[1] as depicted in Murasaki Shikibu's *The Tale of Genji*, was another site of fashion in the pre-industrial, pre-modern world. *Imamikashi*, meaning "up to date," was high praise for style in Heian Japan.

Cultural Heritage and Popular Culture

In the twenty-first century, Japanese popular culture and cultural heritage manifests itself through Japan's global leadership in street style and subcultural fashion, such as gothic and lolita dress. Several designers have also incorporated traditional Japanese *yokai*, or spirits, into their collections, including global brands such as Moschino (Jeremy Scott), Louis Vuitton (Virgil Abloh), Sarah Liang, and Maison Kitsune, and Japanese brand Written Afterwards.[2]

I hope that this book provides a compelling case that the twenty-first century is indeed the Asian century, especially in terms of cultural soft power, and in particular, fashion. In the introduction that follows, the rise of the Asian economies, particularly that of China, will be chronicled in further detail.

Amanda Sikarskie

Notes

1 For a discussion of the disambiguation of the terms dress and fashion, please see: Joanne B. Eicher and Mary Roach-Higgins, "Describing Dress: A System of Classifying and Defining," in Ruth Barnes and Joanne B. Eicher (eds), *Dress and Gender: Making Meaning in Cultural Context*, Oxford and Washington, DC: Berg, 1993, 135–47.

2 Chloe Foussianes, "Liberté, Egalitié, ANIME!," *Town & Country*, October 2020, 51.

Acknowledgments

First and foremost, many thanks to Georgia Kennedy, our wonderful acquisitions editor at Bloomsbury, who was supportive of this project from the beginning. A big thank you also to Bloomsbury's Eve James, who handled the logistics and general herding of cats for us.

Thanks also to Sun Jingru, one of the authors featured in this book, for graciously offering to switch sections during the editorial process of this volume.

Thanks to my husband, Matthew Sikarskie, for the idea to add "in the New Millennium" to the subtitle of this book, helping prospective readers know that the Asian century is now.

I would also like to thank the Korea Society for putting together the series of lectures on hanbok by dress historian Dr. Minjee Kim in 2022, which was very helpful in the research process for this book. I'd also like to thank Dr. Kim for her advice in the planning stages of this book project.

Thank you to the American Quilt Study Group for granting a seminar fellowship in 2023 for presentation on *hyungbae* and *buzi*.

Finally, many thanks also to the Metropolitan Museum of Art, New York, the Philadelphia Museum of Art, and the Los Angeles County Museum of Art for donating images of works that appear in this book to the public domain. And thank you to Getty Images for facilitating the publication of images for this book.

Introduction: Fashioning the Asian Century

As a means of introducing this book, I wanted to touch upon a topic that not only incorporates the themes of media aesthetics, sustainability, and cultural heritage that unify and organize the essays contained within *Fashioning the Asian Century* (as does the story of Pengsoo in the afterword to this volume), but also to dispel some of the colonial myth-making that still informs much of the Western understanding of culture in the Asian century. After some thought, I settled upon the idea of the "invention" of the color orange.

Western history generally has it that orange was invented, or conceived of as a color, in Europe sometime during the Renaissance. Ian Lawson writes, "'Orange'" began its career as a color term around the late sixteenth century and went through a long phase as a 'transparent' term that referred to the hue by direct analogy with the object, the way we still might use 'salmon' or 'copper.'"[1] Waller, Boyle, and Hooke all wrote in this way—to them it was still more fruit than color."[2] Lawson tells this story of the invention of orange as follows:

> Most philosophers in the seventeenth century, from Savot and de Boodt to Waller and Hooke, retained the painterly idea that yellow and red needn't be mixed together. Materially, this color space was filled by any number of orpiments, ochres and lakes. These belonged to one or the other group but the boundary between red and yellow was so fluid that they themselves were not uncommonly merged into two varieties of the same color. Certainly

> no separate hue lay between them. The elevation of orange to a broad color group covering a range of specific shades seems to have been due initially to philosophers abstracting away from painterly practice and requiring a new color term to describe the mixture of red and yellow their schemes included. Also, as early as the 1670s, Newton had also identified orange as an "original or simple" color lying between red and yellow in the prismatic spectrum.[3] His ideas were notoriously unpopular in the seventeenth century but later, in the eighteenth, he succeeded in focusing attention on color mixing ideas that had their basis in his observations of light, not pigment, and this also very likely played a significant role in stabilizing this shift.[4]

The following passage details a seventeenth-century experiment using saffron. Hooke, like his contemporaries, believed that blue and red were the only primary colors. Yellow was thought to be a derivative of red. The secondary color orange had not yet truly been "invented" in the European imagination:

> Robert Hooke (1635–1703) took this approach one year later in his Micrographia. Hooke explained the way in which pulses of light from the sun were disturbed by reflection or refraction, causing changes that resulted in them being perceived as either red or blue.[5] His theory allowed for only these two possible modifications to white light, and all other colors he explained as mixtures of these as they struck the retina. Both primaries could be either dark or pale depending on the strength of the light, and he described yellow as a pale red. The dark primaries mixed to make purple, the paler ones to make green. Orange was nowhere to be found. Hooke found evidence for his theory in his experiences with certain substances. Saffron, for example, would produce a deep red when applied thickly and a yellow when applied more thinly. Hooke assumed this to be the rule not the exception and sought an explanation of why it was not the case for all red pigments.[6]

So, historians of science and technology can, and do, differ on whether orange was invented in the European imaginary in the 1500s or the 1600s, or even as late as the early 1700s. But much like the Western notion that Johannes

Gutenberg invented the printing press in 1440 (it was actually invented nearly simultaneously in Song Dynasty China and Goryeo Dynasty Korea around the early 1200s), this belies the story that orange had been an extant—and, more importantly, recognized—color in South and East Asia for centuries. This is in part because Buddhist monks wear orange dress and have traditionally produced orange dye.

And this tradition of orange as a color in Asian dress continues today. For the September 2015 New York Fashion Week, Nepalese-born designer Prabal Gurung invited thirty Nepalese Buddhist monks to attend his runway show and offer prayers in the wake of an earthquake which had just devastated a portion of the country in April of that year. Gurung's collection featured looks informed by Buddhism, such as a light, flowing, sleeveless chiffon dress in a color that may be described as Buddhist orange, high-fashion fabrics dyed in imitation of the jackfruit-, saffron-, and spice-based dyes traditionally used to dye Buddhist monastic robes in parts of South and Southeast Asia.[7]

The increasingly global, and in particular increasingly Asia-focused, nature of the Fashion Week movement is a theme to which we will return in this book, in the "Global Fashion Capitals" interstitial and in Aishwarya Pureti's chapter on Lakme Fashion Week.

If some historians categorize the nineteenth century as Britain's imperial century, and the twentieth century as the American century, then the twenty-first century may well be understood as the Asian century. In terms of not only economic and demographic growth, but also cultural dissemination of genres like manga and anime, *Hallyu* or the Korean wave, and Bollywood, the global reach and soft power of Asia is undeniably accelerating. Asia is now home to the tallest buildings in the world and more than half of European luxury goods are destined for consumption in China. What does Asian ascendency mean for fashion? This volume seeks essays that address one or more aspects of this question, such as: Asian fashion designers, Asian fashion consumer behavior, fashion shows and fashion weeks in Asia, fashion trends disseminated through Asian popular culture, Asian garment workers' rights, and sustainability and greenwashing in Asian fashion.

"Three tigers, one mountain" is a Chinese idiom that represents the idea that three major powers—China, Japan, and Korea—coexist within the same

Figure 0.1 *A model walks the runway at the Prabal Gurung Autumn/Winter 2014 fashion show during New York Fashion Week, New York, USA, February 8, 2014.*
Photo: Catwalking/Getty Images

general area of the world. Each of these "tigers" necessarily influences the others, and this is true in both economics and fashion, as we will see in this book. This idiom dates back centuries, however, and in the last few decades, a few other "tigers" have ascended the proverbial mountain. Alternately, Hong Kong, Singapore, South Korea, and Taiwan are still sometimes collectively dubbed the "Four Asian Tigers,"[8] all having experienced rapid industrialization and economic growth from the 1950s to the 1990s. And India, too, with its growing economy, population, soft power, and role in Brics+ deserves to be recognized as a "tiger" in the Asian century. Economies in Southeast Asia are also growing, and poised for further growth, perhaps most notably in Vietnam.

Although some have observed that the [long] Asian century began as early as the 1980s,[9] it may be safer to argue that it truly began in 2009, when Western economies were rocked by the global recession. Liam Byrne succinctly described the effects of the global recession in the United Kingdom as follows:

> The great global crash of 2009 did not do as much damage as the second world war. But here in Britain, it destroyed one million jobs and £400 billion of wealth. Now, just as in 1945, we have to rebuild by trading our way back to prosperity. The problem is this: the friends who helped us in 1945 are in as much trouble as we are. America is mired in slow growth and fierce arguments about how to pay its debts; Europe is trapped in disagreements about how to save its currency.[10]

And then after the global financial crisis came the European Union (Withdrawal) Act of 2018, with the United Kingdom finally "Brexiting," or leaving the European Union, on January 31, 2020. Laws that operate within the European Union directly affect fashion, such as regulations concerning trade and freedom of movement, so the effects that Brexit is already having upon the fashion industry are great. Besides legal uncertainties, Brexit also creates logistical challenges in terms of design, production, supply chain, and marketing.

China, in particular, has benefited from the West's misfortunes in the first two decades of the twenty-first century. And China's ascent was indeed meteoric. The rise of China as a soft power can be traced largely to the father of socialism with Chinese characteristics, Deng Xiaoping. Writing in 1977,

Deng observed that "We are so poor and backward, that, to be frank, we fail to live up to the expectations of our people. Foreigners are questioning how long the Chinese people can endure. We should pay attention to such remarks." Deng was not wrong. In 1978, China accounted for 1 percent of the world's output. Its wealth per head ranked 190th in the world and was on par with Zaire.[11] By 2009, a mere thirty-two years later, China was poised to become the world's second-largest economy. Both Winston Churchill and Richard Nixon anticipated this global shift.

> It was long predicted that China would be the giant of the 21st century, and the crash has not dimmed its rise. Far from it. "Beware the sleeping dragon," said Winston Churchill, "for when she wakes the Earth will shake." In 1967, searching for a way out of Vietnam, Richard Nixon wrote, "We simply cannot afford to leave China outside the family of nations, there to nurture its fantasies, cherish its hates and threaten its neighbours. There is no place on this small planet for a billion of its potentially most able people to live in angry isolation." It was nine years ago [in 2004] that economists at Goldman Sachs forecast that China could become the world's richest nation by 2041. Last year [2012], China became the world's number two economy. It will be number one within a decade.[12]

Had the extended lockdown caused by the COVID-19 pandemic of 2020 not occurred in China, this likely would have come to pass. "It is a decisive shift in the globe's balance of power which could mean by 2050 China, together with India, Brazil, Egypt, the Philippines, Indonesia, Iran, Mexico, and a few others will control 60 percent of the world's wealth in a revolutionary shift that could push 2 billion people into the global middle class."[13] China, India, Brazil, and Russia founded the "Bric" group in 2006. South Africa joined the four founding countries in 2010, making it "Brics," with Egypt, Ethiopia, Iran, Saudi Arabia, and the United Arab Emirates entering the group on January 1, 2024, to create "Brics+." As Julian Weiss noted in his introduction to *The Asian Century*, it is this global realignment, rather than simply trade or GDP, that makes the rise of Asia so significant. "The Asian Century *has* arrived. It is an unexpected shooting star in the night sky of world events from which great possibilities emerge. The 'Asian Century' concept embodies far more than economics. It is the kernel of a new geopolitics, a basic realignment in an information age and postindustrial era."[14] In short, Asia has changed, economically, politically, and socioculturally. As an example, in *Fashion in Altermodern China*, Feng Jie noted that the #flauntyourwealth challenge was quite popular among Chinese social media users in 2018. This would have been unthinkable even thirty years ago.[15]

Of the new Asian century, Liam Byrne, author of *Turning to Face the East*, writes:

> The well-spring of worry for the "China bears" is a political system that is very different to ours, without democracy, strong human rights, free speech or consistent rule of law. Confucius plus communism gives you a very different politics to Christ and Kant. The "China bears" worry that this has fostered a political class that is incapable of leading change.[16]

As of the writing of this introduction, China's economy is slowing down, to be sure, especially its real estate market, and China is increasingly confronted with a declining birthrate. The gloominess on China's economy[17] that has dominated 2022 and 2023 in the West, however, does not take into account future enterprises in which China currently excels and will continue to excel, such as rare earth excavation (which is needed for the production of microchips) and government investment in AI (the country currently leads the world). Simply put, in the short term, yes, China's economy is contracting, but in the long term, I will believe it when I see it. If I were the CFO of a luxury brand, I would not be looking to move my global marketing strategy away from China anytime soon. Rather, global luxury houses might well take advantage of a growing appetite in Asia for homegrown fashion talent and look to the Asian tigers to fill the positions of future creative directors.

About This Book

The intention of this volume is to show how Asia will impact and innovate in the fashion industry in the twenty-first century, featuring topics such as Asian designers of global significance, the increasing importance of Asian cities as sites for fashion weeks and couture runway shows, and innovations in sustainability taking place in Asia. This book began with a preface encapsulating 1) sustainability, 2) media and aesthetics, and 3) cultural heritage and popular culture in the history of Japanese dress, and ends with the same themes all embedded within the story of a Korean celebrity penguin. The chapters are also arranged thematically within these three divisions. Within these themes, the essays feature a range of subject countries: China, India, Japan, South Korea, and Thailand.

We hope that this book will be novel and useful in its exploration of fashion from a Pan-Asian context, especially a context that emphasizes political, economic, demographic, and cultural soft power changes. There are books that do this for a single country, like Sara Liao's *Fashioning China* or our (with Peng Liu and Lan Lan) own Bloomsbury book *Male Idols and Branding in Chinese Luxury*. Authors for the present volume hail from China, England, India, Japan, Romania, and the United States, and represent a multidisciplinary approach, covering topics in Chinese, Indian, Japanese, Korean, and Thai fashion, making this a truly international collection of essays.

One final thread running throughout this book is Asia's preference for the preservation of tradition in the face of globalization and late modernity. We see this in various chapters on *boro* and the turn back towards heritage mending techniques, and through the connection of *hanfu*, *kimono*, and K-drama and K-pop with traditional spirits across three of the essays in this volume. That is, Asian ascendancy does not mean a loss of Asian-ness to Westernization, but rather the opposite: a reaffirmation of what makes Asian dress and textiles Asian.

Notes

1 Robert Hooke, *Micrographia, or Some Physiological Descriptions of Minute Bodies Made by Magnifying Glasses, with Observations and Inquiries Thereupon,* London: J. Martyn and J. Allestry, 1665, observation 9, 39.

2 Ian Lawson, "Pigments, Natural History and Primary Qualities: How Orange Became a Color," in Bettina Bock von Wulfingen, *Science in Color: Visualizing Achromatic Knowledge*, 2019, 146.

3 Hooke, 35.

4 Lawson, 145.

5 Hooke, 23.

6 Lawson, 141–2.

7 Just what exact color constitutes Buddhist orange today? For reference, Prabal Gurung's dress is: HEX #f5901c; RGB rgba (245,144,28,255) and the orange in the Buddhist flag is: HEX #fc9c04; RGB rgb(252,156,4). The hex code for marigold is #EAA221 (richer hue), or #FCC006 (lighter hue). Jackfruit is hex code #F7C680. Saffron is given variously as #F4C430, #FF7722, and #FF9933 (for deep saffron).

8 Julian Weiss, *The Asian Century*, New York: Facts on File, 1989, vii.

9 Ibid.

10 Ibid.

11 Liam Byrne, *Turning to Face the East*, London: Guardian Books, 2013, 23.

12 Byrne, 21.

13 Ibid., 231.

14 Weiss, vi.

15 Feng Jie, *Fashion in Altermodern China*, London: Bloomsbury, 2023, 96.

16 Byrne, 242.

17 As an example, see: Yuen Yuen Ang, "The Moral of the China Story," *The Japan Times*, December 29, 2023, https://www.japantimes.co.jp/commentary/2023/12/29/china-story-gilded-age/

Part One

Fashioning Sustainability: The Animate World of the Hani-Akha

For the Hani-Akha people of Xishuangbanna, Yunnan Province (an area of southern China that borders Myanmar and Laos in the Mekong River region), the natural world is animate, with spirits residing in forests and mountain, lakes and rivers, and animals from elephants and tigers to lorises and pangolins.[1] China has a complicated history in its relationship with animals. According to the *Book of Songs* (also known as *The Classic of Poetry*, circa eleventh–seventh century BCE), the country boasted one of the first zoos in the world, the Park of Intelligence, founded under the auspices of Wu Wang circa 1050 BCE.[2] Nicholas J. Saunders, in his book *Animal Spirits*, notes that several Chinese animals once thought to be legendary or mythical have turned out to be real. Saunders wrote:

> In 685 AD the imperial Japanese accounts describe a gift of two white bears and 70 white bear skins sent to the *tenno* (emperor) of Japan by the Chinese emperor. It was assumed by naturalists that these were polar bears, although

> a Chinese chronicle from 621 BC mentions the white bears as coming from the bamboo forests of Yunnan province, and describes them as having black markings. It was not until 1869 that Pere Armand David rediscovered the giant pandas in the hills of Szechuan.[3]

The Classic of Mountains and Seas, a Han-Dynasty era travelogue, mixes actual and legendary animals, generally making no distinction between them. It serves as a guided tour of China and its neighbors by an anonymous narrator, the core of which dates to at least 50 BCE,[4] if not a century or two earlier.[5] Book XV of *The Classic of Mountains and Seas*, "The Classic of the Great Wilderness: The South," describes land likely to the south of modern-day China, such as Laos, Myanmar, and Vietnam, as well as southern territories of the PRC, such as Xishuangbanna. Book XV includes descriptions of such civilizations as the Mushroom People near Mount Southtype: "There are small people here. Their name is the Mushroom People. There is Mount Southtype. This is the place where the legacy jade, the green horses, the triple-grey horse, the look-flesh creature, the sweet-bloom tree, and the hundred grains are all to be found."[6] These descriptions of the lands to the south of classical China are largely favorable, describing the local inhabitants without fear, though noticeably still "other," and the region's flora and fauna as colorful and pharmacologically valuable.

Book XV closes with the mention of the sweet-bloom tree and the legacy jade. Of these, Birrell notes that the sweet-bloom, or *kanhua*, is a "fabled tree. Kuo describes it as having scarlet branches and trunk, with yellow blossom."[7] And she notes that regarding the legacy jade, or *yi yü*, "Some translators see this as a presentation jade, from the meaning of *yi*, 'to give as a gift.' Since it also means 'to leave behind,' the translation here reflects that sense."[8] Thus, the reader's final impression of the southernmost lands visited in the text is of a utopia that the narrator was loath to leave. The culture of Tai-speaking peoples (to which the modern Thai belong) during the Han Dynasty, the period in which *The Classic of Mountains and Seas* was first written, was likely similar to that of present-day Xishuangbanna in that life revolved around both hunting and gathering and agriculture and making offerings to an animate world filled with both benevolent and malevolent spirits.

The essays in this section of the book explore traditional, natural, sustainable, and authentic practices in Asian fashion design. Nandini Gopalarathinam's

Chapter 1 is a study in contrasts, beginning with the Ambani wedding, one of the biggest global social events of 2024 and one of the most lavish and decadent weddings staged in recent memory. This Indian mega-wedding, which drew A-list celebrity guests such as Kim Kardashian and former British Prime Minister Tony Blair, represents conspicuous consumption in contemporary fashion culture in Asia, and in Gopalarathinam's essay serves as a foil for traditional, artisanal, and sustainable dress and textile craft still very much practiced in India, such as *kantha*.

Mori kei, or forest style, represents a tendency in contemporary Japanese dress towards earthy simplicity in fashion, embracing nature in an often whimsical manner. *Boro*, and mending generally, serves as an emblem of the sustainable "make do and mend" nature of Japanese material culture going back for centuries. In Wang Shuhua's Chapter 2, readers are introduced to both *boro*, the forest style, and traditional *baina* and *nianbei* clothes in China, and how Chinese young people are embracing these sustainable practices from Japan.

Queen Sarkar's Chapter 3, on greenwashing in the fashion industry in Thailand, uses textual analysis to examine the extent to which the portfolios of various Thai designers are guilty of greenwashing and introduces the reader to concepts such as green skepticism and negative green word of mouth.

Notes

1 Jianhua "Ayoe" Wang, Assistant Professor & Chair, Department of Anthropology, Yunnan Minzu University, "Ecology of Sacred Landscapes: Akha Traditional Management System of Natural Resources," talk given via Zoom, Asian Studies Center, Michigan State University, March 24, 2021.

2 Nicholas J. Saunders, *Animal Spirits*, Boston: Little, Brown, and Company, 1995, 164.

3 Ibid.

4 Anne Birrell, "Introduction," *The Classic of Mountains and Seas*, trans. Anne Birrell, London: Penguin Classics, 1999, xiii.

5 Author's note: This dates the core of the text to the Han Dynasty, 202 BC–220 CE.

6 *The Classic of Mountains and Seas*, 170.

7 Birrell, "Notes," 262.

8 Ibid., 235.

1

Crafting Authenticity: The Evolution of Indian Slow Fashion in Digital Transnational Space

NANDINI GOPALARATHINAM

Introduction

The wedding of Anant Ambani, the son of Mukesh Ambani, one of India's richest men, prompted a frenzy of press coverage in 2024. On July 12, 2024, the *New York Times* ran an article with the headline "A Wedding Puts India's Gilded Age on Lavish Display" and went on to say that the wedding "signaled the arrival of the unapologetic billionaire on the global stage and introduced the world to the country's Gilded Age." The article noted that India now has 200 billionaires who "collectively hold about one trillion dollars in wealth . . . nearly a quarter of the country's 2023 gross domestic product."[1] *Vogue* magazine secured the exclusive rights to the wedding festivities, the culmination of a month-long series of events that boggled the mind and, in the age of social media, became an international spectacle.[2]

The Ambani wedding may have put India's "Gilded Age" on display but that is not the whole story. India's population surpassed that of China's at the end of

2023, though the exact figure remains unknown as there has not been a census there since 2011. However, according to the Pew Research Center, India's population has grown by more than one billion people since 1950, and the growing middle class is expected to reach 580 million people by 2025. A significant fact for consumer markets is that more than 40 percent of the population is under the age of 25. One in five people globally under the age of 25 live in India, and it is expected that people in this age group will outnumber people aged 65 and older until at least 2078. In comparison, the two other most populous countries, China and the United States, have aging populations—the median age is 39 and 38 respectively.[3] This young segment of the Indian population has grown up in the post economic-liberalization era and has more disposable income than their parents, courtesy of jobs in new sectors like media, consulting, IT, and finance. While the billionaire class is important to the luxury market, it is these young digital natives that are expected to be the primary drivers of luxury consumption in the coming decades.

In thinking about Indian luxury fashion and how it is influencing both domestic and global markets for this chapter, I observed that my initial encounters with Indian brands of all kinds was happening on social media and primarily on Instagram (IG). Many of these brands, luxury or otherwise, are not readily available in brick-and-mortar spaces outside of India but it was simple to scroll, click, and purchase, link to brand websites or send direct messages (DM) through IG and chat with the brand directly. Often, after encountering these brands on IG, I would make it a point to search for them on trips to India. In this way, digital transnational spaces like IG have opened up worlds of possibilities for how we connect to fashion, in both digital and physical spaces. IG has developed functionalities since its inception in 2010 that allow brands of all sizes to link their product to posts on their IG accounts, create video, and have direct relationships with consumers. IG has created a seamless shopping experience for consumers globally, what Rocomora defines as "the mediatization of retail, that is, of the transformation of retail from an activity located in three-dimensional spaces—physical shops—to one tailored to, enacted through, and indeed turned into, a media interface."[4] This has completely disrupted established retail models and created new digital transnational circulations.

Anthropologist Arjun Appadurai locates the transnational in public culture, and specifically its confluences of economy and culture. Significantly, his idea of transnational spaces emphasizes the idea that objects themselves hold a central place in shaping human worlds, through movement across traditional borders. In his view, material objects are inscribed with meaning; movement and change shape how material objects function and what they mean.[5] If we think of this digital world as a new kind of transnational space and material objects are inscribed with meaning, as Appadurai says, how does circulation within this new digital transnational space affect the function and meaning of these objects? What kinds of circulations and exchanges are created?

IG has changed our visual culture with its tools and format and that in turn is disrupting both consumption and production within the fashion system. These new digital transnational spaces, such as IG, have created accelerated, and irreversible forms of global interconnectedness, the effects of which are just beginning to be studied. In terms of fashion, there is an ever increasing importance placed on the ideas, values, ethical concepts, creativity, and human dialogue behind products and brands. Consumers, especially digitally savvy millennial and Gen Z consumers, want products that have a sense of purpose, are aesthetically pleasing, and have a story to tell about how and why they were made, what could be called a new kind of "authenticity." They are seeking a connection to the material, the tactile, and the tangible, even in digitally mediated space.

This chapter presents a case study of how Indian luxury brand 11.11/eleven eleven is creating new digital transnational circulations of "radically quiet" luxury through the dissemination of their brand philosophies and production methods on social media platforms such as IG. These new circulations recontextualize many of the hallmarks associated with traditional Western luxury brands such as heritage, provenance, and craftsmanship and demonstrate how 11.11/eleven eleven represents the natural evolution of luxury fashion. Their "radically quiet" luxury is one that is particularly suited to the unique terroir offered by Indian craft, design education, and the vast resources provided by India's living cultural heritage, contained within the physical bodies of its craftspeople. In the offering of maximal craft and a sustainable "seed-to-stitch" philosophy, 11.11/eleven eleven clothing is an example of how Indian designers are attempting to resolve many of the inherent conflicts that exist in the designer/craftsperson relationship and create a sustainable luxury lifestyle brand that taps into the kind of "authenticity" the global consumer is looking for.

An exploration of how luxury consumption habits have changed in the twenty-first century, the development of the "aspiration economy," and a brief history of the Indian fashion industry offers a framework to discuss how 11.11/eleven eleven is creating new digital transnational circulations of "radically quiet" luxury in the digital age for those in search of the "authentic." Studying selected posts from their IG account allows for a discussion of how these new ways of producing, marketing, and consuming allow brands like 11.11/eleven eleven to fashion a radical new era in luxury, and fashion the Asian century.

It is important to note that I am taking a qualitative approach to studying IG. In January of 2024, India had the largest IG audience in the world with 362 million users, versus 169 million in the United States. This level of audience engagement in India makes IG an important site of study, especially for consumption purposes. The goal in this chapter is to apply a historical perspective to the work being crafted in this digital transnational space by brands like 11.11/eleven eleven.

From Transnational to Digital Transnational Space

Expanding the definition of transnational networks has been explored extensively by Crang et al. in their work.[6] Based on Appadurai's idea to "follow things themselves," they "adopted a more expansive conception of transnational space that understood social spaces themselves as constitutive of transnationality . . . our focus upon the transnational spaces of commodity culture [is] a topography produced through the notion of *emporium*—or commerce—which creates 'not a world of boundaries that separate but of routes that connect.'"[7]

They posit "that transnational fashion cultures must be understood not only through the material geographies of transnational flows of labour or goods but also through the symbolic and imaginative geographies that accompany these circuits of production."[8] Claire Dwyer positions these "symbolic and imaginative geographies" within a British-South Asian transnational space that has looked to the "East" for inspiration since the Industrial Revolution as well as Asian fashion in Britain, created by different kinds of transnational circulations, defined by Parminder Bhachu as "diaspora economies." Bhachu contends that the economies of the Asian diaspora give rise to unique hybrid fashion cultures, shaped by both transnational and local influences.[9]

As a way to think about how these transnational circulations have influenced fashion within India itself, Dwyer discusses Delhi-based Indian designer Ritu Kumar, one of India's first luxury designers. Kumar is a key figure in the development of ethnic revivalist fashion, incorporating elaborate beading and surface embellishments in ethnic chic designs that look back to the glory of India's royal past for inspiration. Kumar has also written books on craft and has played a significant role in the dissemination of textile and design education through her connections to the Delhi Crafts Council and the National Institute of Fashion Technology (NIFT) in Delhi.

Kumar has visited the Victoria and Albert Museum in London many times in order to look at designs and textiles that are no longer produced in India in order to research and revive lost techniques and traditions. She adopts designs that may have been influenced by "symbolic and imaginative geographies" of the "East" within the British-Asian transnational space and creates a new transnational circulation, one that Arti Sandhu characterizes as self-Orientalizing. In this kind of exchange, the reclamation of Indian heritage and looking to one's own past can be seen as positive "when the knowledge and background the wearers and designers bring to them is taken into consideration."[10] In this way, transnational fashion in postcolonial cultures that "retain the resonances of histories of empire within which cultural and economic imperatives and imaginaries were entwined" can be recontextualized.[11] Indian designers like Kumar can be seen as offering a new "perspective around the inception and reception of re- or self-Orientalizing design methods [that] hinges on collective historic, vernacular and ongoing social and cultural contexts within which they are practiced."[12] Though Kumar's work looks to a royal past and craft that would have been influenced by movements such as the nineteenth-century British Arts and Crafts movement, her revival and adoption of colonial era craft techniques creates a new transnational circulation that challenges the "imaginative geographies of 'East' and 'West,' 'India' and 'Britain'" that Dwyer argues "are mobilized and deployed in ways that evoke a fixing in place."[13]

Dwyer's work highlights how these transnational fashion circulations are a way "to illustrate how transnational fashion cultures might be understood as the complex geographies within which clothes are designed, manufactured, retailed and consumed."[14] While she is rooting these geographies in transitional circuits of production connected to urban centers such as London, Delhi, and Mumbai, this chapter positions the digital transnational spaces of the present, such as IG, as the space within which these "symbolic and imaginative geographies" are being recontextualized. 11.11/eleven eleven are utilizing these new digital transnational spaces to challenge the "imaginative geographies of 'East' and 'West,' 'India' and 'Britain'" and beyond to create new digital transnational circulations of what Made in India represents in the twenty-first century.

The Rise of Quiet Luxury and the Aspiration Economy

Since the early 2000s, there has been a noticeable shift in consumer behavior from conspicuous to inconspicuous consumption, reflecting deeper societal changes and evolving values. Conspicuous consumption, which Veblen described as the display of wealth through overtly branded goods, was dominant in the early part of the century.[15] However, following the 2008 financial crisis, a growing preference for inconspicuous consumption emerged, characterized by the acquisition of high-quality, subtly branded products that emphasized craftsmanship and sustainability over blatant displays of wealth.[16]

This trend towards inconspicuous consumption is also reinforced by a cultural movement toward the new kinds of "authenticity" discussed above. The rise of the "quiet luxury" movement exemplifies this shift. Studies indicate that this preference for subtle signals of status is particularly prevalent among affluent consumers who do not feel the need to flaunt their wealth.[17]

Further, the democratization of the luxury market has led to the diminishment of the perceived value of luxury brands. As luxury goods become more accessible to a broader audience, the exclusivity and status associated with these brands are diluted. This phenomenon is driven by the proliferation of entry-level luxury products, widespread distribution channels, and aggressive marketing strategies aimed at expanding the consumer base. Scandals surrounding Armani clothing and Dior handbags that retail for $2,600 being produced for $58 in Italian sweatshops has "threaten[ed] the luxury sector's most precious asset—brand image—calling into question the veracity of the craftsmanship-soaked marketing narrative luxury players routinely use to bolster the perceived quality of their products, while painting labor exploitation as a mass market problem."[18]

Sociologist and branding expert Ana Andjelic divides this dilution of luxury into two categories. The first she calls "Big Luxury," which is "commercial, and its goal is to push consumers to buy more. Big Luxury is the domain . . . which emphasize[s] merch[andise] and logos that turn everyone willing to spend $600 on a t-shirt, a branded hat, or a belt into a luxury consumer." The second category is epitomized by brands like Hermès and Loro Piana who within "this domain of aspiration, champions displays of human creativity; algorithm-free, analog taste; and admiration for well-made things." This is the kind of luxury favored by the "quiet luxury" consumer, one who values knowing who the makers are behind the products. As Andjelic says, "Both Big Luxury and its retro-new counterpart revolve around collecting. In the first scenario, we are prompted to collect and resell commodities; in the second, to accumulate cultural, social, environmental, and spiritual information and knowledge . . . In the new economy, the more connected we and our possessions can afford to be with nature and culture, the more valuable they are."[19]

It's worth thinking about a new definition of what a brand is and how it is related to the new trends discussed by Andjelic. As Sarah Banet-Weiser defines it, "the term 'brand' refers to the intersecting relationship between marketing, a product, and consumers. 'Brand cultures' refers to the way in which these types of brand relationships have increasingly become cultural contexts for everyday living, individual identity, and affective relationships."[20] Increasingly, consumers are involved in a brand's success by voluntarily choosing to share information on social media about a brand they feel personally involved with or that they think speaks to their values and choices. What is considered authentic in this sense may no longer be the product itself but the making and selling of immaterial things—feelings and affects, personalities and values—rather than actual goods.

The intersection of "brand cultures" and this aspirational space has led to the creation of what Andjelic calls the "aspiration economy." What a consumer in the "aspiration economy" is interested in is not how much something costs but what it says about their own taste and what it is signaling to others, primarily on social media sites like Tik Tok and IG. The creation of "taste communities" within the "aspiration economy" allows consumers to seek out and engage with a far more diverse array of subcultures in digital transnational spaces like IG, creating niche "taste verticals." The key to the "aspiration economy" is tapping into these "taste communities." In Andjelic's view, smaller lifestyle brands with a highly curated point of view, strong storytelling, and an engaged micro audience will lead the way forward in the twenty-first century.[21] This challenges traditional notions of what makes a brand successful, especially within the fashion industry, where "Big Luxury" is involved in mass democratization. The cycle of seasonal trends, multiple runway shows, and the churn of goods that count as success for many luxury brands feels increasingly irrelevant as more and more brands, especially those that are outside of the Western fashion system, have access to the "aspiration economy" through digital transnational spaces like IG.

This also demonstrates how in the age of "brand cultures" and the "aspiration economy," a brand like 11.11/eleven eleven is uniquely positioned to tap into increasingly niche global taste verticals and engage the aspirational consumer—one searching for a brand that allows them to signal their own social, cultural, and environmental priorities and values.

The Evolution of the Indian Fashion Industry

In her discussion of the development of the Indian fashion industry from the 1980-2005, Mukti Khaire offers one of the only comprehensive histories of the early years of the industry. The establishment of training institutes, the creation of domestic fashion magazines, and the development of multi-designer stores are the key factors in how the Indian fashion industry gained legitimacy in that time period.

The development of training institutes, such as the National Institute of Design (NID) in 1968 followed by the National Institute of Fashion Technology (NIFT) in 1986, under the aegis of the Ministry of Textiles and aided by the Fashion Institute of Technology, were some of the first educational institutions for those interested in textile and fashion design. Educational initiatives there made the integration and promotion of indigenous textile weaving and craft industries a key part of the program.[22]

As fashion programs developed, magazines like *Femina,* established in 1959 as a women's lifestyle magazine, transitioned into fashion. *Verve,* India's first true fashion magazine, was modeled on *Vogue.* US and European titles like *Elle* were circulating by the late 1990s and Fashion TV was available by 2001. Stores like Ensemble, opened by designer Tarun Tahiliani in 1987, carried the work of a new class of merging designers and paved the way for other stores. By the 1990s, the emergence of more organized retail within India offered designers access to new markets.[23]

The establishment of the Fashion Design Council of India (FDCI) in 1999 was the final step in creating the system within which Indian luxury designers are operating today. Based on existing models like the Council of Fashion Designers of America (CFDA) and the Chambre Syndicale de la haute couture, over 400 designers are currently members. The FDCI is responsible for seasonal Lakmé fashion weeks in New Delhi and Mumbai. Initially, this adherence to established Western models was helpful in forging boundaries between those who were operating as designers and the parallel and equally thriving tailoring industry that existed in India. In their effort to distinguish themselves from tailors, this first generation of Indian fashion designers, like the aforementioned Ritu Kumar, focused on creating value through the use of ornate embroideries and embellishment.[24] Inspired by Mughal and Rajput royal history, their designs appealed to a new generation of elite Indians and the country's increasing economic power and visibility on the global stage.

However, the transnational circulations created by this first generation of fashion designers of what Indian fashion looks like, characterized by heavy embellishments, craftsmanship, hand-woven textiles, and more traditional silhouettes, has evolved. A new generation of fashion designers who started their careers in the late 2010s have embraced a more minimal aesthetic. These designers were educated at Indian designs schools like NIFT or NID and in European and US design schools and bring the melding of these influences to an aesthetic Arti Sandhu terms "new-Swadeshi," defined as an approach to design that is "subversive and empowering," as they not only reconfigure Western fashion for Indian tastes (and vice versa) and suit the nature of indigenous resources, but also act as powerful mediums for the maintenance of difference and the assertion of distinction—in some cases through the production of intentional "anti-Western fashion."[25]

Rahul Mishra, one of these designers, won the International Woolmark Prize in 2014. Educated at NID, he was one of the first non-European designers to be awarded a scholarship to pursue an MA in fashion at Milan's Instituto Marangoni.[26] His early collections reinterpret handloom through minimal embellishment and innovative draping. He won the International Woolmark Prize in 2014 and he is currently one of the few Indian designers who has a regular slot on the Paris haute couture calendar.

While Mishra's win was important, Ruchika Sachdeva, who won the International Woolmark Prize in 2018, truly epitomizes this shift to a minimal aesthetic in Indian fashion. She started at the Pearl Academy in Delhi but moved to London in 2007 and studied womenswear at the London College of Fashion. Her label, Bodice Studio, established in 2011, offers premium everyday clothing versus Mishra's more expensive occasion wear. Sachdeva utilizes elements of men's tailoring, androgyny and a signature hand-bound pleating technique in her designs. Her work "shatters many stereotypes of Indian design as shaped by its Bollywood-influenced bridal market."[27] While handcraft and handloom textiles are utilized, the execution is radically different. Other than the hand bound pleating, there are no embroideries or prints, and the color palette is muted neutral tones with the occasional bold blue or orange.

Even though Bodice Studio does not show in Paris like Mishra, many of its designs have quietly made their way into the diaspora, raising visibility for the brand outside of India. Actress Poorna Jagannathan has mentioned the brand as a favorite and has worn several of the brand's dresses on season 3 of the Netflix show *Never Have I Ever*.[28] This is a new kind of global visibility, offered by the endless churn of content flowing through the digital transnational spaces of the twenty-first century. While previous generations of designers relied on Bollywood and traditional runway shows as a vehicle for exposure and influence, this new generation of designers is able to look beyond that, given the development of these digital transnational platforms. This generation of designers has had access to social media platforms like IG that offer a steady stream of images, information, and inspiration that flows from East to West, North to South, and everywhere in between.

Taking these developments into account offers a glimpse into the very complex nature of luxury Indian fashion and how it has evolved over time. The evolution of the Indian fashion industry and the shift to a more minimal aesthetic is key to understanding 11.11/eleven eleven's "radically quiet luxury."

11.11/eleven eleven: From Jugaad to Jugalbandi: Bringing New Value to Made in India

> "My question has always been, 'Why is 'Made In Italy' such a big deal while 'Made in India' isn't? I have since realized that it's the passion of the maker which gives soul to the product. Industrially produced fashion lacks soul in India: there has never been a dialogue between the consumer and maker. The consumer needs to respect how things are made and craftsmen need to understand what they're doing and for whom it's being done. That exposure and link is critical."[29]

At a time when the value of traditional Western luxury brands has been diluted through democratization and the "aspiration economy" is increasingly important, the above quote from Shani Himanshu, one of the founders of 11.11/eleven eleven clothing, seems particularly relevant.

Educated at NIFT Gandhinagar, Himanshu won competitions that allowed him to travel to Japan and Korea and eventually to the Domus Academy in Milan for a MA in fashion design. His 2003 thesis with Nokia revolved around how to connect lifestyle and fashion with the mobile phone—work that was well ahead of its time, as mobile phones were not ubiquitous at that time. He formed his first company CellDSGN in Milan and consulted for Renato Montagner, an architect, as well as other brands, eventually working on a project for 55DSL and meeting Renzo Rosso. He moved back to Delhi and continued to consult with Diesel, starting 11.11/eleven eleven, the prêt arm of CellDSGN, in 2009. Co-founder Mia Morikawa, a graphic design graduate from Central Saint Martins University of the Arts London, joined the brand in 2010.[30]

At the heart of the brand is a purist's approach to all aspects of production that highlights their "seed-to-stitch" "new-Swadeshi" approach. Their philosophy is summed up by the Hindi word *jugaad*—"using whatever is to hand to fashion solutions to everyday problems."[31] *Jugaad* can be difficult to translate, but another way to define it could be thinking outside the box to create innovative solutions with limited resources. Himanshu has also referred to the approach as "*jugalbandis* of techniques that come together with the handspun-handwoven narrative."[32] The word *jugalbandi* means "entwined twins" in a number of Indian languages, and was originally used to describe an Indian classical music performance that features the duet of two solo artists. In his analysis of innovation in Indian businesses, Sanjay Jain uses the term "*jugalbandi* to denote ways in which Indian organizations combine practices and mindsets that are reflective of a local approach to innovation, as exemplified by *jugaad*, with more systematic modes … it involves synthesizing what appear to be two different genres of organizational practice."[33] He "view[s] the term *jugalbandi* as generative in that it will . . . inspire innovation initiatives by organizations that are creative combinations of local and global practices focused on addressing the . . . societal challenges prevalent across the planet."[34]

The concept of *jugalbandi,* a combining of the local with the global, and how this is being translated to social imagery in digital transnational space by 11.11/eleven eleven, offers unpredictable exchanges and fusions. This social imagery connects the aspirational luxury consumer to the physical making landscapes, processes and people behind the brand, forming the links that Himanshu sees as necessary to create new value around what Made in India means.

Since the inception of the brand, Himanshu and Morikawa have engaged with local analog processes such as the cultivation of indigenous kala cotton, hand-spinning on a Peti *charkha* (a portable hand-spinning wheel), hand-weaving, and experimenting with khadi, in an effort to create new value chains for khadi and reposition it as a luxury fabric. Their approach to the production of cotton and khadi embodies Gandhi's philosophies of self-reliance, sustainability, and social equity in the twenty-first century. Khadi, a hand-spun and hand-woven fabric, was championed by Gandhi as a symbol of India's struggle for independence advocating for a decentralized, village-based economy that empowered local artisans. Khadi production and distribution are regulated primarily by the Khadi and Village Industries Commission (KVIC). It ensures that khadi remains true to its traditional roots by setting standards for the production process, including the hand-spinning and hand-weaving techniques that define authentic khadi. Only cotton produced in this way can be called khadi.

Kala cotton is a traditional, indigenous variety of cotton native to the Kachchh region in Gujarat, India. It is known for its hardiness and ability to thrive in arid, drought-prone areas with minimal water and does not need pesticides or synthetic fertilizers. As a rain-fed cotton, the ecological footprint associated with its cultivation is reduced.

In addition to reintroducing indigenous cotton textiles and recontextualizing khadi, natural dyes, particularly indigo, are being developed. Their surface designs incorporate kalamkari, block printing, kantha embroidery, and bandhani. These are not techniques that change from one season to the next. Each collection represents ongoing dialogues and evolutions between the designers and the artisan communities they work with hand in hand.

Himanshu and Morikawa have been careful in how they, as designers, interact with the artisanal process, but as Himanshu says,

> "When we say hand-spun and handwoven, it is often confused with handloom for instance. That is why it is important for us to tell our story in a tighter, simpler way. I feel the dialogues that take place when we visit craftspeople at their homes and talk about impact of the right display, new technology while retaining craft and culture must also be shared.[35]

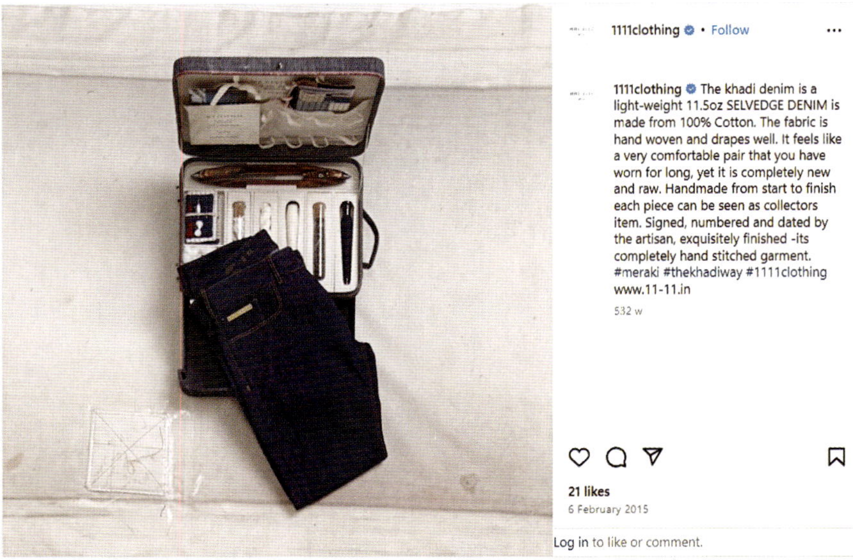

Figure 1.1 *Screenshot of the 11.11/eleven eleven Route Case, which narrates the journey of the brand's khadi denim from @1111clothing.*

Source: 11.11/eleven eleven clothing, "The Khadi Way," Instagram, *February 6, 2015.*

One of their ongoing innovations is yarn-dyed indigo khadi denim. An IG post on February 6, 2015 states: "The khadi denim is a lightweight 11.5 oz SELVEDGE DENIM . . . Handmade from start to finish each piece can be seen as a collectors item. Signed, numbered and dated by the artisan, exquisitely finished . . . #thekhadiway."[36]

The image accompanying the text is of a neatly folded, rich indigo pair of jeans placed atop a small open suitcase, also wrapped in a light blue khadi. Inside the case and inlaid on an ecru textile wrapped insert are, amongst other items, an assortment of hand-spun yarns in indigo, a glass tube with cotton seeds, fluffy natural cotton from the plant, threads for mending and a beautiful wooden weaving shuttle. Tucked into the lid of the case are what look like denim samples and a booklet. This is the Route Case, designed to narrate the journey of 100 percent khadi denim. Every element that goes into the production of the textile is deconstructed and broken down to its basic components and presented as a collection of covetable objects in their own right. In this way, the brand is recontextualizing the Indian terroir: the cotton seeds, the bolls from the cotton plant, the yarn and dye, and transforming this terroir into an art object, an "unexpected fusion" of the local and global, and in its execution, an example of the *jugalbandis* of techniques at the heart of the brand's "new-Swadeshi" philosophy. In this fusion, khadi itself is recontextualized as a new kind of luxury heritage object, as a collector's item in the form of that most universal of garments: a pair of blue jeans. In one simple image, in the digital transnational space of IG, the brand has revealed what radically quiet luxury looks like and created a new digital transnational circulation that provides the kind of "authenticity" the aspirational luxury consumer of today is looking for.

The Route Case as well as pieces of the brand's handloom khadi denim, yarns, and textiles were also a part of the State of Fashion's 2018 exhibition, *Searching for the New Luxury*, reinforcing the brand's place in creating the kind of future-facing luxury the fashion industry needs. 11.11/eleven eleven was featured in the section titled "The Product and Maker in the Spotlight." The brand posted its display of objects from the exhibition on IG on May 31, 2018. In the catalogue for the exhibition, the lead-in to this section states:

> The internet has made it possible to make all the layers within the production chain visible . . . The product is the materialization of the relationship between us and the producer: knowing the maker can create pride, trust, or a caring bond for the garment. This approach reveals a shift in focus from the "star designer" to the value of the garment itself, or the professionals behind it.[37]

This shift of focus from "star designer" to a more collaborative approach is key to how 11.11/eleven eleven operates. The designer interventions Himanshu and Morikawa engage in is as "intermediaries . . . to selectively disentangle provenance properties, decouple them from the entirety of the context of production . . . and frame those anchors as legitimate points of attachment for others' evaluations of authenticity and craft."[38] Examining how the brand utilizes text captions on IG to add an extra dimension to its posts demonstrates how Himanshu and Morikawa are creating visibility for the brand's complex production processes in innovative ways, and "the representational work of rendering things available as craft" in digital transnational space.[39]

The core values of the brand can be seen in the hashtags they repeatedly use to communicate to the consumer that encounters them in digital transnational space: #madeinmeditation, #handspun, #handwoven, #bandhani, #natural dyes, #handmade, #thekhadiway. These hashtags allow the "taste communities" of the aspiration economy to find the brand in digital transnational space and gather with others who are members of the niche "taste verticals" a brand like 11.11/eleven eleven is connecting with. Once they are scrolling through the brand's feed, there is a wealth of information to be found about the artisans, craft, and techniques that go into the creation of the garments and textiles. In this way, Himanshu and Morikawa are creating texture and context for the textiles and techniques that are being encountered in digital transnational space. This is evident in two related posts from July 2020 regarding the technique of hand painting textiles.

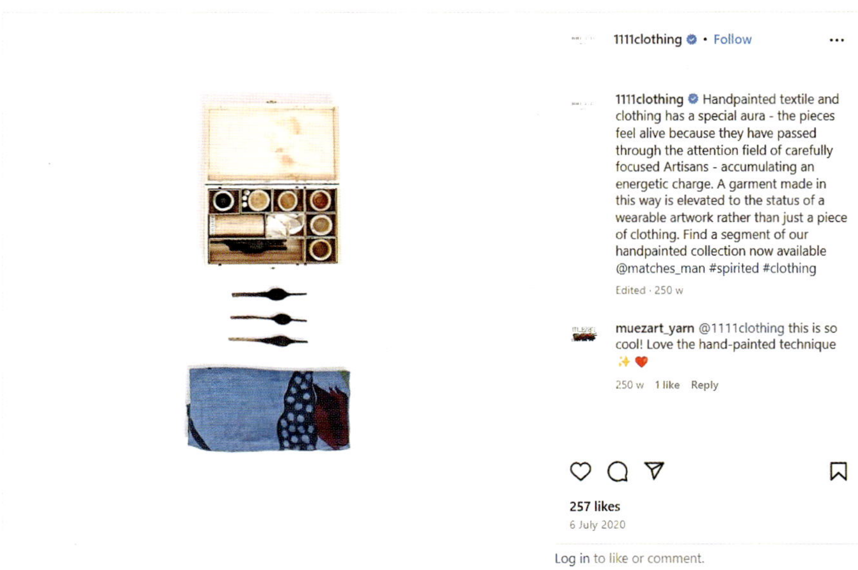

Figure 1.2 *Hand painting and the tools of artisanship from @1111clothing.*
Source: 11.11/eleven eleven clothing, "Hand Painted," Instagram, July 5, 2020.

Figure 1.3 *Hand painted shirt from @1111clothing.*
Source: 11.11/eleven eleven clothing, "Hand Painted Shirt," Instagram, July 6, 2020

In the first post, an image of a wooden box with pigments, tools, and a carefully folded blue textile with a partial print is visible. The text states:

> that "Hand painted textile[s] and clothing ha[ve] a special aura—the pieces feel alive because they have passed through the attention field of carefully focused artisans—accumulating an electric charge. A garment made this way is elevated to the status of a wearable artwork rather than just a piece of clothing.[40]

The text brings the artisans involved in the creation of the garment into our "attention field" in an innovative way by using words like "aura" and "electric" connecting to the process of making without the obvious cliché of showing the artisan at work. Instead, the handcrafted tools, the brushes and pigment represent the "aura of the analogue" in the digital world and let the viewer into the process of making in a way that allows them to deepen their own knowledge and develop a "caring bond" with the garment.[41]

In the second image, the textile from the first post is shown from the back, with large painted flora visible. The text reads:

> This relaxed fit gender fluid silk shirt is the ultimate expression of luxury leisure wear. Social equity is embedded in this garment, investing in this piece means participating in creating conditions which are conducive to life and planetary health. This is not a digital print—each piece is individually hand painted with natural indigenous color for you.[42]

The shirt is silk, but the luxury woven and painted into and onto the garment "selectively disentangle[s] provenance properties" through the use of words such as "indigenous" and "planetary health," and "anchors" the garment's inherent qualities of social equity as "legitimate points of attachment for others' evaluations of authenticity and craft."

Representing craft visually is powerful because images can capture the embodied sensory, aesthetic, and emotional qualities of craft, but the addition of symbolic text paints another layer onto the story being told by the brand in digital transnational space. Morikawa has spoken about the importance of creating new language around textiles similar to the kind of vocabulary used to describe wine:

> The language used to describe wine can seem high-brow and can add a sort of reverence for the fact that growing, fermenting grapes, and transforming them into wine is a slow process that requires skill and knowledge. When we speak to the qualities and properties of a textile, our zero-count hand-spun yarn has a low twist, a lofted character, and a dry hand. Increasing our textile lexicon to find more nuanced ways of describing the characteristics of fabric is definitely part of our practice.[43]

In this way, the brand is using the digital transnational space of IG to create "an additional space for the production of desire," and "a storehouse of signs, images, connections, and significations for consumers, producers, and intermediaries to work through and with."[44]

One final piece to consider in thinking about how the brand is creating a uniquely Indian quiet luxury is how it has empowered the artisans they work with. For example, the brand has developed application-based software that allows for full transparency into the production process, allowing every artisan, from farmer to tailor, to record their personal information, what they have worked on, and the time they have contributed to the finished product. A visitor to the brand's website can click on a product, see the hours that went into crafting a product, and click on the "Meet the Makers" box to connect to the human hands behind the products. Interestingly, there are no pictures of Himanshu and Morikawa on the website, nor are there many on the brand's IG. In this way, they are truly embracing their role as the intermediaries, not interventionists, and letting go of ideas of the "star designer" as being of utmost importance.

In addition, while they continue to work with artisan clusters throughout India on the *jugalbandis* of techniques that are deployed in their work, in 2021 they founded Kalakhoj, an 11.11/eleven eleven initiative in partnership with the Good Earth Heritage Foundation. Kalakhoj is a for-profit producer company headquartered in the village of Khambra, in Kachchh, Gujurat. Kachchh is known as a hub of Indian crafts and the artisans are the directors and shareholders, with all getting a share of the profits along with the wages they earn. The brand has its own IG account and one of its earliest posts, from August 10, 2022, is an illustration of the infinite circularity of production possibilities offered by the seed-to-stitch process (Figure 1.4).

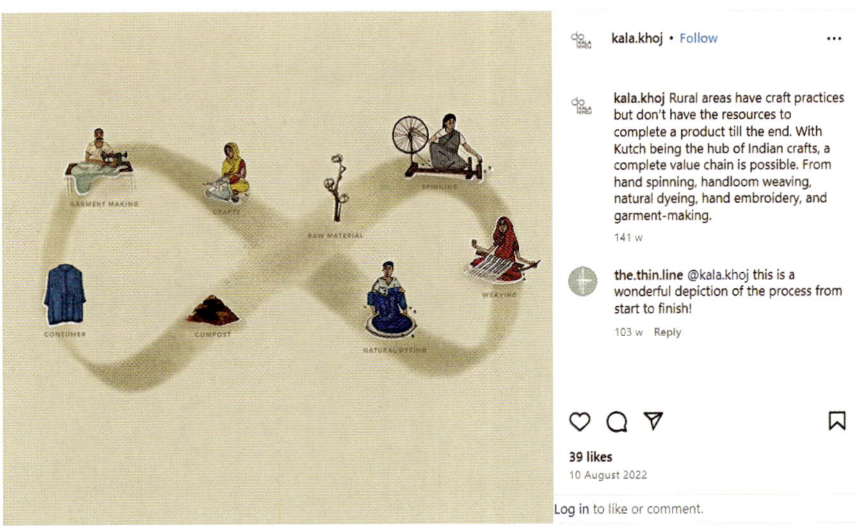

Figure 1.4 *Creating a circular value chain through the Kalakhoj initiative from @kalakhoj.*

Source: Kalakhoj, "The Circular Value Chain," Instagram, August 10, 2022.

Much of the kantha work 11.11/eleven eleven produces is now created by the artisans of Kalkhoj. In an effort to move to a zero waste model of production, the brand creates kantha jackets, coats, and pants created from textile remnants. Each piece is unique, featuring a curvilinear pattern reminiscent of ripples on water. The fine kantha features such close stitches that many of the pieces can look embroidered. Any smaller textile remnants are made into paper which is used for hangtags as well as in the stationery the brand creates.

In this way, the circular value chain seen on Kalakjoh's IG post is realized. By creating a village-based value chain and empowering the artisans to operate independently, the brand is recontextualizing idealized transnational circulations of "the Indian village . . . as a utopian version of an earlier pre-capitalist stage of Britain's own evolution to modernity" within which the Indian village "served as an imaginary in which the fluidity of craft time was performed, and which served as a focal point for discussions around craft and community since early colonial rule."[45] Kalakhoj is an example of how the brand has repositioned the Indian village as a site of innovation and experimentation. A new transnational circulation that challenges postcolonial fashion systems that "retain the resonances of histories of empire within which cultural and

Figure 1.5 *Kantha jacket by @1111clothing.*

Source: 11.11/eleven eleven clothing, "Kantha Work," Instagram, July 27, 2024.

economic imperatives and imaginaries were entwined" has been created by 11.11/eleven eleven and challenges the "imaginative geographies of 'East' and 'West', 'India' and 'Britain'" and beyond to create new digital transnational circulations of what Made in India represents in the twenty-first century.

Conclusion

Contemporary approaches in both fashion and craft practice act as a means to identify an evolving connection between the new digital transnational spaces of IG and established analogue processes, creating new circulations of the "complex geographies within which clothes are designed, manufactured, retailed and consumed." Brands like 11.11/eleven eleven are crafting radically quiet luxury as an anti-industrial expression and resistance movement that offers a sustainable solution to the fast, faster, fastest cycles of production that characterize modern consumption. Their slow fashion, small-batch production model stands in opposition to "Big Luxury" and offers the niche "taste communities" of today connections to the kinds of "authenticity" they are seeking in digitally mediated space. As Morikawa says, "11.11 clothing feels good to wear; the pieces reconnect us to what it means to be human and alive, to be complex and imperfect."[46] By embracing the humanity behind the garments, this quietly radical brand is paving a path forward for how we think about luxury—as a continuous and beautiful cycle of craftsmanship, that reveals in its complexities the responsibilities we all have to create something more responsible and long-lasting for this planet and its people. They, and all who will take inspiration from what they do, are truly fashioning a new Asian century.

Notes

1 Anupreeta Das, "Ambani Wedding Shows Off India's New Gilded Age," *New York Times*, July 12, 2024. https://www.nytimes.com/2024/07/12/world/asia/india-ambani-wedding-billionaire.html

2 Elise Taylor, "Inside Anant Ambani and Radhika Merchant's Final Wedding Celebration in Mumbai," Vogue.com, July 14, 2024. https://www.vogue.com/slideshow/anant-ambani-radhika-merchant-wedding-exclusive

3 Laura Silver, Christine Huang, and Laura Clancy, "Key Facts as India Surpasses China as World's Most Populous Country," Pewresearch.org, February 9, 2023, https://www.pewresearch.org/short-reads/2023/02/09/key-facts-as-india-surpasses-china-as-the-worlds-most-populous-country/

4 Agnes Rocamora, "Mediatization and Digital Retail," in *The End of Fashion: Clothing and Dress in the Age of Globalization,* Adam Geczy and Vicki Karaminas, eds, London: Bloomsbury Visual Arts, 2019, 109.

5 Arjun Appadurai, *Social Life of Things: Commodities in Cultural Perspective,* West Nyack, NY: Cambridge University Press, 1986.

6 Philip Crang, Claire Dwyer, and Peter Jackson, "Transnationalism and the Spaces of Commodity Culture," *Progress in Human Geography* 27 (4): 2003, 438–56. doi:10.1191/0309132503ph443oa. Also Philip Crang and Sonia Ashmore, "The Transnational Spaces of Things: South Asian Textiles in Britain and the Grammar of Ornament," *European Review of History: Revue Européenne d'Histoire,* 16 (5): 2009, 655–78.

7 Crang, Philip, and Dwyer, "*Transnationalism,*" 446–8.

8 Claire Dwyer, "Fabrications of India: Transnational Fashion Networks," in *Fashion's World Cities,* Christopher Breward and David Gilbert, eds, *Cultures of Consumption Series*, Oxford: Berg, 2006, 220.

9 Dwyer, "Fabrications of India," 220.

10 Arti Sandhu, "Introduction: Indian Fashion," in *Indian Fashion: Tradition, Innovation, Style*, London: Bloomsbury Academic, 2015, 21.

11 Dwyer, "Fabrications of India," 220.

12 Sandhu, "Introduction: Indian Fashion," 21.

13 Dwyer, "Fabrications of India," 233.

14 Ibid.

15 Thorstein Veblen, *The Theory of the Leisure Class*, New York: Penguin Books, 1994.

16 Giana M. Eckhardt, Russell W. Belk, and Jonathan A .J. Wilson, "The Rise of Inconspicuous Consumption," *Journal of Marketing Management* 31 (7–8): 2015, 807–26. doi:10.1080/0267257X.2014.989890.

17 Jonah Berger and Morgan Ward, "Subtle Signals of Inconspicuous Consumption," *Journal of Consumer Research* 37 (4): 2010, 555–69. doi:10.1086/655445.

18 Sarah Kent, "Is Luxury Finally Set for a Sustainability Reckoning?" Businessoffashion.com, July 19, 2024, https://www.businessoffashion.com/articles/sustainability/luxury-sweatshop-reckoning-armani-dior-italy-investigation/

19 Ana Andjelic, "The Decade of Two Luxuries," andjelicaaa.medium.com, December 11, 2019, https://andjelicaaa.medium.com/luxurys-great-bifurcation-2010-2020-fff3c468efb4

20 Sarah Banet-Weiser, *Authentic TM: Politics and Ambivalence in a Brand Culture,* New York: New York University Press, 2012, 4.

21 Ana Andjelic, *The Business of Aspiration,* New York: Routledge, 2021.

22 Mukti Khaire, "The Indian Fashion Industry and Traditional Indian Crafts," *Business History Review* 85 (2): 2011, 353.

23 Ibid., 354–5.

24 Ibid.

25 Sandhu, "Introduction: Indian Fashion," 21.

26 Rahul Mishra, *Business of Fashion,* December 17, 2024, https://www.businessoffashion.com/people/rahul-mishra/

27 Phyllida Jay, "An Alternative to Bollywood Style," *New York Times,* August 22, 2018, https://www.nytimes.com/2018/08/22/fashion/bodice-woolmark-prize-winner.html

28 Snigdha Sur, "The Fierceness of Poorna Jagannathan," the juggernaut.com, August 8, 2022, https://www.thejuggernaut.com/poorna-jagannathan-never-have-i-ever-interview

29 "Himanshu Shani," Border & Fall, accessed April 15, 2024, https://www.borderandfall.com/people-spaces/himanshu-shani/

30 Ibid.

31 Phyllida Jay, *Fashion India,* New York: Thames and Hudson, 2015, 109.

32 Sanhati Baerjee, "Shani Himanshu's New Khadi Way," thevoiceoffashion.com, August 6, 2019, https://www.thevoiceoffashion.com/fabric-of-india/features/shani-himanshus-new-khadi-way--2974/

33 Sanjay Jain, "From Jugaad to Jugalbandi: Understanding the Changing Nature of Indian Innovation," *Asia Pacific Journal of Management* 39 (1): 2022, 6.

34 Ibid.

35 Shefalee Vasudev, "Untold Stories of Fashion," Platform-mag.com, accessed June 20, 2024, https://www.platform-mag.com/fashion/untold-stories-of-unfashion.html

36 11.11/eleven eleven clothing, "The Khadi Way," *Instagram,* February 6, 2015, https://www.instagram.com/p/ywYTyqL-2S/

37 "State of Fashion: Searching for a New Luxury," issuu.com, August 23, 2018, https://issuu.com/stateoffashion/docs/stof_07_2018_catalogus_interactive__84d6b3f0f988ec

38 Jennifer Smith Maguire, "Wine, the Authenticity Taste Regime, and Rendering Craft," in *The Organization of Craft Work: Identities, Meanings, and Materiality,* Emma Bell et al., eds, New York: Routledge, 2018, 60–81. The chapter reframes the narrative around the mythical status of the vigneron as the sole creator of artisanal winemaking and argues that all involved in the production of wine, from the farmers to the consumers, are valuable in creating narratives of authenticity.

39 Maguire, "Wine, the Authenticity," 80.

40 11.11/eleven eleven clothing, "Hand Painted" *Instagram,* July 5, 2020, https://www.instagram.com/p/CCSF4uwBH95/?img_index=1

41 Susan Luckman, *Craft and the Creative Economy*, London: Palgrave Macmillan, 2015, 68–75. Luckman discusses how the "aura of the analogue" in our digital age is closely connected to consumer fascination with processes of making and makers. She centers her discussion around handcrafted items available for sale on the internet platform Etsy but it is equally applicable to IG.

42 11.11/eleven eleven clothing, "Hand Painted Shirt" *Instagram,* July 6, 2020, https://www.instagram.com/p/CCSlxUnBf6L/?img_index=1

43 Charles MacFarlane, "Interview with 11.11's Own Mia Morikawa," standardandstrange.com, January 6, 2024, https://standardandstrange.com/blogs/standard-strange-stories/interview-with-mia-morikawa-of-11-11.

44 Rocamora, "Mediatization," 109.

45 Sria Chatterjee, "Postindustrialism and the Long Arts and Crafts Movement: Between Britain, India, and the United States of America," Britishartstudies.ac.uk, accessed March 15, 2024, https://doi.org/10.17658/issn.2058-5462/issue-15/schatterjee/p26 https://. Chatterjee discusses the Long Arts and Crafts Movement and how key advocates of craft such as Coomarasway and even Gandhi had overly idealized and unrealistic views influenced by British Arts and Crafts advocates.

46 MacFarlane, "Interview."

Bibliography

Andjelic, Ana. *The Business of Aspiration*. New York: Routledge, 2021.

Andjelic, Ana. "The Decade of Two Luxuries." andelicaaa.medium.com, December 11, 2019. https://andjelicaaa.medium.com/luxurys-great-bifurcation-2010-2020-fff3c468efb4

Appadurai, Arjun. *Social Life of Things: Commodities in Cultural Perspective*. West Nyack, NY: Cambridge University Press, 1986.

Baerjee, Sanhati. "Shani Himanshu's New Khadi Way." thevoiceoffashion.com, August 6, 2019. https://www.thevoiceoffashion.com/fabric-of-india/features/shani-himanshus-new-khadi-way--2974/

Banet-Weiser, Sarah. *Authentic TM: Politics and Ambivalence in a Brand Culture*. New York: New York University Press, 2012.

Berger, Jonah, and Morgan Ward. "Subtle Signals of Inconspicuous Consumption." *The Journal of Consumer Research* 37 (4): 2010, 555–69.

Chatterjee, Sria. "Postindustrialism and the Long Arts and Crafts Movement: Between Britain, India, and the United States of America." Britishartstudies.ac.uk. https://doi.org/10.17658/issn.2058-5462/issue-15/schatterjee/p26 https://

Crang, Philip, and Sonia Ashmore. "The Transnational Spaces of Things: South Asian Textiles in Britain and the Grammar of Ornament." *European Review of History: Revue Européenne d'Histoire* 16 (5): 2009, 655–78.

Crang, Philip, Claire Dwyer, and Peter Jackson. "Transnationalism and the Spaces of Commodity Culture." *Progress in Human Geography* 27 (4): 2003, 438–56. doi:10.1191/0309132503ph443oa.

Das, Anupreeta. "Ambani Wedding Shows Off India's New Gilded Age." *New York Times*, July 12, 2024. https://www.nytimes.com/2024/07/12/world/asia/india-ambani-wedding-billionaire.html

Dwyer, Claire. "Fabrications of India: Transnational Fashion Networks." In *Fashion's World Cities*, Christopher Breward and David Gilbert, eds. Oxford: Berg, 2006, 217–34.

Eckhardt, Giana M., Russell W. Belk, and Jonathan A. J. Wilson. "The Rise of Inconspicuous Consumption." *Journal of Marketing Management* 31 (7–8): 2015, 807–26.

Jain, Sanjay. "From Jugaad to Jugalbandi: Understanding the Changing Nature of Indian Innovation." *Asia Pacific Journal of Management* 39 (1): 2022, 1–26.

Jay, Phyllida. *Fashion India*. New York: Thames and Hudson, 2015.

Jay, Phyllida. "An Alternative to Bollywood Style." *New York Times*, August 22, 2018. https://www.nytimes.com/2018/08/22/fashion/bodice-woolmark-prize-winner.html

Kent, Sarah. "Is Luxury Finally Set for a Sustainability Reckoning?" Businessoffashion.com, July 19, 2024. https://www.businessoffashion.com/articles/sustainability/luxury-sweatshop-reckoning-armani-dior-italy-investigation/

Khaire, Mukti. "The Indian Fashion Industry and Traditional Indian Crafts." *Business History Review* 85 (2): 2011, 345–66.

Luckman, Susan. *Craft and the Creative Economy*. London: Palgrave Macmillan, 2015.

MacFarlane, Charles. "Interview with 11.11's Own Mia Morikawa." standardandstrange.com, January 6, 2024. https://standardandstrange.com/blogs/standard-strange-stories/interview-with-mia-morikawa-of-11-11.

Maguire, Jennifer Smith. "Wine, the Authenticity Taste Regime, and Rendering Craft." In *The Organization of Craft Work: Identities, Meanings, and Materiality*, Emma Bell et al., eds. New York: Routledge, 2018, 60–81.

Rocamora, Agnes. "Mediatization and Digital Retail." In *The End of Fashion: Clothing and Dress in the Age of Globalization*, Adam Geczy and Vicki Karaminas, eds. London: Bloomsbury Visual Arts, 2019, 99–112.

Sandhu, Arti. "Introduction: Indian Fashion." In *Indian Fashion: Tradition, Innovation, Style*. London: Bloomsbury Academic, 2015, 1–24.

Silver, Laura, Christine Huang, and Laura Clancy. "Key Facts as India Surpasses China as World's Most Populous Country." Pewresearch.org, February 9, 2023. https://www.pewresearch.org/short-reads/2023/02/09/key-facts-as-india-surpasses-china-as-the-worlds-most-populous-country/

Sur, Snigdha. "The Fierceness of Poorna Jagannathan." thejuggernaut.com, August 8, 2022. https://www.thejuggernaut.com/poorna-jagannathan-never-have-i-ever-interview

Taylor, Elise. "Inside Anant Ambani and Radhika Merchant's Final Wedding Celebration in Mumbai." Vogue.com, July 14, 2024. https://www.vogue.com/slideshow/anant-ambani-radhika-merchant-wedding-exclusive

Vasudev, Shefalee. "Untold Stories of Fashion." Platform-mag.com. https://www.platform-mag.com/fashion/untold-stories-of-unfashion.html.

Veblen, Thorstein. *The Theory of the Leisure Class*. New York: Penguin Books, 1994.

2

Between Traditional and Modern: The New Popularity of boro Patchwork Clothing Among Chinese Youth

WANG SHUHUA

Although the term "boro" originates from modern Japan, rag clothing did not solely emerge from Japan. The "boro" phenomenon garnered attention in the fashion world after Japanese folklorist and archaeologist Tadanori Tanaka exhibited the rag clothing he had collected over forty years. Boro is a transliteration of the Japanese word ぼろぼろの (pronounced as boroboro no), which originally means "ragged" or "worn-out." It refers to the traditional folk textiles of Japan's Edo period (1600–1868) and the early Showa era (1926–45), crafted by stitching together hundreds of different, worn-out cotton and linen patches with rugged thread and needles—a practice known as recycling old fabrics. China's ancient "baina clothes" (hundred-patch cloak) and patchwork quilt covers resemble boro in appearance and share some cultural origins, but they also have differences. Both are clothing cultures stemming from frugality and sustainability among ancients, but Japanese boro pursues the aesthetics of wabisabi, while Chinese baina clothes emphasizes "work with the heart can only accept everything." In history, boro was once viewed as a symbol of poverty, as it was only chosen by people when they could not afford new clothing or textiles and resorted to stitching together old items for use. However, as time passed, boro gradually came to be regarded as a unique cultural heritage and art form. Today, it has become an important component of Japanese traditional handicrafts and is loved and appreciated by an increasing number of people.

Despite slight cultural differences in boro clothing between China and Japan, the design aesthetics of boro have sparked Chinese youth's interest in traditional baina clothing culture. New boro and baina clothing are typical cultural symbols explored by young people amidst the collision of traditional and modern cultures. They integrate traditional creation ideas with modernist propositions, satisfying the younger generation's psychological desire to both inherit Chinese culture and pursue innovation. Since 2013, influenced by brands such as Louis Vuitton and Japanese streetwear labels Kapita, Kuon, Porter Classic, Visvim, 45R, and Junya Watanabe, boro has emerged as a stylistic element in luxury brands including Dior, Chanel, Etro, and Loewe, as well as in street fashion brands such as Visvim, FDMLT, and Beams.

Some designers and brands do not view boro merely as a fashion appearance but adopt boro aesthetics as a design principle.[1] In recent years, China has witnessed the emergence of several handmade boro clothing brands, such as Baopu, FINITEMADE, and Leshou. Chinese boro brand designers are not only tracing back to China's traditional baina culture but also exploring new boro fashion trends. China's new boro brands are growing together in harmony with their consumer base.

The First "New boro" Brand: "Baopu"'s Commitment to "Sustainable Living" and "Genderless Dressing"

Chinese youth fashion designer Hong Dan founded the clothing brand Baopu in Kaili, Guizhou, inspired by the Japanese boro style. Hong Dan began consuming Japanese boro brand items in 2013, when he was running a tea room and homestay in Guangzhou, China. In the process of running his business, Hong Dan encountered a group of young people who loved Chinese Chan (Zen in Japanese) tea culture. Sharing common interests with this group, including a passion for traditional Chinese culture and a preference for a natural lifestyle, they were striving to find clothing that resonated with their inner feelings. However, most of the clothing available in the market was fast fashion, lacking sustainable wearability. A more serious issue was that fast fashion clothing produced more pollutants during the manufacturing process, affecting people's living environments. Therefore, when this group of young people encountered Japanese boro clothing, they were moved by its natural texture and nostalgic style. They quickly became loyal users of boro clothing brands. After consuming Japanese boro clothing for some time, this young group deeply realized that Japanese boro products still could not meet their subtle inner needs. They wanted a simpler and more natural "boro" clothing that was more aligned with the humanistic spirit of China. Based on his decade-long feelings about traditional Chinese fabrics and unconscious pursuit, Hong Dan founded the patchwork clothing brand Baopu.

The name Baopu (bàopŭ) originates from Chapter 19 of Laozi's "Tao Te Ching," which reads, "Maintain simplicity and embrace unadorned purity; reduce selfish desires and avoid excessive ambitions; renounce learning to attain tranquility." "Pu" refers to plainness, naturalness, and the original state without any adornment. Baopu represents the pursuit of preserving one's true self, embracing simplicity, not being entangled in material desires, and remaining uninfluenced by natural and social factors. Initially established as a small studio in Guangzhou, Baopu moved its studio and exhibition hall to the urban area of Kaili, Guizhou, during the COVID-19 pandemic, with Kaili becoming the main development base for the brand.

Kaili, located in the southeast of Guizhou Province, is known as an "Ecological Museum of Traditional Chinese Culture." The clothing culture of thousands of years ago in China has been preserved in Guizhou. In the urban area of Kaili, there is a market for old embroidered clothing of southwestern ethnic minorities, surrounded by numerous Hmong villages. These villages retain rich traditional festivals, and the embroidered costumes worn during these festivals are renowned worldwide. Starting in the 1990s, many Hmong vendors traveled to rural areas in provinces such as Guizhou, Yunnan, Hunan, and Sichuan to purchase old embroidered clothing. A large distribution center for old embroidery spontaneously formed in Caoping New Village, Kaili City, attracting old embroidery enthusiasts from all over China and even abroad to search for embroidery. In 2021, Hong Dan opened his brand studio next to the old embroidery market in Kaili, where he not only collected old embroidered clothing but also gathered a large amount of traditionally handwoven ancient fabric as raw materials for patchwork clothing.

The Baopu brand encompasses two design concepts. Firstly, it advocates a sustainable lifestyle. Hong Dan believes that the ancient Chinese patchwork clothing, known as baina yi, involved reassembling used and torn cloth into new clothing items, demonstrating that fabric can be recycled and reused, presenting different charming appearances at each stage. Baopu also creates new clothing from ancient fabric, focusing on innovative patchwork designs to create unique styles and patterns. Secondly, Baopu advocates "genderless dressing." Genderless design differs from neutral style, which falls between male and female clothing without obvious gender characteristics. Genderless encompasses not only neutral but also androgynous and gender transformative.

Concept of Sustainable Living

In China, where agricultural culture has persisted for thousands of years, people value cultural continuity, particularly in clothing and accessories. To this day, in the underdeveloped regions of southwest and northwest China, a vast amount of patchwork handicraft items, such as quilts and children's clothing, are still preserved among the people. In Majiang County, Guizhou Province, there is an ethnic subgroup called the "Raojia" who have a custom of sewing torn indigo-dyed fabric into quilts, with each generation adding their own worn-out fabric to the quilt. Therefore, during my field research, I saw numerous quilts sewn together by several generations. These quilts are largely composed of deeply and shallowly hand-dyed, handwoven indigo fabric, with some wax-printing patterns. Sometimes, when lifting up the torn areas, one can faintly see embroidery hidden within the layers. People have given such

Figure 2.1 *Wan Nianbei from the Raojia Ethnic Group in Guizhou. Collected by Hong Dan*

quilts a very vivid name: "Wan Nianbei" (Ten Thousand Years Quilt) ((As shown in Figure 2.1).). This does not mean that the quilt is ten thousands years old, but rather conveys two meanings: first, such quilts have been passed down through many generations within the family, with "ten thousands" being an exaggeration for "long duration"; second, descendants sleeping on such quilts can enjoy continuous prosperity and longevity for ten thousands years. Imagine, if modern industrial textiles had not been introduced into the mountainous regions of southwest China for widespread use, local women would continue to sew worn-out fabric onto the "Ten Thousand Year Quilt," and the quilt would continue to "grow."

To protect the Earth's environment and reduce waste, fashion brands worldwide are seeking effective and sustainable ways of dressing. The brand Baopu, founded by Hong Dan, makes continuous use of old fabric, or finds new uses for old fabric. In his earlier years, Hong Dan was moved by boro clothing made from these old indigo-dyed cotton fabrics. He said:

> For those like us who know what we want very early on, fast fashion clothing does not match our spiritual needs. The ancient, hand-spun, and handwoven fabric contains a strong vitality that deeply touches me. I can feel the fabric's breath and its state of life. When I understand the life characteristics of each piece of fabric, I cannot help but think of establishing a deep connection with them and presenting their charm once again in clothing. Although I have not specifically conducted consumer market research, I run a homestay and meet many people, learning that many friends have the same clothing needs as me. Based on my own needs, I know what kind of clothing this group would pay for. Then, I can use my designs to connect more deeply with this group.[2]

In the Baopu design studio, a vast collection of ancient cotton and linen fabrics sourced from ethnic minority villages is stored. Most of these fabrics are used quilt covers, bedsheets, and skirt materials. Hong Dan and his design team clean, sort, cut, and piece together these old fabrics. To ensure wearing comfort, they also incorporate a small portion of modern, industrially produced fine cotton fabric into their designs and production. By recycling traditional old fabrics and combining them with new fabric, they breathe new life into them, allowing them to shine in new ways through patchwork designs.

Genderless Dressing

The Baopu design studio is established in Kaili, a small city in southwest China, and its creative concept is closely related to the traditional clothing culture of "unisex attire" preserved in the southwest region. In the traditional societies of ethnic minorities in the southwest, there is no significant binary division between men's and women's clothing in style or decoration. That is, they did not strictly distinguish between men and women in terms of social roles, and both genders shared the social and familial responsibilities of their ethnic group and branch. During my investigation in Hmong communities, it was found that local women, besides engaging in female crafts such as embroidery and weaving, also participated in some of the same work as men, such as farming, buying and selling daily necessities, and transporting goods. When guests come to their homes, the women sit at the table and drink alcohol and sing duets with the guests. As Confucian culture has not fully integrated into the southwest region, the boundaries between men and women are not as strictly drawn as in Han society. In most Han areas of old China, women were not allowed to sit at the table and entertain guests during meals, but such strict gender segregation does not exist among ethnic minorities in the southwest, and their traditional clothing does not strictly delineate gender boundaries. This reflects an unconscious state in the societies of ethnic minorities in the southwest: regardless of gender, individuals exist as "human beings" rather than presenting themselves to others as "male" or "female." That is, their awareness of gender is not as clearly defined as in developed civilized societies, and they do not use labels such as "delicate" and "masculine" to differentiate between women and men. This is a very simple and primitive gender outlook based on "unity." Therefore, it is quite normal for women to do men's work and for men to wear the same clothing as women.

In the Western fashion world, "genderless fashion" has been trending for several years. This trend can be traced back to the minimalist and gender-neutral aesthetic of "Normcore." As Normcore evolved, its neutral style escalated into "genderless fashion," though there are distinctions between genderless design and the neutral style emphasized by Normcore. "Neutral" refers to a design style that falls between men's and women's clothing and lacks distinct gender characteristics, while "genderless" encompasses not only neutral but also androgynous and gender-fluid styles. The design style is no longer exclusively minimalist but also favors the recombination of design elements with obvious gender characteristics. This unified design concept, rooted in philosophy, aligns with the simple gender outlook of ethnic minorities in southwest China. Hong Dan, the founder of Baopu, defines the brand's design concept similarly. The fabrics he uses originate from the southwest region, and the design concepts and methods also stem from the same place. These materials and ideas are inherited from ancient China. When discussing the original intention behind his "genderless dressing" design, he said:

> Over the years, I've harbored a thought that differs from the past: Should a person's disposition be defined by their gender? Both men and women possess an easygoing nature in their bones. Men can have a vulnerable side,

and women can have a masculine side. The clothes we wear can bring out our inner qualities, reflecting our disposition rather than defining our gender. Gender should not be used to distinguish between people; for example, some women possess immense energy, while some men may have less. "Genderless dressing" can break the binary opposition caused by gender labels, expressing one's true disposition more objectively and helping society overcome gender discrimination and biases.[3]

Figure 2.2 *Baopu's genderless dressing, boro product*
Photos provided by Hong Dan

Initially, Hong Dan's Baopu was positioned to design patchwork clothing for male groups. Surprisingly, around 80 percent of his customers were women (as shown in Figure 2.2). This data prompted him to reassess his designs and gauge the psychological needs of his clientele. He discovered that women's aesthetic demands for clothing are increasingly high, and their definitions of social roles are no longer confined to traditional concepts. Under the multiple pressures of society, they have more self-awareness and greater freedom in choosing their attire compared to men. However, most men in society cannot match women in terms of aesthetics, and the few men with high aesthetic accomplishments tend to prioritize spiritual needs and refuse to be swayed by fast fashion. They still face a dilemma: finding suitable clothes to match their inner needs is challenging, and even finding a suitable hairstylist is difficult, so some men let their hair grow longer, including Hong Dan himself.

"True androgynous clothing will eliminate the respective shortcomings of men's and women's clothing while combining their respective advantages."[4] Paoletti and Kidwell wrote in their conclusion to Kidwell and Steele's book *Men and Women: Dressing the Part* that "genderlessness is a form of freedom and personal expression. It is not just an aesthetic revolution but also a change in thinking. The popularity of genderlessness indicates that this era is becoming increasingly inclusive and equal."[5]

The Second "New boro" Brand: FINITEMADE's "Denim Cultivation Culture"

The founder of FINITEMADE, Zhou Sha, is a young post-90s girl whose university major was pharmaceutical sciences. Due to her love for handmade leather crafts, after graduating from university in 2016, she was attracted to boro products. She then began collecting old indigo-dyed cotton fabrics from ethnic minority regions in Guizhou and old pattern-dyed cotton fabrics from Japan, preparing to make her favorite handmade clothing accessories. By 2019, she had established her own small "Ancient Fabric, New Creations" studio, FINITEMADE. When talking about why she quit her formal job at a hospital to return to her hometown Hubei to establish a handmade clothing studio, she said:

> I was instantly captivated by the aura of the indigo-dyed old fabric. It was truly moving. The simplicity and warmth of the ancient fabric are invisible but strike a chord in my heart. While fascinated by them, I also hope they can return to our daily lives, taking on a new "identity" as everyday items and continuing their journey through time.[6]

For Zhou Sha herself, her initial intention in founding the studio, much like Hong Dan, was to design sustainable boro clothing made from antique fabrics. However, after operating for some time, customers started coming to her to customize vintage-style shoes, jeans, and backpacks using old fabrics, as shown in Figure 2.3. These customers belonged to the "Wear in Jeans Vintage Trend" group, which has a particular fondness for vintage and classic trends and is mostly male. The "Wear in Jeans Culture" specifically refers to the culture of "raw denim" care, which originated in the United States and was initially formed unintentionally by gold miners. Due to limited living conditions, the miners often wore their blue jeans without washing or replacing them, leading to unique creases and wear patterns over time. This unique appearance,

Figure 2.3 *Boro patchwork products by FINITEMADE.*
Photo provided by Zhou Sha

possessing a special aesthetic, gradually gained popularity in the fashion world, evolving into a systematic "'Wear in Jeans Culture" and maintenance methods. The key to denim care lies in allowing raw denim to undergo natural friction and oxidation during wear. Through daily wear and activities, the denim develops natural fading and wear on joints and friction areas, with colors and textures changing over time and with the wearer's activities, creating a unique visual effect. In recent years, the "'Wear in Jeans Culture" has also gradually risen in popularity in China. With the prevalence of Japanese boro style, an increasing number of jeans enthusiasts tend to collage ancient fabrics with ancient patterns and special textures onto their jeans for added decoration, such as using sashiko stitching with indigo-dyed handwoven cotton, tie-dyed fabrics, wax-printed fabrics, pattern-dyed fabrics, or Japanese printed cotton. The "'Wear in Jeans Culture" reflects people's pursuit of vintage and classic styles. Many denim enthusiasts prefer red-edged denim jeans woven on old-fashioned looms, a fabric technique so rare that it adds to its preciousness.

Zhou Sha is an independent female designer who consistently creates indigo-dyed patchwork clothing in styles she loves, resulting in a relatively tough and rugged aesthetic. In stark contrast to Hong Dan, Zhou Sha's boro products primarily attract a male consumer base, while 80 percent of Hong Dan's baopu consumers are female. This intriguing contrast seems to remind me that a segment of contemporary young people is no longer constrained by society's established gender norms. When choosing clothing that reflects their inner spirit, they opt for products with gender ambiguity.

To further validate this viewpoint, ducted an in-depth interview with Yongheng, the designer and head of another "new boro" handmade brand, Leshou.

The Third "New boro" Brand: Leshou

Yongheng, the designer of Leshou, is also a post-90s male who majored in graphic design at university. During his student days, he became deeply interested in indigo dyeing after encountering hand tie-dyeing techniques. After working for three years in the Planning and Design Institute of a Chinese listed company after graduation, he quit his job as a graphic designer to study traditional Chinese indigo dyeing techniques. During his work, he frequently visited Japan for research and was exposed to the indigo dyeing culture that spread from ancient China to Japan. Since most boro clothing in Japan is made of naturally indigo-dyed fabrics, Yongheng developed a keen interest in boro clothing. In 2016, his mother in his hometown in Fujian Province happened to give him a batch of ancient indigo-dyed clothes left by his great-grandmother. The beautiful colors deeply moved him and inspired him to start collecting traditional Chinese indigo-dyed fabrics and Japanese ancient fabrics to create the indigo-dyed patchwork products he wanted to explore.

The brand name Leshou expresses a lifestyle attitude of "gladly accepting and enjoying oneself." This name originates from Chinese Chan (Japanese Zen) Buddhism, whose purpose is "no self, no attachment, no distinction, accepting everything." Yongheng sees a Chan-like (Zen-like) state of life in indigo dyeing, as the entire process of indigo dyeing demonstrates the transformation of various life states, all presenting a vague and inclusive appearance, expressing that "passing away is the beginning of another new life." For example, indigo dyeing begins with the planting of a Polygonum tinctorium seed, which grows leaves; the leaves are beaten into indigo mud used to ferment dye vats, which produce bacteria that turn fabrics blue; the blue fabrics are worn on people's bodies and gradually worn out by friction, either turning into dust or being restitched into a new boro garment. This is a journey of constant life transformation filled with uncertainty and vagueness. This vagueness points to the inclusiveness and acceptance of life's fluidity. For instance, first, the normal operating temperature of the dye vat is controlled around 26 degrees Celsius, and it can work as long as it stays within this range; second, the pH level of the dye solution in the vat is controlled around a value of 11, and it can also work normally within this range; third, the indigo mud and nutrients added to the vat are related to local produce and vary, with indigo plants being divided into several types, such as wood indigo, Japanese indigo, Polygonum tinctorium, and woad, each with different colors but capable of producing beautiful blue hues.

Due to the ambiguity and inclusiveness of indigo dyeing colors, the emergence of boro had a solid foundation. The blues on ancient boro were diverse, with old pieces of fabric sewn together to present a comprehensive

Figure 2.4 *Yongheng (first left) exchanges ideas on patchwork culture with Shin Tatsumi, curator of AMUSE MUSEUM (second right) and others.*
Photo provided by Yongheng

appearance of varying depths, shades, and textures, capable of expressing both profoundness and subtle elegance. Boro boasts numerous color gradients, each expressing different feelings yet harmonious overall. This is similar to people's fascination with the worn and oxidized effects on blue jeans; although its appearance is vague and indistinct, its texture presents a rich and subtle tension and balance. This characteristic is the secret behind its appeal.

The unique temperament of boro deeply attracted the young designer. Yongheng stated that at the Boro and Baina Invitation Exhibition held by the AMUSE MUSEUM in Tokyo at the Shenzhen Academy of Fine Arts Museum in 2019, he saw a large collection of boro from Aomori Prefecture, Japan, gathered by the Japanese folklorist Tanaka Chuzaburo (see Figure 2.4). These boro items included delivery blankets, quilts, and clothing. Although made of

Figure 2.5 *Handcrafted dragon pattern, boro handbag product by Leshou brand.*
Photo provided by Yongheng

ragged fabrics, the stitching was meticulous and careful, indicating that people at that time sincerely treated every worn-out piece of fabric and seriously faced their own lives. It is said that girls in the Aomori area learned sewing skills from a young age and, after marriage, presented their sewn clothing to their parents-in-law for inspection to prove their ability to care for their families. This is consistent with customs in traditional Chinese society. The earnestness of women towards life inadvertently gave boro a natural style. Its temperament is elusive, difficult to generalize, and hard to replicate in identical boro products. In Aomori Prefecture, Japan, there is a bodoko (a nickname given by locals), similar to a quilt, which is the most symbolic fabric among the locals. Bodoko is used during childbirth for pregnant women. Each generation of women in the family carefully sews and cares for this blanket, passing it down from one generation to the next. Children are born on this cloth, with their birth blood coagulating on it, as if blessed and protected by their ancestors, enabling them to grow up healthy and strong. The family bloodline is thus transmitted. On the walls of the museum, there are handwritten notes by Tanaka Chuzaburo:

> At that time, the method of childbirth was "sitting delivery." A rope was tied to the beam of the house, and the pregnant woman held the rope to support her body in a squatting position for delivery. Bodoko was sewn from the old clothes of grandparents and parents. That is why it has been passed down through generations, with patches added layer upon layer. Each child is not born by the strength of one person alone. It requires the strength of parents, grandparents, and ancestors connected by blood. Even if we only trace back ten generations, each of their blood contains the blood of thousands of others. Without any of these individuals, we would not be here today.[7]

Due to its significant weight, boro requires great physical strength for transportation and ample space for storage. This underscores the immense effort Tanaka Chuzaburo must have put into collecting these fabrics, driven solely by his profound love for boro. The origin of boro also deeply moved Yongheng:

> When I embarked on making the Hundred Patchwork Bag Series, this boro exhibition unexpectedly presented itself to me, as if everything in life is meant for you. It's truly fascinating! When people were stitching together each piece of fabric in the past, they could never have imagined that decades later, these fabrics would be exhibited worldwide, becoming nostalgic stories. Just as we don't know what lies beyond time in every moment, it can turn out so wonderful. In the face of the unknown, we embrace it with a brave and resilient heart, driven by the persistence of life and the desire for love. My brand "Leshou'" has always adhered to the life attitude of 'accepting with joy and finding pleasure in it,' and patchwork is also a process of complete acceptance and introspection. In my designs, I aim to express the most primitive and natural state of integration within human unity."[8]

According to Yongheng, the consumer group for the Leshou brand does not specifically define the gender of its customers, but in reality, it is primarily dominated by women from the post-1980s and post-1990s generation. (The products of Leshou are shown in Figure 2.5.) This consumer group is characterized by its members' independent thinking, a clear understanding of what they want and don't want, a love for handmade products, a particular fondness for traditional artifacts with signs of use, and a unique pursuit of aesthetics and art.

Comparing Japanese boro with Chinese patchwork, we find many similarities, yet each with its unique cultural background. Japanese folk boro originated mainly from the necessity of life, a connection to the source of life created through mending and patching under past harsh living conditions. In China, besides being used in folk necessities, the concept of "patchwork" was also adopted by the aristocracy to sew quilted clothing as a way to pray for the well-being of the collective. However, in terms of humans' discovery of beauty, understanding of life, and connection to the natural universe, there is a profound resonance between China and Japan, sharing an identical essence that presents a sustainable, natural, and unintentional beauty.

Conclusion

In the transition between tradition and modernity, Chinese boro clothing has gradually evolved into a style with gender ambiguity. The three brands mentioned earlier uphold their respective philosophies: Baopu's "sustainable living" and "genderless dressing," FINITEMADE's "denim culture," and Leshou's "natural integration" and "acceptance of all." On the surface, although the clothing presented by these three brands has different characteristics, I see from their philosophies a dynamic and ongoing trend Compared to the previous generation, there have been some changes in gender awareness regarding the clothing consumption attitudes of young Chinese people. They tend to choose clothing that aligns with their inner temperament to express themselves, rather than selecting items with obvious gender-specific characteristics. The female designers in the cases studied have male audiences as their primary target, while the male designers' boro products, initially designed for men or without gender restrictions, are actually consumed mainly by women. This conveys a signal: independent women are eager to break free from gender constraints, and men also need to transcend the limitations imposed by gender awareness. As Hong Dan previously stated, a person's temperament is not determined by gender but by their energy. Chinese modern society's values are becoming increasingly diverse, and young people have shed ideological constraints. With the gradual rise of women's power and the transformation of men's mindset, both are breaking through themselves and striving to experience the state of freedom attainable as a "human." In this state, they have no internal gender restrictions, accept the diversification of life states, and thereby balance their yin and yang energy states, which is what Yongheng refers to as "the most primitive and natural state of integration within human unity."

Here, I must mention an exciting phenomenon: this group of young people who love boro have had awakening consciousness very early on, and their consumption of boro patchwork clothing reveals their state of cultivation. More surprisingly, the female group is larger than the male group, with earlier awakening and more advanced aesthetic awareness. The emerging female economy in China may be a pivotal force in promoting the upward shift of social collective consciousness in the twenty-first century.

Notes

1 Leren Li, "Reviving boro: The Transcultural Reconstruction of Japanese Patchwork," Ph.D. diss., History of Design, Royal College of Art/Victoria and Albert Museum, June 2020, 26.

2 Hong Dan, Interview with Wang Shuhua, Personal Interview, Kaili, China, July 15, 2024.

3 Hong Dan, Interview with Wang Shuhua, Personal Interview, Kaili, China, July 15, 2024.

4 Claudia Brush Kidwell and Valerie Steele, *Men and Women: Dressing the Part*, Washington, DC: Smithsonian Institution Press, 1989.

5 J. B. Paoletti and Claudia Brush Kidwell, "Conclusion," ibid.

6 Zhou Sha, Interview with Wang Shuhua, Personal Interview, Xiaogan, China, July 25, 2024.

7 Tanaka Chuzaburo, Exhibition Introduction, BORO&BAINA Invitation Exhibition, Special Exhibition in the Museum Collection of AMUSE MUSEUM "BORO" in Tokyo. December 14, 2019–March 1, 2020. Shenzhen Academy of Fine Arts Museum, Shenzhen, China.

8 Interview with Yongheng, Conducted by Wang Shuhua, Personal Interview, Dali, China, July 30, 2024.

Bibliography

Chuzaburo, Tanaka. Exhibition Introduction. BORO&BAINA Invitation Exhibition, Special Exhibition in the Museum Collection of AMUSE MUSEUM "BORO" in Tokyo. December 14, 2019–March 1, 2020. Shenzhen Academy of Fine Arts Museum, Shenzhen, China.

Kidwell, Claudia Brush, and Valerie Steele, eds. *Men and Women: Dressing the Part*. Washington, DC: Smithsonian Institution Press, 1989.

Li, Leren. "Reviving Boro: The Transcultural Reconstruction of Japanese Patchwork." Ph.D. diss., History of Design, Royal College of Art/Victoria and Albert Museum, June 2020, 26.

Paoletti, J. B. and Claudia Brush Kidwell. "Conclusion." In *Men and Women: Dressing the Part*, ed. Claudia Brush Kidwell and Valerie Steele. Washington, DC: Smithsonian Institution Press, 1989, 158.

3

From Roots to Runways: Unveiling Greenwashing Trends in the Thai Fashion Industry—a Melange of Tradition and Contemporary Consciousness

QUEEN SARKAR

Introduction

The fashion industry has increasingly recognized the importance of sustainability and environmental responsibility, driven by a growing consumer demand for environmentally friendly products. As fashion brands strive to adopt sustainable practices within their supply chains, they face the dual challenge of meeting consumer expectations while navigating the complexities of production and marketing.[1] However, the growing interest in sustainability has also given rise to greenwashing, a practice whereby companies employ marketing strategies to portray their products or operations as eco-friendly, despite a lack of substantive environmental benefits.[2]

Greenwashing is prevalent across various industries, including cosmetics, food and beverages,[3] energy,[4] electronics,[5] retail,[6] and notably, fashion.[7] The fast fashion sector, in particular, has garnered significant attention for its contributions to clothing waste and environmental degradation.[8] Some fast fashion brands have faced allegations of greenwashing, asserting the use of organic cotton and recyclable materials in select garments while adhering to a business model predicated on rapid consumption and disposability.[9] The actions of a few brands can undermine the credibility of the entire industry.[10]

Fast fashion is characterized by efficient and rapid supply chains designed to create stylish goods that meet consumer demand within a limited timeframe.[11] These products often have short life cycles, as retailers frequently update their inventory to satisfy consumer desire for new designs, resulting in a high turnover of products.[12] Despite claims of sustainability—such as labels indicating "100% recycled polyester"—it is essential to recognize that polyester is a plastic material that is not biodegradable and contributes to microplastic pollution.[13] The practice of greenwashing fosters consumer distrust and skepticism.[14] Green skepticism emerges as a significant factor influencing consumer behavior, particularly in assessing the credibility of sustainability claims. When consumers perceive inconsistencies in claims or lack supporting evidence, they may develop skepticism toward corporate sustainability messaging.[15] This skepticism can lead to negative word-of-mouth recommendations, further undermining a brand's reputation.[16]

The concept of green word-of-mouth (GWOM) remains a compelling area of study, as consumers tend to regard information shared through GWOM as more credible than direct marketing assertions from companies.[17] Experiences and recommendations from peers often carry more weight, encouraging companies to innovate in developing environmentally friendly products and services.[18] However, previous research has established that greenwashing can severely damage a brand's reputation and diminish consumer trust in its sustainability claims.[19]

In Thailand, the rapid growth of the fast fashion sector has a significant impact on the environment. International brands like H&M, Zara, and Uniqlo have expanded their presence in major cities, becoming increasingly popular due to their latest designs and affordability. However, this growth contributes to rising waste levels, which pose environmental challenges. According to the Ministry of Environment and Forestry, textile waste accounted for 2.8 percent of the total waste volume in Indonesia in 2023.[20] Although this percentage may seem small, the trend in clothing disposal is expected to increase, subsequently heightening the volume of clothing waste.

As some companies claim to be "green" or "eco-friendly," research on greenwashing becomes critical in evaluating whether these claims are substantiated by real actions or simply marketing ploys. This research aims to investigate the intricate dynamics between greenwashing, green skepticism, and negative green word-of-mouth (NGWOM) within the Thai fashion industry. The primary focus is to assess whether greenwashing influences NGWOM, particularly by examining how exaggerated or false sustainability claims lead to consumer distrust and negative brand perceptions. Additionally, the study explores the role of green skepticism, investigating whether consumer doubt over sustainability claims further exacerbates NGWOM, potentially impacting a brand's reputation. Beyond the consumer behavior aspect, the research also delves into the broader tensions between tradition and modernity within the fashion industry. It examines whether traditional Thai craftsmanship can coexist with contemporary sustainability practices, balancing cultural authenticity with the demands of a globalized and eco-conscious market. Finally, the study seeks to discern how genuine sustainability efforts can be differentiated from greenwashing, offering a path forward for the Thai fashion industry to maintain cultural heritage while moving toward a more transparent and sustainable future.

Attitudes and Behaviors Towards Sustainable Fashion

Sustainable fashion encompasses a range of terms, such as eco-fashion, ethical fashion, green fashion, conscious fashion, and responsible fashion. This diversity of terminology has contributed to consumer confusion regarding what constitutes a truly sustainable fashion brand. As a result, the concept of 'sustainability' has become overly generalized, leading to misunderstandings among consumers.[21] Despite this confusion, there exists an expectation among consumers for companies and governments to adopt socially and environmentally responsible practices. However, this expectation often conflicts with their own commitment to responsible consumption. This discrepancy has been identified as the "attitude-behavior gap," a phenomenon whereby positive attitudes toward sustainability do not translate into actual purchasing behaviors. In the fashion industry, this gap is frequently referred to as "the fashion paradox," reflecting a disconnect between consumer intentions and actions.[22] Research indicates that many consumers possess limited knowledge of sustainable fashion, making it challenging for them to differentiate between sustainable and non-sustainable brands.[23] Additionally, studies suggest that positive attitudes toward sustainability and increased awareness of the fashion industry's environmental impact do not necessarily influence purchasing decisions for sustainable products. In fact, some scholars argue that consumer behavior is more heavily influenced by established habits than by awareness of sustainable practices employed by brands.[24]

A significant barrier to purchasing sustainable fashion products is the perception that these items are priced higher than conventional alternatives. Furthermore, consumers often perceive sustainable fashion as less fashionable or stylish, which further deters them from making such purchases. Research has demonstrated that consumers are reluctant to compromise on style or comfort for the sake of sustainability.[25] Additionally, trust issues surrounding companies and their sustainability claims contribute to consumer skepticism. This lack of trust, coupled with the perception of higher prices and limited availability, often leads consumers to favor second-hand options or rental services over new sustainable purchases.[26]

The Phenomenon of Greenwashing

The term "greenwashing" was introduced by environmentalist Jay Westerveld in 1986 to describe deceptive marketing practices used by companies to exaggerate their environmental efforts.[27] Scholars define greenwashing as the practice of falsely promoting an organization's environmental initiatives, often investing more in marketing claims than in sustainable practices. It encompasses various misleading communications and actions that create false perceptions of an organization's environmental performance.[28]

Greenwashing can manifest at two levels: the product/service level, where misleading claims about ecological benefits are made, and the execution level, where visual or auditory elements evoke nature to mislead consumers. Such vague communication strategies can generate confusion, mistrust, and consumer disloyalty. It represents an implicit form of deception, as consumers may misinterpret sustainability claims, leading to positive inferences about products that do not reflect their actual environmental impact.[29]

Greenwashing in the Fast Fashion Industry

Fast fashion is characterized as readily available, affordably produced fashion that encourages a culture of disposability.[30] This business model stands in stark contrast to sustainable practices aimed at combating textile waste and promoting the longevity of clothing. Despite the push for sustainability, many fast fashion brands have launched marketing campaigns that highlight their use of organic materials or promote eco-friendly sub-brands. However, these efforts have not entirely alleviated consumer skepticism. Despite positive marketing strategies, many consumers remain doubtful of fast fashion companies' sustainability claims. Between 2019 and 2022, the frequency of greenwashing-related discussions in traditional media and social networks has significantly increased, with the fashion industry being a primary target of scrutiny. Recent reports highlight greenwashing as one of the foremost challenges facing the fashion sector, especially among fast fashion brands.[31] The growing complexity of misleading environmental claims has drawn attention to the negative impacts of greenwashing on corporate reputation and consumer trust.[32]

In response to these challenges, the European Commission has introduced measures to curb greenwashing practices, mandating that sustainability claims made by companies must be substantiated and verified by independent authorities. This regulatory shift raises important questions about consumer perceptions of greenwashing and whether these perceptions correlate with specific attitudes and behaviors regarding sustainability and media consumption.

Methodology

This study employs a multidimensional methodology to explore the intricate relationships between greenwashing, green skepticism, and negative green word-of-mouth in the context of the Thai fashion industry. The primary objectives of this research include assessing whether greenwashing affects NGWOM, examining the influence of green skepticism on NGWOM, and exploring the tensions between tradition and modernity, as well as authenticity and commercial viability within the realm of sustainable practices in fashion. The methodology comprises several key components.

Comprehensive Analysis of Sustainable Initiatives

The research begins with a thorough examination of existing sustainable initiatives within the Thai fashion industry. This involves an analysis of various brands and designers that have publicly committed to sustainable practices. Thailand, with its long-standing membership in the World Trade Organization (WTO) since 1995, is transitioning toward a bio-circular green economic model, moving away from conventional manufacturing techniques. This shift is supported by the latest trade policy review conducted by the United Nations Environment Programme (UNEP), titled *Sustainable and Circular Textile Value Chains: Linkages with Trade and Trade Policy*.[33] The UNEP study underscores the critical role of trade policy instruments in fostering a more sustainable and circular textile sector. Notable strides have been made in this direction, particularly with the removal of tariffs on clean technologies aimed at encouraging the adoption of environmentally friendly practices among textile manufacturers. For instance, the elimination of tariffs for waste water treatment machines in January 2013 and solar cells in 2007 has significantly contributed to their affordability and widespread use. Additionally, the policy extends zero tariffs to worn clothing, although it highlights the need for more consistent support for energy-efficient products, particularly noting the existing high tariffs on LED products at 40 percent.[34]

In addition to tariff adjustments, Thailand has implemented a series of environmental standards and regulations tailored to the manufacturing industry, including specific guidelines for textile factories. These measures are designed to enhance energy efficiency, foster energy conservation, and minimize pollution. The UNEP study details technical regulations on the use of dyes that align with the Thai Industrial Standards for synthetic dye stuffs, ensuring compliance with environmental norms.

The adoption of eco-labels has also seen an uptick among Thai textile exporters, leveraging voluntary sustainability labels such as the Global Organic Textile Standard (GOTS), Green Label: Thailand, the EU Ecolabel, and the Bluesign standard. These eco-labels are commonly known as "eco-label jungle."[35] These certifications significantly facilitate access to the global market for Thai producers, despite challenges such as a limited certification range, complex processes, and insufficient awareness of the benefits associated with these labels.

Further enhancing its commitment to sustainable textile production, Thailand has embraced non-tariff measures for imported textile products, including stringent labeling requirements for medical textiles to ensure safety and quality. The country's proactive investment management policies, including incentives offered by the Board of Investment (BOI) and Special Economic Zones (SEZs) such as the Eastern Economic Corridor (EEC), aim to attract foreign investments in high-tech and innovative textile industries. These policies not only support the country's environmental goals but also its ambition to become a regional hub for textiles, fostering innovation in areas such as functional textiles, biomass energy, and compliance with international environmental standards.

Thailand's integration into the global value chain is further supported by its participation in the Regional Comprehensive Economic Partnership (RCEP), the world's largest free trade agreement, which simplifies trade rules and fosters economic cooperation within the block. Through these initiatives, Thailand is positioning itself as a leader in sustainable textile production while preserving its rich cultural heritage. Thai sustainable fashion brands are making significant contributions to these initiatives. Brands such as Taktai,[36] FolkCharm,[37] and Bhukram[38] exemplify how traditional craftsmanship can coexist with sustainability practices.

Taktai is known for using bamboo fibers, a sustainable alternative to conventional textiles, promoting eco-friendly production processes. FolkCharm specializes in handwoven organic cotton produced by local artisans, emphasizing fair trade and ethical production practices. Bhukram integrates natural dyes and traditional weaving techniques with modern designs, contributing to eco-conscious fashion while preserving local craftsmanship. Other notable brands include Rotsaniyom,[39] which incorporates recycled fabrics and materials into its designs to reduce waste, and Patapian,[40] which focuses on handcrafted products made from natural materials like bamboo and rattan. These brands demonstrate Thailand's ability to merge traditional techniques with modern sustainable practices, positioning the country as a leader in eco-conscious fashion.

Additionally, Thailand is increasingly recognized not only for its traditional textile mills but also for its innovations in developing new types of materials. Among these advancements are solar-powered fabrics and textiles designed to be resistant to dust and mites, positioning Thailand as a pivotal player in the textile industry. Significant investments are being funneled into the creation of new synthetic fibers, while exciting combinations of natural ingredients are emerging in textile production. For instance, some fabrics harness the antimicrobial properties of coconut and charcoal, showcasing the country's commitment to blending innovation with sustainability.

Trend Analysis

Growth of Sustainable Fashion in Thailand

The rise of sustainable fashion in Thailand has been gradual but significant. Urban consumers, especially in cities like Bangkok, are becoming increasingly aware of the environmental and social impact of their fashion choices, reflecting global trends of ethical consumption. This shift is fueled by a combination of factors, including rising consumer awareness, global environmental movements, and the Thai government's initiatives aimed at fostering sustainability across various industries, including textiles.

One prominent example is Thailand's move towards embracing the Bio-Circular-Green (BCG)[41] economy model. The BCG model, which is part of the country's national agenda, encourages industries to adopt practices that are not only economically viable but also environmentally and socially responsible. This framework has had a direct influence on the textile and fashion sectors by promoting the use of recycled materials, reducing waste, and encouraging sustainable production processes.

Consumer and Greenwashing Awareness

A survey by Mintel in 2022 reveals that 60 percent of Thai consumers expressed concern about the environmental impact of their clothing choices. However, only 20 percent felt confident in identifying genuinely sustainable products, pointing to widespread confusion caused by greenwashing. Mintel also reports that younger consumers (aged 18–34) are particularly influenced by sustainability claims, but they are also the demographic most critical of superficial greenwashing practices.[42] Moreover, it has also been noted that nearly 40 percent of Thai consumers expressed frustration with brands that falsely advertise sustainability. They prefer transparent communication regarding sourcing, production, and labor practices. The lack of clear certification systems adds to the complexity, as many consumers rely on brand marketing rather than third-party verification to assess sustainability claims.

Fashion Week and Public Perspective

Siam Paragon solidifies its status as a "World-Class Fashion Destination" by showcasing Thai fashion, a vital aspect of the country's soft power. This achievement is celebrated through the prestigious Siam Paragon Bangkok International Fashion Week 2023 (BIFW2023). Under the theme "The Future of Fashion," this event highlights sustainability as a crucial driver for the flourishing future of the fashion industry. BIFW2023 was a remarkable success, featuring twelve captivating shows from leading Thai brands, held from October 5–8, 2023, at Parc Paragon, Siam Paragon. The lineup included top

Thai fashion brands showcasing their creative talents, such as Absolute Siam x Holy Number 7 x 789, Flynow, FRI27NOV, presented by SCG, Greyhound Original x TikTok, ISSUE presented by Purra, Kloset, Leisure Projects presented by Crocs, MOO, Nagara, PAINKILLER Atelier presented by Seiko 5 Sports, TUBE GALLERY presented by TAT, and VATANIKA presented by AION – AIONIC AUTO. Each of the twelve shows debuted exclusive collections, with many Thai designers actively embracing the sustainability concept, reflecting a significant trend and essential goal in the global fashion landscape.[43] However, according to a post-event analysis by Elle Thailand, some participating brands were found to engage in greenwashing. While they claimed to use sustainable materials, independent analysis revealed that a significant portion of these materials were synthetically blended, negating much of the environmental benefit.

Survey

To give the research a cosmopolitan perspective, we designed a survey with the undergraduate students of the School of Economics & Commerce (KSEC), Kalinga Institute of Industrial Technology (KIIT), Bhubaneswar, India. The decision to survey undergraduate students from KIIT regarding the sustainability trends and greenwashing in Thai fashion stems from several pertinent factors that connect Indian consumers and future professionals to the global fashion industry, particularly in Southeast Asia. Indian consumers, including students, have become increasingly aware of sustainable fashion due to the global fashion industry's influence, proximity to Southeast Asia, and their exposure to fast fashion and high-end sustainable brands. Thailand and India share cultural and geographical proximity, which enhances cross-border consumption of fashion trends and sustainability discourses. Undergraduate students, particularly those studying commerce, fashion, and related disciplines, represent the next generation of consumers and professionals who will either drive or challenge these trends in both domestic and global contexts. Their awareness, perceptions, and attitudes toward greenwashing and sustainability in fashion offer critical insights into emerging consumer behavior, industry expectations, and potential educational gaps in understanding sustainability. The survey was designed with fifteen questions focusing on three primary areas:

Awareness of Sustainable Fashion: Questions aimed to measure students' understanding of sustainable practices and greenwashing within the fashion industry.
Perception of Thai Fashion: Questions to gauge how students perceive Thai fashion, especially regarding its sustainability claims.
Consumer Behavior: Questions to assess how sustainability influences students' purchasing decisions, including their ability to differentiate between genuine sustainability and greenwashing.

Table 3.1 Awareness of Sustainable Fashion Among Undergraduate Students

Awareness Level	**Percentage**
Very familiar	25%
Somewhat familiar	50%
Not familiar at all	25%

Analysis: A majority (75%) of students were at least somewhat familiar with the concept of sustainable fashion, reflecting the growing global awareness of sustainability issues among the younger generation. This suggests that students are well positioned to critically engage with the fashion industry's sustainability claims, including those made by Thai brands.

Table 3.2 Perception of Difficulty in Identifying Greenwashing

Difficulty Level	**Percentage**
Very easy	5%
Somewhat easy	15%
Difficult	45%
Very difficult	25%
Impossible	10%

Analysis: The results show that most students (80%) found it difficult to identify greenwashing in fashion. This aligns with industry observations that consumers, especially younger ones, struggle to differentiate between genuinely sustainable practices and misleading marketing efforts. This emphasizes the need for clearer labeling and transparency in sustainability claims, both in Thailand and internationally.

Table 3.3 Importance of Traditional Craftsmanship in Sustainable Fashion

Response	Percentage
Yes	70%
No	10%
Maybe	20%

Analysis: A significant portion (70%) of students believe that traditional craftsmanship should be preserved within modern sustainable fashion. This resonates with the research's focus on the interplay between tradition and contemporary practices in Thai fashion, suggesting that students value the preservation of cultural heritage alongside modern sustainability efforts. Thai fashion, with its rich tradition of craftsmanship, stands at a critical juncture where balancing both elements can distinguish genuine sustainability from mere marketing tactics.

Table 3.4 Frequency of Purchasing Sustainable Fashion

Frequency	Percentage
Always	10%
Often	30%
Sometimes	40%
Rarely	15%
Never	5%

Analysis: The majority of students (70%) sometimes or often purchase sustainable fashion, suggesting a growing market for such products among young consumers. This finding is particularly relevant to the Thai fashion industry, where sustainability is increasingly marketed. However, the relatively low percentage of students who always purchase sustainable fashion (10%) indicates that greenwashing might still affect their confidence in making consistent eco-friendly choices.

Table 3.5 Role of Educational Institutions in Raising Awareness

Agreement Level	**Percentage**
Strongly agree	40%
Agree	30%
Neutral	20%
Disagree	5%
Strongly disagree	5%

Analysis: A majority of respondents (70%) believe that educational institutions should play an active role in raising awareness about sustainable fashion. This underlines the importance of incorporating sustainability education into university curricula to equip future consumers and professionals with the skills to critically assess sustainability claims and combat greenwashing.

Textual Analysis of Designer Portfolios

This section outlines a systematic textual analysis[44] of prominent Thai fashion designers, focusing on their sustainability claims and practices. As noted in our earlier trend analysis, there is increasing consumer demand for eco-conscious fashion in Thailand. However, the gap between claims and practices raises concerns about greenwashing in the industry. This textual analysis provides a clearer picture of the extent to which these brands genuinely adhere to sustainability principles. By analyzing public portfolios, websites, and marketing materials, we seek to evaluate their transparency, alignment with sustainable fashion practices, and potential greenwashing. The findings from this textual analysis are contextualized using data and reports from reputable sources such as the Fashion Transparency Index 2022[45] and Global Fashion Agenda.[46]

The selection of sustainable designers was guided by multiple considerations. A primary factor was the purchasing behavior and inclinations of our study participants—the undergraduate students, specially from the KIIT School of Fashion Technology, Bhubaneswar—who actively engage with these brands as consumers. Their exposure to and perception of sustainability in fashion played a crucial role in determining the relevance of these designers to the study. Moreover, the designers chosen have established significant market visibility through strategic branding, eco-labeling, and aesthetic markers associated with sustainability, such as the frequent use of green hues, floral motifs and nature-inspired imagery, and website (content). This performative sustainability, which aligns with broader industry trends in greenwashing, provided a compelling basis for investigation. Additionally, direct engagement with these brands at the Thailand Shopping Festival, held annually in Mumbai and Hyderabad, further informed the selection. This festival serves as a commercial and cultural exchange platform, featuring a diverse range of Thai products, including garments, accessories, Thai silk, herbal cosmetics, and decorative items. First-hand exposure to these designers' offerings and marketing strategies underscored the necessity of critically examining the gap between sustainability claims and actual practices. Here are some brands to look at:

Sretsis

Sretsis[47] claims to draw inspiration from nature, using eco-conscious narratives in their branding. However, our analysis of their publicly available materials shows little detail on sustainable sourcing or third-party certifications. According to the Fashion Transparency Index (2023),[48] Sretsis indicated poor transparency about their supply chain, use of materials, and environmental impact.

Greenwashing indicators: The brand makes broad sustainability claims without sufficient verification. No certifications such as GOTS[49] were mentioned in their disclosures, reflecting potential greenwashing.

Asava

Asava markets its brand as one of sustainable luxury, citing the use of high-quality, long-lasting materials.[50] However, the lack of detailed data on material sourcing or production processes raises questions. Asava also received a low transparency score in the Fashion Transparency Index (2023), which further emphasizes the opacity of their environmental practices.

Connection to greenwashing: Despite promoting sustainable luxury, Asava's claims are largely unsupported by external audits or data. This mirrors a broader trend identified in Eco-Business 2022, where many brands emphasize sustainability but offer little substantiation.

Disaya

Disaya distinguishes itself by highlighting its use of locally sourced organic materials and traditional craftsmanship.[51] Our analysis reveals that the brand does provide more detailed sustainability efforts than most Thai designers. Disaya's transparency score of 38 percent in the Fashion Transparency Index (2023) places it ahead of competitors, though gaps remain regarding external certification.

Partial authenticity: Disaya's portfolio includes tangible sustainability efforts, particularly in promoting local artisanship. However, the absence of comprehensive third-party certifications like Fair Trade raises questions about the overall impact of their sustainability efforts.

TANACHIRA Group[52]

The TANACHIRA Group, which manages brands like Pandora, prominently advertises its use of recycled materials. However, despite these claims, their transparency score in the Fashion Transparency Index (2023) is below average, at 30 percent. The lack of detailed reports on labor practices and material sourcing further suggests that their sustainability claims may be overstated.

Greenwashing trend: TANACHIRA's claims of using eco-friendly materials are not consistently backed by verifiable data or external audits—a common issue seen across global fashion brands.

Janesuda

Unlike other brands, Janesuda shows a stronger commitment to sustainability, utilizing GOTS-certified organic cotton and collaborating with local artisans. This brand demonstrates genuine efforts toward environmental responsibility and earned a higher transparency score of 45 percent in the Fashion Transparency Index (2023).

Authentic sustainability: Janesuda's portfolio reflects a more serious commitment to sustainable practices, including the use of certified organic materials and transparent communication about production processes.[53]

The textual analysis[54] reveals a mixed landscape in Thai fashion. While some brands like Janesuda exhibit genuine sustainability efforts, others, such as Sretsis and Asava, seem to capitalize on the demand for eco-friendly fashion without providing sufficient transparency or third-party verification. The Fashion Transparency Index (2023) results align with global concerns about greenwashing, where only 17 percent of global brands disclose their entire supply chains, indicating that much of the industry still lacks accountability in its sustainability claims. These findings emphasize the need for more rigorous standards and transparency to address the growing issue of greenwashing in fashion.

Findings and Summary: Textual Analysis of Designer Portfolios

The textual analysis of designer portfolios within the Thai fashion industry presents a nuanced landscape, where brands increasingly capitalize on sustainability narratives. However, many of these claims lack the depth and transparency needed to substantiate their environmental responsibility, indicating greenwashing tendencies. This analysis, aligned with the earlier trend analysis, reveals that while Thai fashion designers such as Sretsis and Asava employ eco-friendly rhetoric, their practices are often superficial.

In contrast, brands like Janesuda show more tangible efforts toward sustainability, with a higher score on the Fashion Transparency Index.

Janesuda's use of GOTS-certified materials and its collaboration with local artisans demonstrate an authentic commitment to sustainable fashion. However, even Janesuda's efforts are not without gaps, particularly in areas such as labor rights transparency and third-party audits, as noted in the GOTS public database. This variation in commitment to sustainability underscores the complex relationship between fashion, culture, and environmental responsibility in Thailand.

When these findings are connected to the KIIT student survey, a clearer picture emerges of how global perceptions of greenwashing impact consumer behavior in neighboring markets like India. The survey, conducted among undergraduate students, revealed that 75 percent of respondents were aware of greenwashing in fashion, and the rest had experienced brands whose sustainability claims they perceived as exaggerated or misleading. This level of awareness is crucial because it illustrates how even consumers outside Thailand, particularly younger, more environmentally conscious demographics, are directly influenced by global fashion trends. According to Statista's 2023 Consumer Insights, a similar trend has been observed worldwide, where younger generations, particularly in South and Southeast Asia, increasingly demand transparency and accountability from fashion brands. The alignment between the KIIT student survey and the findings from the textual analysis of Thai designer portfolios highlights the broader issue of greenwashing in the fashion industry. While the demand for sustainable fashion is growing, both in Thailand and globally, the lack of verifiable, transparent practices undermines consumer trust. As demonstrated by the Thai fashion industry's engagement in superficial sustainability claims, it becomes clear that a shift towards more authentic and accountable practices is needed to meet the expectations of both local and global consumers.

Navigating the Tensions in Thai Fashion: Tradition, Sustainability, and Globalization

The Thai fashion industry finds itself at a pivotal moment where traditional craftsmanship, modern sustainability initiatives, and the pressures of globalization converge. This study explores how these seemingly divergent forces can coexist and lead to a more conscious and transparent industry that both preserves Thailand's cultural heritage and charts a path toward a greener future. We address key questions: Can traditional craftsmanship coexist with contemporary sustainability practices? How does Thai fashion reconcile the demands of a globalized market with local cultural values? And how can we distinguish genuine sustainability from greenwashing in the evolving landscape of Asian fashion?

The integration of traditional craftsmanship within sustainable frameworks is exemplified by DoiTung, a brand embedded in the social enterprise model of the Mae Fah Luang Foundation. For over three decades, DoiTung has sought to transform perceptions of Thai handwoven fabrics through its latest "Everyday" collection, which marries cultural heritage with modern aesthetics. This collection not only underscores a commitment to sustainability but also embodies a distinctive and contemporary design ethos. The brand's guiding philosophy, "An Enterprise for a Better World," is predicated on the inquiry, "What do the community, society, and the environment gain?" This approach exemplifies how traditional craftsmanship can be revitalized to meet modern consumer demands without sacrificing cultural authenticity.[55] As Thai fashion navigates the complexities of globalization, maintaining local cultural values is paramount. Designers such as Chai Jiamkittikul highlight the importance of artisan collaboration in preserving local craftsmanship. By engaging directly with artisans, Jiamkittikul ensures that traditional techniques are not only maintained but also innovatively adapted for contemporary audiences. This collaborative approach serves as a model for the Thai fashion industry, demonstrating how cultural integrity can coexist with commercial viability.[56]

Additionally, Her Royal Highness Princess Sirivannavari Nariratana Rajakanya plays a pivotal role in promoting Thai textiles among younger generations.[57] Drawing inspiration from the legacy of Her Majesty Queen Sirikit, the Princess actively supports local artisans and fosters a new mindset among villagers, urging them to create versatile designs suitable for all ages. Collaborating with prominent designers such as Polpat "Moo Asava" Asavaprapha and Kullawit "Ford" Laosuksri, the Princess's initiatives are crucial for bridging the gap between traditional techniques and contemporary fashion demands.[58]

Distinguishing Genuine Sustainability from Greenwashing

The quest for sustainability in fashion often encounters the challenge of distinguishing authentic practices from greenwashing. The Thai fashion industry is not exempt from this scrutiny. Brands must transparently communicate their sustainability efforts to avoid misleading consumers. Stella McCartney,[59] while not Thai, exemplifies best practices in sustainability. Since establishing her eponymous brand in 2001, McCartney has championed ethical fashion by eschewing leather and fur, instead opting for eco-friendly materials such as organic cotton and regenerated cashmere.[60] Her commitment to reducing the carbon footprint through circularity and transparency sets a benchmark for the fashion industry. In the same vein, Christopher Raeburn has emerged as a leading advocate for sustainable practices through his focus on upcycling military surplus materials. By repurposing discarded textiles into contemporary menswear, Raeburn demonstrates that sustainability and creativity can coexist, significantly minimizing waste in the process. His emphasis on ethical manufacturing practices further underscores the importance of transparency in the fashion supply chain.[61]

The inquiry into whether traditional craftsmanship can coexist with contemporary sustainability practices reveals that such integration is not only possible but essential for the evolution of the Thai fashion industry. Traditional Thai craftsmanship, characterized by intricate handwoven textiles and artisanal techniques, carries deep cultural significance. However, as the global fashion landscape shifts toward sustainability, these practices must adapt to meet contemporary demands without losing their authenticity. By merging traditional methods with sustainable practices, Thai fashion can create a unique niche that respects cultural heritage while addressing environmental concerns.

As the demand for sustainable fashion rises, consumers must be vigilant against greenwashing, in cases where brands exaggerate or misrepresent their environmental efforts. Key indicators of greenwashing include vague or misleading language and irrelevant claims. Terms like "natural" or "eco-friendly" are often used without clear definitions, making it essential for consumers to seek specifics.[62] A brand that asserts its products are "eco-friendly" without providing concrete data or certifications from recognized sustainability organizations raises a red flag. Additionally, brands may promote being "cruelty-free" for products that never involved animal testing in the first place, indicating that such claims may be irrelevant to the product's actual environmental impact.

Consumers should also be cautious of hidden trade-offs: a product made from "recycled plastic" may still contribute to overall plastic pollution if it does not address its entire life cycle.[63] This necessitates a holistic consideration of a product's environmental impact, from sourcing raw materials to disposal. The visual appeal of products, often enhanced by images of nature, can be misleading. While aesthetically pleasing packaging featuring breathtaking landscapes or pictures of leaves may suggest sustainability, it does not inherently equate to genuine eco-friendly practices. Therefore, delving deeper into a company's environmental initiatives is critical to discerning the truth behind its claims.[64]

Lack of transparency is another significant warning sign. Companies genuinely committed to sustainability are typically eager to share detailed information about their practices, certifications, and goals. Brands that make ambiguous claims without readily available supporting evidence should be approached with skepticism. On the other hand, reputable companies publish comprehensive sustainability reports that outline their environmental and social impact, detailing progress toward established goals and highlighting ongoing initiatives.

Implications for Future Research

The exploration of traditional craftsmanship and contemporary sustainability in the Thai fashion industry invites a range of dynamic and innovative avenues for future research. One promising area is the impact of technological advancements on traditional textile production methods. As digital technologies, such as 3D printing and AI-driven design tools, emerge, researchers could investigate how these innovations can be integrated with traditional practices to create sustainable solutions. This includes examining how technology can enhance efficiency, reduce waste, and preserve artisan techniques while appealing to a modern consumer base.

Conclusion

In an era where the fashion industry faces increasing scrutiny over its environmental and social impacts, the demand for transparency has never been more critical. As consumers become more discerning, they seek not just products but narratives—stories that resonate with their values and reflect a genuine commitment to sustainability. This transformation challenges brands to move beyond superficial eco-labels and engage in authentic dialogues about their practices and impacts. Transparency is not merely a compliance measure, it is an ethical imperative that fosters trust and loyalty. It compels brands to disclose their supply chains, share their sustainability metrics, and engage openly with the communities they affect. Such openness empowers consumers to make informed choices and supports artisans who pour their heart and soul into their craft. When brands embrace transparency, they not only demonstrate accountability but also celebrate the rich tapestry of traditions that define their heritage. Moreover, in the fight against greenwashing, the responsibility lies with both producers and consumers. Brands must be held accountable for their claims, while consumers should cultivate a critical eye and seek authenticity in the products they support. This reciprocal relationship can reshape the marketplace, driving demand for genuine sustainability over mere marketing gimmicks.

Notes

1 F. Lemke and J. P. P. Luzio, "Exploring Green Consumers' Mind-set Toward Green Product Design and Life Cycle Assessment: The Case of Skeptical Brazilian and Portuguese Green Consumers Lemke and Luzio Exploring Green Consumers' Mind-set Toward Design and LCA," *Journal of Industrial Ecology* 18 (5): 2014, 619–30. https://doi.org/10.1111/ jiec.12123

2 Y.-S. Chen, C.-L. Lin, and C.-H. Chang, "The Influence of Greenwash on Green Word-of-Mouth (Green WOM): The Mediation Effects of Green Perceived Quality and Green Satisfaction," *Quality & Quantity* 48 (5): 2014, 2411–25. https:// doi.org/10.1007/ s11135-013-9898-1

3 J. Guerreiro and M. Pacheco, "How Green Trust, Consumer Brand Engagement and Green Word-of-Mouth Mediate Purchasing Intentions," *Sustainability* 13 (14): 2021, 7877. https://doi.org/10.3390/su13147877

4 Y. Farooq and H. Wicaksono, "Advancing on the Analysis of Causes and Consequences of Green Skepticism," *Journal of Cleaner Production* 320: August 2021, 128927. https://doi.org/10.1016/j.jclepro.2021.128927

5 Chen, Lin, and Chang, "The influence of greenwash."

6 S. B. Junior, M. P. Martínez, C. M. Correa, R. C. Moura-Leite, and D. Da Silva, "Greenwashing Effect, Attitudes, and Beliefs in Green Consumption," *RAUSP Management Journal* 54 (2): 2019, 226–41. https://doi.org/10.1108/RAUSP-08-2018-0070; E. Keller and B. Fay, "Word-of-mouth advocacy," *Journal of Advertising Research* 52 (4): 2012, 459–64. https://doi. org/10.2501/JAR-52-4-459-464

7 S. Munir and V. Mohan, "Consumer Perceptions of Greenwashing: Lessons Learned from the Fashion Sector in the UAE. *Asian Journal of Business Ethics* 11 (1): 2022, 1–44. https://doi.org/10.1007/s13520-021-00140-z

8 T. Mysirli and D. Axarli, "Effects of Greenwashing on the Markets of the Western World," HAPSc *Policy Briefs Series* 2 (2): 2021, 95. https://doi.org/10.12681/hapscpbs.29496

9 The Changing Markets Foundation, "Licence to Greenwash," 2022. *https://changingmarkets.org/report/licence-to-greenwash-how-certification-schemes-and-voluntary-initiatives-are-fuelling-fossil-fashion/*

10 Munir and Mohan, "Consumer Perceptions of Greenwashing."

11 S. Byun and B. Sternquist, "Fast Fashion and In-store Hoarding: The Drivers, Moderator, and Consequences," *Clothing and Textiles Research Journal* 29 (3): 2011. https://doi.org/10.1177/0887302X11411709

12 L. McNeill and R. Moore, "Sustainable Fashion Consumption and the Fast Fashion Conundrum: Fashionable Consumers and Attitudes to Sustainability in Clothing Choice," *International Journal of Consumer Studies* 39 (3): 2015, 212–22. https://doi.org/10.1111/ijcs.12169

13 Greenpeace, "Greenwash Danger Zone Report: 10 Years After Rana Plaza Fashion Labels Conceal a Broken System," 2023. https://www.greenpeace.de/publikationen/Greenpeace_Report_Greenwash_Danger_Zone.pdf

14 H. M. Aji and B. Sutikno, "The Extended Consequence of Greenwashing: Perceived Consumer Skepticism," *International Journal of Business and Information* 10 (4): 2015, 433–69. http://52.68.60.251/ojs/index.php/ijbi/article/ view/127

15 L. Zhang, D. Li, C. Cao, and S. Huang, "The Influence of Greenwashing Perception on Green Purchasing Intentions: The Mediating Role of Green Word-of-Mouth and Moderating Role of Green Concern, *Journal of Cleaner Production* 187: 2018, 740–50. https://doi.org/10.1016/j.jclepro.2018.03.201

16 C. N. Leonidou and D. Skarmeas, "Gray Shades of Green: Causes and Consequences of Green Skepticism," *Journal of Business Ethics* 144 (2): 2017, 401–15. https://doi. org/10.1007/s10551-015-2829-4

17 E. Keller and B. Fay, "Word-of-Mouth Advocacy," *Journal of Advertising Research* 52 (4): 2012, 459–64. https://doi. org/10.2501/JAR-52-4-459-464

18 Chen, Lin, and Chang, "The influence of greenwash."

19 M. Zhang et al., "Greenwashing: Consumers' Skepticism and Attitude," *Sustainability* 10 (7): 2018, 2485.

20 Ministry of Environment and Forestry, 2023. https://sipsn.menlhk.go.id/ sipsn/public/ data/timbulan#

21 N. D. Beard, "The Branding of Ethical Fashion and the Consumer: A Luxury Niche or Mass-market Reality? *Fashion Theory* 12 (4): 2008, 447–67. https://doi.org/10.2752/175 174108X346931

22 M. Wiederhold and L. F. Martinez, "Ethical Consumer Behaviour in Germany: The Attitude-Behaviour gap in the Green Apparel Industry," *International Journal of Consumer Studies* 42 (4): 2018, 419–29. https://doi.org/10.1111/ijcs.12435

23 S. Blas Riesgo, M. Lavanga, and M. Codina, "Drivers and Barriers for Sustainable Fashion Consumption in Spain: A Comparison Between Sustainable and Non-sustainable Consumers," *International Journal of Fashion Design, Technology and Education* 16 (1): 2023 1–13. https://doi.org/10.1080/17543266.2022.2089239

24 J. M. Kozar and K. Y. H. Connell, "Socially and Environmentally Responsible Apparel Consumption: Knowledge, Attitudes, and Behaviors," *Social Responsibility Journal* 9 (2): 2013, 315–24. https://doi.org/10.1108/SRJ-09-2011-0076

25 E. L. Ritch and M. J. Schroder, "Accessing and Affording Sustainability: The Experience of Fashion Consumption Within Young Families," *International Journal of Consumer Studies* 36 (2): 2012, 203–10. https://doi.org/10.1111/j.1470-6431.2011.01088.x

26 Blas Riesgo, Lavanga, and Codina, "Drivers and Barriers for Sustainable Fashion Consumption in Spain.

27 E. Orange and A. M. Cohen, "From Eco-friendly to Eco-intelligent," *The Futurist* 44 (5): 2010, 28–32.

28 K. Becker-Olsen and S. G. Potucek, "Greenwashing," in *Encyclopedia of Corporate Social Responsibility*, S. O. Idowu, N. Capaldi, L. Zu, and A. D. Gupta, eds, Berlin: Springer, 2013, 1318–23.

29 S. V. De Freitas, M. F. F. Sobral, A. R. B. Ribeiro, and G. R. Soares, "Relationship Between Agricultural Pesticides and the Diet of Riparian Spiders in the Field. *Environmental Sciences Europe* 32 (1): 2020 1–12.

30 R. Bick, E. Halsey, and C. C. Ekenga, "The Global Environmental Injustice of Fast Fashion," *Environmental Health* 19 (92): 2018, 1–14.

31 Onclusive, "Construir la reputación de marca evitando el riesgo greenwashing," 2023. https://onclusive.com/es/recursos/informes/construir-la-reputacion-de-marca-evitando-el-riesgo-de-greenwashing/

32 M. A. Delmas and V. C. Burbano, "The Drivers of Greenwashing," *California Management Review* 54: 2011, 64–87.

33 Y. Zhang and N. S. Pornphrom, "Sustainable and Circular Textile Value Chains: Linkages with Trade and Trade Policy – Case Study: Thailand," Vanessa Finaughty, ed., One Planet Network, 2020. https://www.unep.org/resources/case-study/sustainable-and-circular-textile-value-chains-linkages-trade-and-trade-policy

34 Global Value Chains in ASEAN: Textiles and Clothing, Paper 14, ASEAN-Japan Centre, 2020, 194. https://www.asean.org/wpcontent/uploads/images/archive/22692.pdf

35 A. Halatsch, "The German Ecolabel Blue Angel: Environmental Standard for Green Public Procurement (GPP)," German Environment Agency, 2015.

36 Tamsin Blanchard, "COP26: Meet Nine Fashion Designers Making Real Change," *Guardian*, October 29, 2021. https://www.theguardian.com/fashion/2021/oct/29/cop26-meet-nine-fashion-designers-making-real-change.

37 FOLKCHARM, "A.I. Angels of Impact," n.d., accessed October 23, 2024. https://www.angelsofimpact.com/folkcharm.html.

38 Blanchard, "COP26: Meet Nine Fashion Designers Making Real Change."

39 Kupluthai, Pungkanon, "Where Talent Shines Through," nationthailand, April 16, 2021. https://www.nationthailand.com/life/30341954

40 British Council, "New for Old: Thai Designers Present Sustainable Craft," May 1, 2016. https://www.britishcouncil.org/contact/press/new-for-old-Thai-Designers-Present-Sustainable-Craft

41 "Bio-Circular-Green Economic Model (BCG)," Royal Thai Embassy, Washington, DC, December 29, 2023. https://washingtondc.thaiembassy.org/en/page/bio-circular-green-economic-mode-bcg?menu=641d7fac4f13e1579a67e3b4

42 "Mintel Announces the Thai Consumer 2022," Mintel, January 10, 2023. https://www.mintel.com/press-centre/mintel-announces-the-thai-consumer-2022/

43 "Siam Paragon Showcases Thailand's Creative Soft Power at Siam Paragon Bangkok International Fashion Week 2023 (BIFW2023)," European Business Magazine, October 27, 2023. https://europeanbusinessmagazine.com/media-outreach/siam-paragon-showcases-thailands-creative-soft-power-at-siam-paragon-bangkok-international-fashion-week-2023-bifw2023/

44 While the study incorporates a rating scale to evaluate sustainability claims, it does not employ a formal statistical validation test. Given the focus on interpretive analysis rather than inferential statistics, a formal statistical validation test was not conducted. The ratings were derived from qualitative assessments and cross-referenced with established sustainability frameworks rather than subjected to inferential statistical analysis. Thus, the ratings are structured assessments rather than statistically tested measures.

45 "Fashion Transparency Index 2022," Issuu, July 14, 2022. https://issuu.com/fashionrevolution/docs/fti_2022

46 "Global Circular Fashion Forum," Global Fashion Agenda, March 18, 2024. https://globalfashionagenda.org/global-circular-fashion-forum/

47 Hafsa Lodi, "Sretsis Autumn/Winter 2015 Collection Lands at S*UCE," *The National*, June 25, 2021. https://www.thenationalnews.com/sretsis-autumn-winter-2015-collection-lands-at-s-uce-1.59955

48 "Fashion Transparency Index 2023: How Transparent are 250 of the World's Largest Fashion Brands?" *Fashion Revolution*, accessed October 23, 2024. https://www.fashionrevolution.org/fashion-transparency-index-2023/

49 "Home – GOTS – Global Organic Textile Standard," accessed October 23, 2024. https://global-standard.org/

50 "Stories," ASAVAGROUP, accessed October 23, 2024. https://asavagroup.com/stories/

51 Kimberly Lauren Bryant, "Disaya," *Times of India Travel*, June 24, 2016. https://timesofindia.indiatimes.com/travel/things-to-do/disaya/articleshow/52895591.cms

52 Tanachira Retail Corporation, "Sustainability at Glance," accessed October 23, 2024. https://www.tanachira.co.th/en/sustainability/home

53 "The First Janesuda X Pomelo Collection Featuring Sustainable Cotton Fabrics," Pamper.My, October 15, 2021. https://www.pamper.my/news/lifestyle/fashion/the-first-janesuda-x-pomelo-collection-featuring-sustainable-cotton-fabrics/

54 Rather than systematically coding and decoding textual data, the research engages in a critical examination of sustainability narratives, branding strategies, and linguistic as well as visual representations within Thai fashion.

55 "Sustainable Fashion: DoiTung Fuses Tradition, and Modernity in the New Collection." nationthailand, January 15, 2024. https://www.nationthailand.com/blogs/lifestyle/fashion/40034720

56 UNESCO Institute for Statistics (UIS), "The Globalisation of Cultural Trade: A Shift in Consumption," accessed October 23, 2024. https://uis.unesco.org/sites/default/files/documents/the-globalisation-of-cultural-trade-a-shift-in-consumption-international-flows-of-cultural-goods-services-2004-2013-en_0.pdf

57 "The Founder," SIRIVANNAVARI, October 4, 2023. https://sirivannavari.com/the-founder/

58 "Reviving Thai Textiles for Modern Sustainability," *Bangkok Post*, July 8, 2024. https://www.bangkokpost.com/thailand/pr/2825214/reviving-thai-textiles-for-modern-sustainability.

59 Naina Bajekal, "Stella McCartney on Wanting to Make Fashion More Sustainable," *Time*, August 9, 2023. https://time.com/6302562/stella-mccartney-sustainability-interview-lvmh/.

60 "Stella McCartney on Pioneering Sustainability in Fashion," *Atmos*, accessed October 24, 2024. https://atmos.earth/stella-mccartney-on-pioneering-sustainability-in-fashion/.

61 Emily Chan, "London's OG Upcycler Christopher Raeburn is Celebrating his 15th Anniversary with a New Retrospective," *British Vogue*, September 14, 2024. https://www.vogue.co.uk/article/christopher-raeburn-15th-anniversary-retrospective

62 Nat Misic, "Greenwashing: A Concerning Trend in Environmental Marketing and How to Stop It," *Medium*, September 18, 2023. https://medium.com/green-code-innovations/greenwashing-a-concerning-trend-in-environmental-marketing-and-how-to-stop-it-d771eebb4e99

63 Christoph Herrmann, Sebastian Rhein, and Katharina Friederike Sträter, "Consumers' Sustainability-Related Perception of and Willingness-to-Pay for Food Packaging Alternatives," *Resources, Conservation and Recycling* 181: June 2022, 106219. https://doi.org/10.1016/j.resconrec.2022.106219

64 Annie Walls, "Uncovering the Truth: What is Greenwashing and How to Spot it?" *The Ethical Futurists*, July 23, 2024. https://www.theethicalfuturists.com/uncovering-the-truth-what-is-greenwashing-and-how-to-spot-it/.

Bibliography

A Practical Guide to Sustainable Fashion. 2020. Bloomsbury Visual Arts.

Black, Sandy. *The Sustainable Fashion Handbook*. London: Thames & Hudson, 2012.

Blanchard, Tamsin. *Green is the New Black: How to Save the World in Style*. London: Hodder Paperback, 2008.

Eicher, Joanne B., ed. *Berg Encyclopedia of World Dress and Fashion, vol. 4: South Asia and Southeast Asia*. London: Bloomsbury Academic, 2015.

Fletcher, Kate. *Sustainable Fashion and Textiles: Design Journeys*. London: Routledge, 2012.

Fletcher, Kate, and Mathilda Tham, eds. *Routledge Handbook of Sustainability and Fashion*. London: Routledge, 2016.

Gardetti, Miguel Angel, and Subramanian Senthilkannan Muthu, eds. *Handbook of Sustainable Luxury Textiles and Fashion, vol. 2*. Singapore: Springer, 2016.

Hethorn, Janet. *Sustainable Fashion: What's Next?* London: Bloomsbury, Fairchild Books, 2015.

Holroyd, Amy Twigger, Jennifer Farley Gordon, and Colleen Hill. *Historical Perspectives on Sustainable Fashion: Inspiration for Change*. 2nd ed. London: Bloomsbury Visual Arts, 2023.

Mahalik, Tanushree. *Life and Livelihood of Pattachitra Paniters of Odisha*. Astral International, 2022.

Thomas, Dana. *Fashionopolis: The Price of Fast Fashion and the Future of Clothes*. New York: Penguin Press, 2019.

Part Two

Fashioning Media and Aesthetics: Global Fashion Capitals

China flirted with the Western high fashion world from the Deng Xiaoping era in the 1970s onward. Yves Saint Laurent famously showed a "Chinese collection" in F/W 1978, and later Thierry Mugler notably went "Maoist" as well. John Galliano for Dior 1997 created a "Chinese" collection on the departure of Hong Kong from British possession, leading to the colonial nostalgia "the sun never sets on the runway."[1]

Today, China currently has two distinct fashion capitals, Shanghai and Beijing—a situation that is, according to Valerie Steele, unsustainable, much like the situation in Italy in the 1920s when Florence, Milan, and Turin all vied for the position of Italy's fashion capital; eventually either Shanghai or Beijing will emerge as China's fashion capital.[2] "Global Fashion Capitals" was a 2015 exhibition at the Museum at FIT, New York, which examined sixteen fashion capitals: the traditional big four—New York, London, Paris, and Milan—along with twelve others, included in which were several fashion capitals in Asia: Tokyo, Seoul, Shanghai, Beijing, New Delhi, and Mumbai.

A 2022 Balenciaga ad, in which "Paris" is crossed out and replaced by "Beijing," succinctly explains the state of the relationship between Western fashion and China in the 2020s. No longer merely an object of exoticism and colonial fascination, China's consumers are now to Balenciaga and other luxury brands what Parisian consumers (and European consumers more broadly) were for much of the twentieth century.

Babette Radclyffe-Thomas's Chapter 4 makes for an excellent point of departure, as it takes on orientalism, and specifically, chinoiserie. Radclyffe-Thomas uses *Vogue China* as a case study and point of departure and highlights trailblazing models, such as Liu Wen and Sui He, and actresses, such as Fan Bingbing, drawing a contrast with Western fashion's ideas of China, which are still largely stuck in the era of 1930s glamour. Rimi Nandy and Mukulika Dattagupta's Chapter 5 on "Ray's Women" looks at women's dress through the lens of the films of Satyajit Ray. Rooted in historical and colonial context, particularly that of the Bengal Renaissance, their essay is rooted in critical theory (particularly Roland Barthes and Ferdinand de Saussure) and explores the rise of a nationalist, modernist dress in Bengal. After moving from China to Bengal, the second chapter of Part Two also looks at India, taking the reader from the northeastern state of Bengal to Mumbai.

Notes

1 Valerie Steele, "The Geography of Fashion," *Fashion and Diplomacy*, December 2, 2021, University of Oslo.

2 Ibid.

4

Fashioning Asia Through Fashion Media: The Modern Chinese Woman in Vogue

BABETTE RADCLYFFE-THOMAS

Introduction

The Chinese luxury market has become one of the world's most significant and valuable markets. The prestige of this growth is reflected in top luxury brands establishing headquarters in China, rapid retail expansion nationwide, the use of Chinese-speaking sales assistants in luxury boutiques worldwide to cater to the traveling shopper, and the usage of Chinese models and influencers in global campaigns and runway shows.

Despite the decades-old predictions of the "imminent" death of print media, fashion media continues to play a pivotal role in the global fashion market by forming identities and communicating the standards of high fashion to a global audience. And none more so than *Vogue*, one of the world's oldest and most prestigious titles in fashion media.

"Within international fashion publishing, no title resonates with authority and history the way that *Vogue* does".[1] An extremely influential and powerful arbiter of style, *Vogue* has earned the accolade "style bible,"[2] acting as a gatekeeper and facilitator for the consumption of global fashion trends. Simply put, when *Vogue* does something, it has an impact.

Within the world of fashion media, *Vogue* is an icon of style and luxury. Founded in 1892 by Arthur Baldwin Turnure and published by Condé Nast, *Vogue* currently has twenty-eight international editions and a global readership. Throughout its over 100-year history, despite its expansion and a passing roster of editors, its focus has remained consistent, i.e. an aspirational high-fashion lifestyle for its readership; a jet-setting world of fashion and luxury consumed and enjoyed in glamorous locations.

Print and digital media are integral to fashion communication and how consumers receive information and knowledge about who and what is in across fashion and beauty. By adhering to *Vogue*'s guidelines, its readers are invited to join its global fashion community.

For over a century, *Vogue* and its cultural capital has dominated global fashion media. Despite the increasing media competition, print decline and many regional editions, *Vogue US* still plays a dominant role. As a North American product, *Vogue* represents the majority fashion system. It creates and represents a North American/Western European hegemony that only invites other cultures to play but does not recognize their cultural capital. The standards and representations created and mirrored in *Vogue US* have not been inclusive, since they are dominated by a Western-centric view that is repeated across the pages of *Vogue*.

The rise of regional *Vogue* editions could posit an interesting challenge to *Vogue US*'s dominance. However, many of the regional editions republish syndicated content, and the only regional issues that have historically been allowed editorial content are the main Western fashion capitals, i.e. *Vogue Paris* and Italy. Recently, an increase in Asia editions, specifically *Vogue China*, has reflected the growing market power and importance of China. Currently China and the US are two global superpowers in fashion: the US as the site of *Vogue*'s birth and China as the largest producer of fashion and a rising force in consumption. Therefore, the rise of *Vogue China* is significant and the magazine itself entertains an interesting space where we can explore to what extent it has managed to challenge this dominance.

This chapter analyzes how *Vogue* has constructed tropes of Chinese women as a mystery that, with *Vogue*'s help, readers can hope to understand. By using a semiotic analysis of several key pieces of content for signs and embedded meanings at the denotative and connotative level, the chapter explores how Chinese identity has been fashioned in the eyes of *Vogue*. Starting with an overview of the market context, it then analyzes how the myth of China has been created in *Vogue US* before positing the rise of *Vogue China* as a possible contender for global fashion dominance.

Orientalism and "the Idea of China"

"What does the modern Chinese woman do about beauty? Does she cling to the old formulae or follow the Western world's?" *Vogue* asked its readers in November 1936.[3] Over ninety years later, at the time of *Vogue China*'s launch in 2005, Chinese fashion, and by extension modern Chinese women, had still not been accepted as part of the modern fashion system. The traditional Western fashion centers still dominated global fashion, and in this system Chinese women were still considered as part of an "old formulae" way to be a Chinese woman in fashion. Western ideas of China have been communicated globally, and this is especially pertinent as China and Chinese creatives did not have a global stage to communicate their identities until very recently (due to isolationism during the twentieth century and a fractured fashion history). In order to understand this phenomenon (of how Chinese women have been shaped in *Vogue US*), we need to examine how these dominant ideas and imagery are underpinned by an unjust, imbalanced global fashion system.

The predominant fashion system has historically been dominated by Western creatives[4] and *Vogue* and its regional editions continue to operate in an inequitable global fashion system and media industry. Said's theoretical argument of Orientalism explores the binary divide between the East and the West. Said's "Orient" was not geographically Asia, yet focused on the unequal power balance and resulting stereotypical depictions created of the East and by the West, especially in art and literature. This critical concept can be a useful lens to analyze global inequities as manifested in other fields including fashion media, i.e. fashion Orientalism.

An Orientalist approach has led to the creation of damaging stereotypes and culturally essentialist views posit dichotomous views of culture, so that the West and East as imagined communities are in binary opposition.[5] "Stereotyping reduces, essentializes, naturalizes and fixes 'difference'" and "is a practice of 'closure' and exclusion";[6] thus fashion media images that use stereotypes are extremely significant. The traditional Western-dominated fashion system is one in which Chinese fashion is Othered and exoticized.[7] It is also a system that sees the Orient as "neither a cultural, religious or linguistic unity."[8] However Orientalist discourses define the East as sharing a unified identity and adopt a "summational attitude."[9] Therefore, this lens is useful to analyze representations of "Eastern" women in *Vogue*, as the symbolic production and discursive construction of Chinese femininity has traditionally been constructed in the eyes of the North American/Western European-centric fashion system.

One of the clearest manifestations of fashion Orientalism is Chinoiserie—a visual and decorative style that whilst it has its roots in an appreciation of Chinese/Japanese design and products, has resulted in inauthentic and static representations of Asia as a magical and mythical place. Chinoiserie reflects a kind of ethnocentricity that comes from admiration and enjoyment of culture but does not permit that culture to become modern or change; it enjoys the static representation of that culture.[10] This phenomenon essentializes Chinese culture, resulting in stereotypical representations and ideas of a modern Chinese identity. Non-Chinese fashion designers often draw inspiration from these static representations, including Imperial-era palaces and 1930s Golden Age Shanghai glamour.

The rise of Chinese models can be seen as a fashion media business strategy and has witnessed a huge increase of Asian models on international catwalks, especially in the 2010s. For example, in 2009 Liu Wen became the first Chinese woman to ever walk in a Victoria's Secret Fashion Show, and in 2011 Sui He was the first Asian model to open a Ralph Lauren show. By 2010, Wen shared: "Chinese models have become a stronger presence. Just a season or two ago, there weren't many models for me to talk with backstage in my native Mandarin. Now I usually have no trouble finding someone at any show."[11] This development was also mirrored in global fashion spreads as Asian models broke boundaries, appearing for the first time on the covers of international

Vogue editions; several years later in January 2013, Fei Fei Sun posed solo on the cover of *Vogue Italia*, marking the edition's first Asian cover model.

The recent rise of China in front of the camera, exemplified by the rise of Chinese models, reflects the growing importance of the Chinese market. The October 2005 *Vogue Paris* edition saw Chinese model Du Juan taking the cover with Gemma Ward, marking the first time an Asian model adorned the cover. Leading on from the perceived success of editor-in-chief Carine Roitfeld's experiences in styling the launch issue of *Vogue China* the month prior, Du Juan and Gemma Ward came together again for the face of the Special Shanghai cover feature. Notably, though, on this cover image, Du Juan's face is mostly covered by Ward's flowing hair, and Ward's body language dominates the image.

Significantly, until March 2017, *Vogue US* had never featured a Chinese model on its cover[12] (excluding foldouts).[13] In fact, Chinese garments had been worn on the cover several times before a Chinese model ever starred: for example, in October 2014 cover star Charlize Theron poses in a qipao. Liu Wen finally took the cover in March 2017, in a group of seven models, all styled identically. Notably, Liu Wen is at the furthest left of the group of models, while Gigi Hadid and Kendall Jenner form the center focus of the cover. Celebrating the 125-year anniversary of *Vogue*, a key coverline stated: "The beauty revolution." In a piece of digital editorial to accompany the shoot, *Vogue* stated: "Each of these cover girls proudly inhabits her own particular gorgeousness in her own particular way. Together they represent a seismic social shift: The new beauty norm is no norm."[14]

Vogue US

As the first edition and still widest-read issue of *Vogue* (8 million monthly readers, 17 million digital and 64 million ssocial media followers in 2022[15]), *Vogue US* plays an important global role. *Vogue US* represents the dominance of the cultural globalization of Western media products, and has played a critical role in shaping representations of fashion.

Fashion images in *Vogue* are important to analyze due to the political consequences of portraying people in a specific way. As Alexandra Shulman, ex-editor-in-chief of British *Vogue* (tenure 1992–2017) said, "The *Vogue* photographer works to create a predestined picture, their efforts combining to realize a preconception about the subject to be conveyed." [16] Shulman acknowledges the power of the one behind the camera: once the photographer is chosen "one is already creating a person rather than simply recording them."[17] The choice of fashion models is undoubtedly linked with the formation and maintenance of beauty ideals, and it is clear to see a continuation of Chinese stereotypes throughout a century of *Vogue US* content.

A fascination for China's "mysticism" started early for *Vogue US*. A search of the *Vogue US* archive for the term "China" returns over 5,000 articles:, with many pieces detailing US brands entering China, "Chinese"-inspired design trends and even state visits. Narrowing the search term to "Chinese beauty" returns over 1,500 articles, leading with articles entitled "Chinese Elegance" (September 1929) illustrated with images of young Chinese women in a range of Chinese robes and Parisian dresses. "The Chinese beauty doctor" feature (September 1923) details a Chinese woman's beauty regimen, stating: "the woman of the Orient is a lover of cosmetics. She was using paint and powder, hair lotions and perfume, when our ancestors were limited to the refining influence of bears' grease and tallow . . . her jewels and flashing eyes have lighted the dull pages of history."

This sense of fascination continues in one of the most notable pieces in the *Vogue US US* archive. The "Chinese beauty" article (November 1, 1936) posits: "What does the modern Chinese woman do about beauty? Does she cling to the old formulae or follow the Western world's?" The article shares insights from Mrs. Russell Sun, whose identity is not made clear except that she is an expert on Chinese beauty. Posing for two dramatic photographs to accompany the article, to give these "fascinating insights while [she] was stopping in New York on a tour around the world that started in her native Shanghai." Mrs. Sun is described as "diminutive, distinguished and chic," and the feature details how "while these native cosmetics have welded amicably with the adoption of European cosmetics, many of the fascinating native devices have been discarded in favour of more modern beautification."

Over seventy years later in editorial content, the *Vogue US* December 2010 issue photoshoot "Asia Major" is of particular note for creating tropes of Chinese women as different, and, notably, a homogenous Asian identity. "Asia

Major" was photographed by Steven Meisel, styled by Grace Coddington, and features eight leading Asian models: Du Juan, Tao Okamoto, Hyun Yi Lee, Hyoni Kang, Liu Wen, Bonnie Chen, So Young Kang, and Lily Zhi. Solely using Asian models, the *Vogue US* editorial team recognizes the increase of Asian models on global catwalks, and it also reflects an appreciation and fascination with Asia and specifically China.

Fashion editorial teams are now significantly larger than in the early years of *Vogue*, seeing many creatives come together to bring fashion stories to life, including the models, photographer, stylist, assistants, make-up artists, hair stylists and more. This photoshoot is significant for its portrayal of Chinese beauty; *Vogue* still posits Chinese, and Asian, beauty as a binary to Western beauty. There are only two images in this piece of editorial, which is unusual, and the opening double page spread references the classic 1948 Cecil Beaton photographs of Charles James evening gowns. Here, the models wear glamorous formal evening gowns by Oscar de la Renta in various pastel shades and adopt classic model poses. Mirroring the original Beaton photograph, the models are scattered around a traditional ballroom with glamorous chandeliers and chaises longues, drinking tea or engaging in conversation, and none of them make eye contact with the camera. It would look like an image straight from the late 1940s, except all the models are Asian and each model has her hair strikingly styled in large Mohican hairstyles.

The shoot is accompanied by an article by Samantha V. Chang reflecting on her own identity as a young Korean American. Chang states that Asian models are "redefining traditional concepts of beauty," describing some of the models as "porcelain faced" with "brows like accent marks" and stating that the models "appear to be redrawing the frontlines of beauty." When this issue was published, many readers took to fashion blogs to vent their frustration at such apparently Orientalist copy, commenting that for centuries Asian women have been seen as beautiful in Asia.

By describing Asian models as creating "new concepts," those in the dominant position (*Vogue US*) are reproducing their power through placing Asian models in opposition to Caucasian models that are commonly found in *Vogue US*. Presenting all models in homogenous styling, as one group, rather than, say, throughout the entire issue's editorial, the Asian models are denied individuality.

The group is placed in binary opposition, and this is further enforced through the Mohican hair styling choices that reference punk subcultures. The juxtaposition of the classic evening gowns with the Mohican hairstyles and the usage of Asian models styled in this unusual way are designed to shock readers. It should be stated here that this styling juxtaposition does not necessarily reflect Orientalist or essentialist motivations, as the styling would retain an impact on a model with different ethnicity and the models in the original Beaton photograph adopt similar poses, none looking directly at the camera.

Interestingly, the imagery also raises issues regarding the imposition of cultures. Beaton took his classic photo in 1948 at a time when China was experiencing huge social and political upheaval just before the establishment of the PRC. The use of Beaton's image is significant because it could be seen that while some Western readers can instantly identify the historical reference, readers from other cultures may not be as familiar with the reference and therefore the imagery does not bear the same resonance.

Less than one year later, another piece of revealing editorial appears in *Vogue US* continuing the myth of China, but this time in the most important issue of the year as the leading feature. The September 2011 issue's "Go East" extended photoshoot by photographer Mario Testino, fashion director Tonne Goodman and world-famous American model Karlie Kloss featured various locations throughout Beijing and China. It is interesting to note the temporal context of the photoshoots. September issues are "the most high-profile issue of the year"[18] globally, showcasing the new Autumn/Winter trends, and are often the largest issue of the year spanning sometimes up to 500 pages in total.

Significantly, here, we can see that almost a century after China first appeared in *Vogue US*, the same stereotypical representations of China are repeated and replicated. China is used as an exotic backdrop upon which American Caucasian women can enact modernity and define fashion. Through the editorial choices, Chinese people are literally used as a backdrop for each image, are Othered and positioned in binary opposition to Caucasian women, and the accompanying text reaffirms *Vogue US*'s tropes of Chinese women as 'inscrutable', mystical, alluring, and different.

Covering over twenty pages of photos, involving over seventeen people, the shoot is also accompanied by a very long article detailing Jonathan Van Meter's recent visit to China, making this an extensive piece of content. By choosing to stage their leading photoshoot of the most important issue of the year in China, the *Vogue US* editorial team reflects an appreciation and fascination with Asia and specifically China, and also the rise of the Chinese market.

At the level of denotation, the photoshoot uses familiar Chinese locations such as the Great Wall, the Pudong skyscraper-filled skyline and the Forbidden City as backdrops. Throughout the shoot, Kloss poses alongside notable Chinese cultural icons including famous jewelry designers, musicians, and actresses in a wide array of outfits. There are multiple images replicating stereotypes of Chinese identity throughout the shoot, from stock images of China that can be perceived as essentially Chinese to China being used as a backdrop.

One notable double-page spread shows a dinner party, where Kloss takes the central focus surrounded by Shaolin monks demonstrating kung fu by jumping in the air. The monks are dressed in a mixture of yellow and orange robes, wearing signature Chinese footwear Feiyue, all complementing Kloss's flowing red dress which is also visibly moving. The monks are her backdrop, but significantly off to one side, nearly hidden by a monk's hand, is an elegantly dressed Chinese woman. Readers would not know that this is in fact top jewelry designer Bao Bao Wan; rather she is presented as a prop in Kloss's backdrop, a filler for Kloss enjoying her evening.

Next, Kloss takes a trip to the factory floor. This double-page spread shows Kloss standing on the Eve NY garment factory floor surrounded by Chinese female factory workers. Kloss is styled in a black wig, she wears a black fashionable dress with white collars, mirroring the white collars on the factory workers' shirts. While Kloss adopts a high-fashion pose in the center of the crowd of workers in uniform, they are denied individuality and identity. It is clear who is allowed to wear fashion and who must wear their uniform. That Chinese women are denied identity outside of their professional roles is a recurring theme throughout this editorial. The image references the trope of China as the factory of the world.

In another image, Kloss poses in a traditional Shanghai market, next to race car driver Han Han. He is styled in his racing overalls, looking off into the distance, while Kloss is at the center of this image making eye contact with the reader. Along with neon signs and market stalls, there is a bicycle in the foreground of the image, another emblem of Chineseness.

Another very notable image is a double-page spread showing director Lu Chuan with his star actor Daniel Wu at the Peninsula Hotel Shanghai. They are shooting on the balcony with the ultra-modern skyscraper-filled Pudong skyline in the background. Instead of wearing high fashion like Kloss, Wu is wearing an ancient military uniform, which we must assume is his recent film costume. Kloss is wearing high-fashion pieces, the glitter on her long evening skirt mirroring the neon background, reinforcing her identity as modern, whereas Wu is literally stuck in the past, a historical Chinese identity, and her direct opposite. Both director and actor are again shown in their professional roles, denying them an identity outside of their jobs. Notably in the article accompanying the shoot, on asking Chuan about his film *The Last Supper,* the author says Chuan is "perhaps trying to employ a Chinese version of the Jedi mind trick."[19]

The Editor's Letter reveals that the photoshoot was inspired by Anna Wintour's trip to China the previous year. She writes: "when I returned home, I knew that this country that I'd found so entrancing – I'd never been anywhere that restless and ceaseless in its pursuit of the new – could act as a powerful and compelling backdrop for a September fashion story."[20] Wintour explicitly states China is a backdrop, and she shares that the production team returned "with pictures that were far, far better than anything I'd imagined in my head," clearly referencing the creation of an idea of China. Wintour says that China is the "epicenter of the twenty-first century," reflecting a fascination with China, and she notably sees Kloss, a tall, slim, Caucasian model, as the "perfect ambassador for America."

The detailed article by Meter that Wintour describes as one that "cleverly and wittily reveals what it is like to spend a week [in China]," is also full of stereotypes of China. One identity is the racist trope of the "inscrutable'" Chinese: Meter writes: "China has been confounding foreigners for centuries. Turns out they are not so 'inscrutable' after all: just like us, they long for $5,000 handbags covered in tiny logos."[21] Another trope is China as terrifyingly advanced: China is the "land of obscene opportunity," Beijing is "Rodeo Drive on steroids," he eats "extravagant" banquets, describes skyscrapers, billionaires, and notes that in China there is "an energy in the air, a feeling that anything is possible."[22] On landing in Shanghai, Meter states that "the overall effect as you fly along is that you have somehow slipped into a video game." These comments hint at what can be seen as techno-Orientalism,[23] an Asian identity that is so futuristic it is a threat.

Replicating the stereotype of Chinese women and Chinese beauty as different, Bao Bao Wan is described as "infamous," "thin as a blade of grass, with spidery long legs and long, straight black hair."[24]

Chinese women are mystical and alluring: on meeting actor Fan Bingbing, Meter states that "there is something very old-fashioned about Bingbing – as if she were playing into an outmoded stereotype: the mysterious, alluring Asian woman. She is old fashioned, too, in how she feels about her country's radical modernization."[25]

The "Go East" photoshoot featuring a Western model in China was the lead photoshoot of the September 2011 issue and covered over twenty pages. The December 2010 issue is smaller and less significant: the "Asia Major" photoshoot that solely used Asian models only merits two pages. Both texts were created and published during the reign of long-term editor-in-chief Anna Wintour (her editorial tenure ran from 1988 to 2025). As the documentary "The September issue" (2009) portrays, Wintour controls the vision of the magazine, and although ultimately the publishers have the final decision, the editorial content is essentially the editor's responsibility. Condé Nast's progress towards equal representation has been especially slow globally, a point widely critiqued, leading to the first public apology by Wintour in light of the Black Lives Matter movement.[26] And as I have written elsewhere, "whilst the western fashion industry has been keen to congratulate itself on the diversity of ethnicities it now showcases, there are many critiques of the lack of true multiculturalism in fashion imagery and a fundamental issue remains as to the extent to which the use of Asian models is less a democratization of fashion, and more a strategic marketing ploy."[27]

Vogue China

Since the first edition of *Vogue US* in 1892, transnational magazines have come to dominate the global print market due to the globalization of media and the cultural globalization of Western media products.[28] *Vogue* is a transnational media product with various regional editions that continue to be launched globally;[29] as of March 2024, there are twenty-eight international editions, including nine Asian editions.[30]

An offshoot of one of the world's most iconic fashion titles, *Vogue* entered the Chinese market in 2005 in cooperation with the state-owned China Pictorial Publishing House. At a time of rapid market growth and China's growing global significance, global media company and publishers Condé Nast decided that the market was ready for *Vogue*.[31] Launching relatively late in comparison to other international fashion titles, *Vogue China*'s offer comprised original Chinese content, featuring Chinese models, and focused on "fashion, beauty, art and the fashionable lifestyle"[32] in a highly luxurious and glossy format. Its slogan "Vogue, Ultimate Fashion in China" denoted the magazine's self-positioning and construction as the country's leading style arbiter and fashion authority.

With over 57 million readers across print, digital and social channels,[33] *Vogue China* plays a key role in offering women outlets for identity formation.[34] Fashion images codify "standards of taste and beauty"[35] and with five times more editorial pages than the US or UK editions, *Vogue China* has the space in which to explore and explain not only the cultural history of the West for an increasingly internationalized readership, but also to promote Chinese fashion including models.[36] China's market rise has been reflected by the rise of *Vogue China* itself, and as a cultural artifact of the Chinese fashion industry, the magazine offers a window into the very important Chinese market, especially during the first decade of its existence under editor-in-chief Angelica Cheung (2005–20).

Within the pages of *Vogue US*, as the analysis has shown, Chinese identity is limited to stereotypical tropes, but in *Vogue China*, Angelica Cheung has recognized the limitations imposed by these stereotypes and instead created multiple and various ways to promote Chineseness and fashion creativity. The gulf between international ideas and the local production team's understanding is exemplified in multiple pieces of *Vogue China* content, the most notable being the September 2005 launch cover image. In this gatefold cover image, five Chinese models (Du Juan, Wang Wen Wen, Liu Dan, Tong Chen, and Ni Ming) pose with one non-Chinese model (Gemma Ward) along the Bund in Shanghai with the modern skyscraper-filled skyline of Pudong in the background. They all wear similar brightly colored print outfits with the same hairstyle featuring a black hairband; all pose similarly, making direct eye contact with the reader, and have similar make-up. Despite the large number of Chinese models, the focal point of the cover image is 2005's most popular model globally, the Australian Gemma Ward.

The launch issue, specifically the cover imagery, highlights problematic issues that arose when an international team imposed a Western creative vision onto a Chinese magazine. The circumstances behind editorial decisions are revealing; Angelica Cheung published a detailed account of her experiences in British *Vogue*.

Cheung described how the make-up artist Peter Philips initially proposed a look inspired by Bernardo Bertolucci's iconic film *The Last Emperor* (1987) and how she had to explain to the team that "young Chinese women want to be modern and chic. Make-up like that . . . would remind them of ancient women" and how the modern Chinese woman, mirroring her fashionista counterparts worldwide, "want[s] to look like Kate Moss."[37] Cheung recognized the conceptual and creative gulf between local and non-Chinese teams: "to me the only concern is to make sure that the all-Western creative team will create a cover that is to the taste of the Chinese market."[38] Cheung had to push back against the visions of the international production team to ensure a more modern depiction of Chinese women, rather than a trope of a traditional, imperial palace ideal.

In addition to the make-up and hair choices for the cover image, there were also disagreements between local and international producers in regard to cultural connotations and knowledge of colors. Cheung described how she encountered problems with French stylist Carine Roitfeld, who was unaware of such cultural connotations. Roitfeld initially planned to dress the models in black, since black has been a staple of European fashion since Chanel's little black dress was introduced in 1926.[39] Cheung was forced to point out how inauspicious black clothing would be for the cover image, being synonymous with misfortune for Chinese people. Such lack of local knowledge shown by non-Chinese creatives builds upon my previous research, which argues that this process "crystallizes the Western fashion industry's misinterpretation of the modern Chinese fashion consumer"[40] and pointedly demonstrates that tensions between creatives from different cultural backgrounds existed since the very first issue.

Western creatives continued to construct Chinese female identity as traditional and in the Western gaze, evidencing how they adopt a mystical vision of China for creative inspiration. In the case of the cover image, the non-Chinese team's initial ideas were scrapped, and a more modern, culturally attuned version was produced. It is significant that from this first issue, local producers such as Cheung resisted the imposition of foreign ideas of Chineseness. Due to Cheung's advice and insights into Chinese culture, the visions of the international team were rejected and instead the models were styled in bright colorful clothing against the more modern setting of Pudong, emphasizing a modern Chinese female identity. Cheung pointed out in the September 2007 Editor's Letter that the launch cover image aimed to show "Chinese models commencing to have international desires and dreams." Cheung clearly links notions of modernity with internationalization, positing that an international female identity is modern. However, the incident demonstrates that non-Chinese producers at *Vogue China* were constructing a visual binary in which Chinese female identity is traditional and static and international identity is constructed as modern. This photoshoot team highlighted how non-Chinese ideas of China differ from the reality experienced by local Chinese producers.

In the same issue, the international creatives who traveled to Shanghai shared how the photoshoots came into being in the "Behind the Cover Story" article. The photoshoot producer believed that *Vogue* is a meeting place for Eastern traditions and Western culture that would become a mainstay for Chinese women. She reinforces an Orientalist viewpoint when she links tradition with Eastern identity, exemplifying cultural imperialism.[41] The viewpoint that "all Chinese people look the same" is problematic and Orientalist. Stylist Roitfeld stated that she chose the Australian model Gemma Ward to appear on the cover of the *Vogue China* launch issue because, despite being Caucasian, Ward's face has a "slight Chinese feel" and that she looks like a "tall, blonde Chinese doll." The non-Chinese hair stylist compared his recent visit to China to the first time he visited China in the 1970s, sharing: "when I first saw these black haired, yellow skinned Chinese models standing in front of me, I found it very difficult to clearly differentiate between them," but over time he was able to tell them apart.

The non-Chinese team demonstrated their lack of cultural knowledge of China or Chinese women. The photoshoot producer stated that she frequently talked to the Chinese team about life in China so that she could better understand the country, but she also said the biggest difficulty she faced in creating the photoshoot was the language barrier due to her lack of Chinese language skills. She stated that "*Vogue* is the world's most influential fashion magazine, and each issue perfectly embodies local culture," without recognizing the team's lack of local cultural knowledge. Through sharing these constructed narratives of how the photoshoots came into being, the non-Chinese creatives reflect and reinforce the unequal distribution of power in the fashion system;[42] despite the team's lack of cultural knowledge about non-Western fashion systems, they still hold powerful positions in the global fashion system.

Since the 2005 launch issue, *Vogue China* has continued to push back on these damaging stereotypes of Chinese women as traditional by profiling successful Chinese women. The magazine showcases a wide range of independent, professional, pioneering women to inspire readers. This is most notably exemplified in one of the most important issues in *Vogue China*'s history: the tenth anniversary issue in September 2015. Ten years is a publishing milestone and a testament to a magazine's success. The gatefold cover image is dedicated to a range of professional female identities: ten women take the cover and are profiled inside the issue (Liu Wen, Fan BingBing, Tang Wei, Li BingBing, Zhang Ziyi, Zhou Xun, Du Juan, Zhao Wei, Carina Lau, and Chris Lee), showing how each woman has changed over the previous decade.

The women are styled in elegant dress, in a mixture of white and gold, in a studio setting with a white fabric background. Two groups pose around a chair in the center of each group, and it is a very sleek and chic image. Each model makes direct eye contact with the reader. Although there is a similarity in their glamorous make-up, hairstyles, and elegant body language, their outfits are quite different, which allows for their individuality to appear: Chris Lee, who is known for a more androgynous style, wears white tailoring.

In the feature, a range of female characteristics are celebrated, showcasing a more diverse array of female social identities for readers, from an androgynous singer to a successful actress. Significantly, each profile focuses on the subject's professional achievements: quotes are included from leading industry figures, such as directors or fellow actors, testifying to their professionalism, and content focusing on their physical attributes is omitted. Personality attributes such as "natural grace" and "persistence" are celebrated: Michael Kors comments that model Liu Wen has "brains and beauty,"[43] highlighting the importance of beauty "inside and out" for Chinese women, as well as the global fashion system's approval of Chinese beauty ideals represented by Liu Wen. A comment from actress Fan Bingbing to a reporter on her acting success is quoted in her profile: "I want to prove that . . . these so-called beautiful female actresses are not just flower vases, she also has acting talent."[44] The "flower vase" comment refers to a woman employed for her beauty, not for her ability, and so Bingbing's statement highlights the empowering stance of *Vogue China* content and the strong rejection of the flower vase stereotype.

Cheung states in her Editor's Letter in the same issue that she wanted to show "Vogue's female spirit . . . [and] extol the praises of the Vogue woman."[45] She shares that all the women featured are "positive, hopeful, self-confident, courageous, compassionate, and are professionally successful,"[46] and she chose ten models for the first time to celebrate their qualities: although they are very different from one another, she wanted to inspire women. Notably Cheung only uses Chinese models, connoting the success of Chinese fashion but also to celebrate Chinese beauty traits. She recognizes the importance of the tenth anniversary, so *Vogue China* makes a significant statement on gender roles with the choice of these women for the special issue. Not only does the content show Chinese beauty as desirable but it also represents a push back against the Western hegemony of beauty ideals. These representations show that by 2015, *Vogue China* constructs female identity that is empowered, self-aware, and professionally successful.

Conclusion

For over a century, *Vogue US* has retained its status as one of the world's most important fashion media titles. Notwithstanding declining print sales and the post-pandemic global luxury industry slowdown, former longtime editor-in-chief Wintour and *Vogue US* still maintain a powerful platform, especially for defining and representing female identity. Despite public calls for increased inclusivity through stereotypical representations, *Vogue US* has continued to promote damaging tropes of Chinese women as markedly different, mystical, and alluring.

Now with the rise of China, and especially the important role Chinese consumers play on the global stage and in the future of most global luxury brands, China has more power than ever before to define its fashion identity. Since its launch two decades ago, *Vogue China* has played a critical role in this development and has attempted to create a more equitable global fashion system in which China plays a greater role with more agency.

Most markedly, *Vogue China* has persisted in promoting a wider, more representative range of female identities. The success of Chinese models on a global stage not only celebrates Chinese beauty, but importantly, challenges the established global Western-centric fashion narrative. Creatives are resisting the Western hegemony of fashion through their celebration and promotion of Chineseness, and as such reveal a shifting power balance in the global fashion industry.

Notes

1 Anna Konig, "Glossy Words: An Analysis of Fashion Writing in British *Vogue*, *Fashion Theory: The Journal of Dress, Body and Culture* 10 (1/2): 2006, 205–24, 205.

2 J. Hartley and L. Montgomery, "Fashion as Consumer Entrepreneurship: Emergent Risk Culture, Social Network Markets, and the Launch of *Vogue* in China," in *Collections of the 2007 China Communication Forum*, National Center for Radio and Television Studies at CUC, China, 2007, 1–23.

3 *Vogue*, November 1936, 72.

4 Valerie Steele and J. Major, *China Chic: East Meets West*. London: Yale University Press, 1999.

5 S. Hall and P. Du Gay, eds, *Questions of Cultural Identity*, Sage Publications, Inc., 1996.

6 Hall and Du Gay, *Questions of Cultural Identity*, 258.

7 Steele and Major, *China Chic*.

8 M. Miyoshi and H. D. Harootunian, "Postmodernism and Japan," Durham, NC: Duke University Press, 1989, 117.

9 Edward W. Said, *Orientalism*, New York: Pantheon Books, 1978, 262.

10 N. Radclyffe-Thomas and B. Radclyffe-Thomas, "From the Steppes to the Runway: Mongolia's Fashion Imaginary," in *Whose Space Is It Anyway? Place Branding and the Politics of Representation*, Pascale Cohen-Avenel and Graham Roberts, eds, Bern: Peter Lang, 2024.

11 S. Chang, "Asia Major," Vogue US.com, 18 November, 2010. https://www.vogue.com/article/asia-major.

12 Throughout the magazine's history, Asian women have rarely featured as *Vogue* cover models; it is even very contested who was the first Asian model on the *Vogue* cover.

13 Three years earlier in September 2014, Fei Fei Sun had appeared on a gatefold cover with multiple models.

14 M. Singer, "How Models Like Ashley Graham and Gigi Hadid are Democratizing Fashion," Vogue US.com, 2017. https://www.vogue.com/article/model-diversity-ashley-graham-gigi-hadid-kendall-jenner-march-cover

15 Vogue Media Kit, 2022. https://web.archive.org/web/20220301012258/https://www.condenast.com/brands/vogue

16 A. Shulman, *Inside* Vogue*: A Diary of my 100th Year*, London: Penguin Books, 2016, 7.

17 Ibid.

18 Terri Agins, *The End of Fashion: How Marketing Changed the Clothing Business Forever*, New York: HarperCollins, 2000, 78.

19 *Vogue US*, September 2011, 754.

20 Ibid., 208.

21 Ibid., 653.

22 Ibid.

23 D. S. Roh, B. Huang, and G. A. Niu, eds, *Techno Orientalism: Imagining Asia in Speculative Fiction, History and Media*, New Brunswick: Rutgers University Press, 2015.

24 *Vogue US*, September 2011, 656.

25 Ibid., 754.

26 S. Lau, "Susie Bubble on Fashion's Oft-obscured 'Bamboo Ceiling.'" British *Vogue*, March 23, 2021. https://www.vogue.co.uk/arts-and-lifestyle/article/susie-bubble-east-asian-representation-fashion

27 N. Radclyffe-Thomas and B. Radclyffe-Thomas, "The New Shanghai Xiaojie: Chinese Fashion Identities," *Journal of Fashion Studies*, 2 (1): 2015, 43–62.

28 W. Ling and S. Segre-Reinach, *Fashion in Multiple Chinas: Chinese Styles in the Transglobal Landscape*, London: Bloomsbury, 2018.

29 M. R. Nelson and H. J. Paek, "Cross-Cultural Differences in Sexual Advertising Content in a Transnational Women's Magazine, *Sex Roles: A Journal of Research*, 53: 2005, 371–83.

30 Philippines, Hong Kong, Thailand, India, China, Japan, Taiwan, Korea, and Singapore.

31 F. Zhao, "China's in Vogue so *Vogue*'s in China," July 21, 2005. http://news.xinhuanet.com/english/2005-07/21/content_3248190.htm

32 A. Cheung, "Visions of China," *British Vogue*, November 2005, 114.

33 Vogue Business Team, "Margaret Zhang and *Vogue China*'s next chapter," February 26, 2021. https://www.voguebusiness.com/companies/margaret-zhang-and-vogue-chinas-next-chapter

34 J. Hermes, *Reading Women's Magazines: An Analysis of Everyday Media Use*, Oxford: Polity Press, 1995.

35 C. Breward, "Fashion on the Page," in *The Fashion Reader*, A. Lillethun and L. Welters, eds, Oxford: Berg, 2007, 399–402.

36 Natascha Radclyffe-Thomas and Babette Radclyffe-Thomas, "The New Shanghai Xiaojie: Chinese Fashion Identities," *International Journal of Fashion Studies* 2 (1): 2015, 43–62.

37 Cheung, "Visions of China," 118.

38 Ibid., 117.

39 J. Craik, *Fashion: The Key Concepts*, Oxford: Berg Publishers, 2009.

40 Radclyffe-Thomas and Radclyffe-Thomas, "The New Shanghai Xiaojie." 47.

41 Said, *Orientalism.*

42 Steele and Major, *China Chic.*

43 *Vogue China,* September 2015, 273.

44 Ibid., 279.

45 Ibid., 118.

46 Ibid., 122.

Bibliography

Agins, Terri. *The End of Fashion: How Marketing Changed the Clothing Business Forever*. HarperCollins, 2000.

Chang, Samantha V. "Asia Major." *Vogue US*, November 18, 2010. https://www.vogue.com/article/asia-major

Cheung, Angelica. "Visions of China." *British Vogue*. November 2005, 113–18.
Craik, Jennifer. *Fashion: The Key Concepts*. Oxford: Berg Publishers, 2009.
Hall, Stuart, and Du Gay, Paul (eds). *Questions of Cultural Identity.* Sage Publications, Inc. 1996.
Hartley, John, and Lucy Montgomery. "Fashion as Consumer Entrepreneurship: Emergent Risk Culture, Social Network Markets, and the Launch of Vogue in China." In *Collections of the 2007 China Communication Forum. National Center for Radio and Television Studies at CUC, China*, 2007, 1–23.
Konig, Anna. "Glossy Words: An Analysis of Fashion Writing in *British Vogue*." *Fashion Theory: The Journal of Dress, Body and Culture*, 10 (1/2): 2006, 205–24.
Lau, Susie. "Susie Bubble on Fashion's Oft-obscured 'Bamboo Ceiling.'" *British Vogue*, March 23, 2011. https://www.vogue.co.uk/arts-and-lifestyle/article/susie-bubble-east-asian-representation-fashion
Ling, Wessie, and Simona Segre Reinach. *Fashion in Multiple Chinas: Chinese Styles in the Transglobal Landscape*. London: Bloomsbury, 2018.
Miyoshi, Masao, and Harry Harootunian. *Postmodernism and Japan*. Durham, NC: Duke University Press, 1989.
Nelson, Michelle R., and Hye-Jin Paek. "Cross-cultural Differences in Sexual Advertising Content in a Transnational Women's Magazine." *Sex Roles: A Journal of Research* 53: 2005, 371–83.
Radclyffe-Thomas, Natascha, and Babette Radclyffe-Thomas. "From the Steppes to the Runway: Mongolia's Fashion Imaginary." In *Whose Space Is It Anyway? Place Branding and the Politics of Representation*. Pascale Cohen-Avenel and Graham Roberts, eds. Bern: Peter Lang, 2024.
Radclyffe-Thomas, Natascha, and Radclyffe-Thomas, Babette. "The New Shanghai Xiaojie: Chinese Fashion Identities." *Journal of Fashion Studies* 2 (10): 2015, 43–62.
Roh, David S., Betsy Huang, and Greta A. Niu, eds. *Techno Orientalism: Imagining Asia in Speculative Fiction, History and Media*. New Brunswick NJ: Rutgers University Press, 2015.
Said, Edward. *Orientalism*. Pantheon Books, 1978.
Shulman, Alexandra. *Inside* Vogue*: A Diary of my 100th Year*. London: Penguin Books, 2016.
Singer, Maya. "How Models Like Ashley Graham and Gigi Hadid are Democratizing Fashion". *Vogue US*, February 8, 2017. https://www.vogue.com/article/model-diversity-ashley-graham-gigi-hadid-kendall-jenner-march-cover
Steele, Valerie, and Major, J. *China Chic: East Meets West*. London: Yale University Press, 1999.
Vogue, November 1936.
Vogue Business Team. "Margaret Zhang and *Vogue China*'s Next Chapter." *Vogue Business*, February 26, 2021. https://www.voguebusiness.com/companies/margaret-zhang-and-vogue-chinas-next-chapter
Vogue Media Kit. 2022. https://web.archive.org/web/20220301012258/https://www.condenast.com/brands/vogue
Zhao, Feifei. "China's in Vogue so *Vogue*'s in China". July 21, 200.5 https://web.archive.org/web/20060825204610/http://news.xinhuanet.com/english/2005-07/21/content_3248190.htm

5

Ray's Women and Sartorial Choices: Exploring Through Colonial and Feminist Perspective

RIMI NANDY AND MUKULIKA DATTAGUPTA

Introduction

Sartorial practices are deeply embedded in our cultural identity, serving as an intricate medium through which personal and collective selves are expressed and negotiated. The concept of "identity" itself is layered and multifaceted, with clothing playing a significant role in shaping how we present ourselves to the world. A garment transforms our outward appearance, signaling not only who we are but also the social, cultural, and spatial contexts we inhabit.

As the Hindi proverb "Jaisa Des waisa Bhes" suggests, attire is intrinsically tied to the cultural spaces we occupy—reflecting the norms, values, and aesthetics of particular regions. This connection manifests in everyday dress codes, which adapt according to the social environments we navigate. For instance, formal clothing may dominate the workplace, while more relaxed or stylish attire might be favored in social settings like nightclubs or dinner parties. In these shifts, garments become more than mere fabric; they act as semiotic markers, symbols that help construct our roles in various spheres of social life.

Our choice of clothing also speaks to our position within the social hierarchy. Modern influencers, such as YouTubers, epitomize this by promoting ways to dress in a manner that reflects wealth or sophistication, thus reaffirming the powerful social currency clothing holds. In this sense, attire can be viewed as both a form of self-expression and a tool of social control, used to categorize and rank individuals based on external appearance.

However, sartorial choices can also be a site of resistance. Clothing may act as a "cage" for the body, adhering to societal expectations, yet it simultaneously holds the potential for liberation. The bra-burning movement during the 1968 Miss America pageant in the United States symbolized a rejection of the objectification of the female body through imposed beauty standards. Similarly, films like *Miss Congeniality* (Dir. Donald Petrie, 2000), in which the protagonist undergoes a makeover, challenge notions of beauty pageants as arenas that commodify women. These examples underscore the complex dialogue between external appearance and societal norms, highlighting how fashion can either constrain or empower the individual.

This chapter aims to explore this nuanced relationship between body and clothing, treating the body as a text written through sartorial choices. By analyzing how garments function as symbols within the broader social order, it offers insights into the ways in which identity is constructed, performed, and, at times, resisted.

Our sartorial choices, whether eccentric, conventional, or stereotypical, play a pivotal role in shaping our identity. The attire that envelops our bodies serves not only to create an external appearance but also to navigate the social norms we engage with. In this sense, clothing possesses a language of its own—a system of signs not confined to verbal communication. As previously mentioned, garments actively contribute to the articulation and framing of the body. This dynamic becomes particularly evident in the visual narratives we encounter in cinema, photography, fashion runways, and other forms of visual representation.

To delve deeper into this phenomenon, this chapter will explore the use of costumes in the films of Satyajit Ray, using Roland Barthes' theory of clothing as a sign system. Barthes, in line with Ferdinand de Saussure's framework of the signifier and the signified, suggests that costumes function as symbols within a broader semiotic landscape. Through this lens, we will examine how Ray's use of costume transcends mere aesthetic choice, instead offering a profound commentary on the characters' identities, social roles, and cultural contexts.

Satyajit Ray, in his films like *Devi* (1960), *Mahanagar* (1963), *Kanchenjungha* (1962), and *Charulata* (1964), among others, has also tried to articulate the female body using the sartorial markers. It could be a matter of investigation whether Ray tried to portray his female protagonists to highlight gender issues as per our current understanding of the same in the twenty-first century. In most of his films Ray has tried to portray various aspects of Bengali life in both urban and rural locations. The on-screen sartorial appearance of his female protagonists also affirm our previous discussion on clothes acting as a social code for the body. Ray's films are often identified as adaptations from various literary manifestations, for example *Pather Panchali* (1955), *Ghare Baire* (1948), and *Jalsaghar* (1958). Along with these rural setups, he also concentrated on the urban setup in films such as *Pratidwandi* (1970), and a few others mentioned earlier, which focuses upon the day-to-day life of the Bengali middle class, their daily struggle to survive, and their dream to climb the social ladder, in context of the colonial past of Bengal and the intricacies of the post-partition era.

Satyajit Ray himself belonged to a Bengali middle-class family with exposure to the Western education system. His family is deeply rooted in the cultural and religious outlook of the Brahmo Samaj. The growth and application of Brahmo ideals played a significant role in the construction of the modern Bengali women. Termed as "bhadromahila," the reconstruction of the role of nineteenth-century Bengali women is intrinsically linked with the changing perceptions of upper-class Bengali men, educated in the Western ways and ideals. According to Devapriya Sanyal, "The *bhadralok* class to which Ray belonged was a Western educated elite whose concern were primarily democracy, nationalism, social equality, and emancipation of women, but they were also brought up on world literature which favored realism and mimesis (representing real life in art) over political rhetoric."[1] Ray is part of a distinct school of filmmakers who engage with the postcolonial elite, utilizing Hollywood cinematic models to explore nationalist concerns. His approach stands out for its focus on the everyday struggles, dreams, aspirations, and downfalls of individuals, all captured through a realistic lens. This method sets his work apart, as it offers a striking contrast to the conventions of Western filmmaking. By blending Hollywood techniques with an intimate portrayal of local realities, Ray creates a cinematic language uniquely attuned to the complexities of postcolonial identity and experience.

Nineteenth-century Bengal that saw the rise of the Bengali 'bhadralok' (gentleman) also saw the rise of the reformist movements that were woven around the issue of women's empowerment along with many other social issues. With the commencement of the twentieth century the Bengali 'bhadralok' became an extremely important aspect of Bengali society at both rural and urban locations. According to J. H. Broomfield:

> At the beginning of the twentieth century Bengali rural and urban society differed in many fundamental respects, yet they shared at least one feature: a common dominant elite. In city, town and village there was one group of Bengalis who claimed and were accorded recognition as superior in social status to the mass of their fellows. These were the *bhadralok*, literally the "respectable people", the "gentlemen". They were distinguished by many aspects of their behavior – their deportment, their speech, their dress, their style of housing, their eating habits, their occupations, and their associations – and white as fundamentally by their cultural values and their sense social propriety.[2]

This "bhadralok" community also acted as a human resource for the British administration by providing people for administrative services. The class of Bengali "bhadralok" was extremely proud to hold such administrative services under British governance. To begin with, they were the pioneers who showed interest in learning the language of their ruler. The establishment of the University of Calcutta in 1857 was an important step towards the introduction of English as the medium of instruction in the newly introduced European education system. Broomfield adds:

> "The enthusiasm with which the Bengali bhadralok accepted and promoted English language education, in marked contrast to the response of the landed elites in the surrounding provinces, gave them the lion's share of the new opportunities for professional, administrative and clerical employment throughout eastern and northern India. They were justly proud of their achievement in creating the educational system that was the key to this success, and the maintenance and development of that system became one of their main preoccupations.[3]

"Bhadralok" as a group developed a completely different sense of cultural identity from their experiences of negotiations since the nineteenth century, while negotiating with the existing social and cultural norms and the newly imported English ones. A small group of Calcutta college-educated "bhadralok" felt the need to analyze and reevaluate the foundation of their traditional belief system, irrespective of their attraction or repulsion for European values. This led to the rise of the reform movements and later nationalist movements. From the above discussion we might deduce why and how the Bengali "bhadralok"—though a product of English education policy and system, with a taste for European lifestyle—initiated the Indian nationalist movements. The following section discusses the birth and growth of the modern ideas and ideologies centered around "bhadramahila."

The Making of the Bengali "Bhadramahila"

The colonial rule affected the cultural constructions across India, and more specifically in Bengal. The upper-class Bengali family with access to the Western education system was exposed to alternative viewpoints regarding the positionality of a woman. Armed with a new set of learnings, the educated "bhadralok" set on a path for women's emancipation. As discussed earlier, the Bengali "bhadralok" adapted the Western understanding of respectability.

Jnanada Nandini Devi is considered to be the woman who pioneered the modern Bengali style of wearing a saree. Having been stopped from entering a club in Mumbai due to the lack of a blouse beneath her saree, she ventured

Figure 5.1 *Jnanada Nandini Devi. https://commons.wikimedia.org/wiki/File: Jnanadanandini_Devi.JPG.*
Published under Creative Commons License

down a path of recasting the saree into a more acceptable and respectable form of attire. Viewed through a colonial lens, the idea of "lajja" or chastity is redefined to include the notion of shame in the context of a Victorian Christian woman.[4]

The traditional attire of a Bengali woman included a saree, which refers to a length of cloth of coarse material wrapped around the body, leaving the shoulders bare. The image in Figure 5.2 on the following page, taken from the collection of Kalighat paintings, depicts a Bengali woman in a traditional form of a saree.

This manner of wearing a saree by virtue of its partial nakedness was perceived by the British colonizers as being uncivilized. Viewed through the Victorian discourse of respectability, it denotes the lack of civilization and propriety among the colonized Bengali class. According to Himani Banerji:

Figure 5.2 *Bengali woman in traditional attire. https://commons.wikimedia.org/wiki/File:Kalighat_pictures_sep_sheets_44.jpg*
Published under Creative Commons License

> This sartorial-moral enterprise is profoundly English nineteenth century in its ethos. Fundamentally distinct from pre-colonial, feudal notions of grandeur or status, this attire is an intrinsic response to and an absorption within a colonial influence. The ideology of Victorian femininity provides the lens through which is perceived and configured the indigenous dominant ideology about womanhood.[5]

Jnanada Nandini Devi pioneered the saree-wearing style termed "brahmika saree" which later also acquired the name of "nivi saree," derived from the Bengali word "naba" meaning new. She combined Western ideas of respectability with Indian ethos by reframing an attire which was rooted in the cultural upbringing of a Bengali woman. She was inspired by the Parsi "gara" or a style of blouse with long sleeves worn by Parsi women. Jnanada Nandini Devi combined this existing form of blouse with a saree draping style with pleats. The use of organized pleats in draping the saree reflected the pleats visible in the gowns worn by nineteenth-century Victorian women. The "brahmika" style of saree (see Figure 5.1), was introduced to accommodate the changing roles of Bengali women to accompany their "bhadralok" husband into the public spaces. Jnanada Nandini Devi chose to amalgamate the traditional Bengali attire with the fashion trends of Victorian England. High collars and lace adornments characterized Victorian women's fashion. With Jnanada Nandini Devi alongside Kadambari Devi (the wife of Bengali playwright, painter, and editor Jyotirindranath Tagore), these aspects of Victorian fashion found their way into the reformed attire for the Bengali "bhadramahila."

The nineteenth- and twentieth-century concept of "bhadramahila" was again transformed in the post-partition era, when women had to venture out into the public space as workers. The sartorial practices underwent another layer of changes in order to accommodate the ease of the working woman. The modern style involves wearing the saree backwards with the "pallav" hanging behind loosely, coupled with a short-sleeved blouse. The changing perception and assimilation of different saree draping styles and fashion trends connected to blouse and petticoats are explicitly featured in the films of Satyajit Ray. The following section connects the ideas of colonialism, nationalism, women empowerment, attire, and the Western notion of respectability through an in-depth analysis of the costumes from select films by Ray, and his attitude to these aspects of sociocultural reformations.

Ray and the Modern Bengali Woman "bhadramahila"

The colonial influence felt during the period of the Bengal Renaissance connects with the nationalist fervor to recreate the saree. This is furthered by the new idea of modernism in the context of India in the post-independence era, through the vision of Pandit Nehru's approach to a modern India. With the Indian independence in 1947, Nehru's understanding of modern India started with another phase of social reformation that was based on developmental models. Nehruvian dreams of modern India were to play a very important role in building the self-esteem of a newly independent nation. Ray's language of films reflected Nehru's idea of modern India. After 1947 under the leadership of Nehru as the first prime minister of India, cultural policies and development of the nation also assumed importance. Such cultural policies promoted arts and literature and started to play a crucial role in shaping public culture and above all recognized its impact on the mass. Ray's films thus gradually found room as a part of this cultural scheme of newly independent India. According to Sanyal, "Ray was doing something that had not been done before in terms of presenting India's social reality to a literate and aware international public."[6] She also adds: "Ray's films … achieved two things: bringing live on screen the life of his people and at the same time addressing the progressive aspirations of the liberal middle class, i.e. the key participant group in Nehru's cultural initiatives."[7] His works seemed to have played a very important role in bringing the culture of Bengal to the big international platform, often referred to as cinema. In his portrayal of characters, though they are mostly adaptations from literature, we may find Indians of post-independence India. We may find members of the Indian intellectual middle class giving us ideas about the nature of post-independence urban Indian citizenry.

Ray's portrayal of women in his films is not indifferent, rather he seems to depict an understanding of the feminine aspects, which probably could be considered as the impact of his upbringing in a Brahmo family. The influence of his mother, Suprabha Ray can be felt in his portrayal of women. Ray's mother worked as a superintendent in the Handicrafts Department at the Vidyasagar Bani Bhawan. Well known for her acumen in knitting and stitching, she also provided lessons to fellow women in different forms of stitching and cutting along with the art of making "shameez," a type of undergarment worn by Indian women in the nineteenth and twentieth centuries.[8]

Ray's portrayal of women seems to be a continuation of the awakened women often becoming a part of the Indian New Wave. Films that were being made at this juncture often negated the commercial entertainment aspect of cinema. This new set of filmmakers were trying their hands at the new experimental genres of film. They were experimenting with all the modernist aspects of filmmaking. Their films were fearlessly questioning the oppressive social structure and the violence ingrained in it, including gender and caste issues. In other words, such films were turning the realist focus of the new wave into reality. Ray, on the other hand, did not seem to be completely walking the same path. While commenting on social issues, he did not neglect cinema's commercial aspect. Through his films he tried to tell a story rather than to re-tell a story. Thus, his experiments were also quite limited, as his work never posed challenges to the understandability of the audience. He tried to reach out to the maximum possible crowd; at the same time, it would be wrong to say that he did not critically comment on contemporary social structure and its practices, as a part of which he focused on gender issues.

Sartorial Objects and 'Bhadramahila' in Ray's Films

The role of objects in the construction of meaning through films is essential to understanding the sartorial practices portrayed in Ray's films. As Shoma Chatterji points out, objects acquire meaning only through their interaction with human beings.[9] The portrayal of human subjectivity in films is directly linked to the use of and reaction to objects such as "saree" and "blouse." The materiality of the objects becomes a marker of social class, ideas, ideologies, and attitude. According to Chatterji, "Ray's films offer a deep and unique insight into the representational qualities of objects, their history, and the socio-political reasons for their presence in his films. The reading they offer sometimes demonstrates the symbiosis between object and subject, and sometimes destabilizes the hierarchies between objects and subjects."[10]

The types of sarees and blouses worn by the characters, of various materials and styles, represent the sense of modernity connected to the women characters in Ray's films. From "Dhakai jamdani" (fine handloom sarees produced in Dhaka) to silk sarees, from "thaan" (a length of borderless white cloth worn by Hindu widows in Bengal) to mass-produced synthetic sarees, ideas concerning a woman's position in nineteenth- and twentieth-century Bengal are conveyed. The presence or absence of blouses and their different styles, such as "jacket" in *Ghare Baire*, "ghoti hata" in *Mahanagar*, and "Kaberi blouse" in *Aranyer Dinratri,* depicts either traditionality or modernity with respect to the women characters.

Charulata, the protagonist in Ray's film of the same name, represents the period during the Bengal Renaissance that saw a movement towards women's emancipation through education and attire. A housewife, trapped within the four walls of her house, peeping outside into the public space, detached from her anglicized husband who is preoccupied with his work, Charulata spends her time reading, writing, and sewing. In presenting her as a Bengali woman modernized in her approach and attitude, the costumes play a major role. Ray's attention to detail is an essential aspect of understanding his films. The frames capturing Charulata show her dressed in "aatpoure" saree (traditional form of Bengali saree without pleats) along with long-sleeved blouses with high collars, adorned with intricate lace around the neck and the wrists. The intricacy of the lace reflects the feminine charm associated with Victorian fashion and the importance of lace in gowns. The closing scene of the film shows Charulata on a beach with her husband. She is wearing a "Dhakai jamdani" with a three-quarters blouse decorated with broad lace intricately designed in white. This attire is quite different to the one Charulata wears while inside her house. Stepping out with her husband in the public space requires her to dress elegantly.

While *Charulata* beautifully portrays the new "bhadramahila," educated and modernised, *Debi* shows the conflicts and contrasts in the views of the existing patriarchy and the modern youth exposed to Western education. In the initial scenes between Doyamoyee and her husband Umaprasad, Doyamoyee is seen wearing a Victorian-style blouse, three-quarter sleeves with lace frills around the neck and the elbows. This is coupled with a traditional "taant" (handloom saree), beautifully adorned with little floral motifs. Through the discussion between Umaprasad and Doyamoyee, the gulf between the traditional and modern thoughts are clearly visible. The colonial influence is reflected in Uma's viewpoints. The exposure to Western education greatly inspires Uma's ideas, especially with respect to English as a source of a new knowledge system. Doyamoyee raises a poignant question: "Is there no knowledge if one does not learn English?" Uma spontaneously answers: "That's old knowledge." This shows the modern Bengali "bhodrolok" with a broader mindset. In contrast, Umaprasad's father represents the old world order of superstitious beliefs, such as his sudden belief that his daughter-in-law,

Doyamoyee, is a goddess incarnate. The later parts of the film, which portrays Doyamoyee as a divine being, worshipped by the various villagers, sees a complete transformation in her attire. The Victorian-style blouses with collars and frills are replaced by a plain white blouse devoid of any decorations. The beautiful "taant" sarees worn in the scenes before her deification are replaced by a plain white saree with broad red border—a quintessential Bengali saree. From the reflection of the Western culture in her attire to a completely Eastern tradition of dressing, the sartorial practices of the character Doyamoyee depict the conflict between the idea of a modern emancipated woman, with a liberal husband, and the tradition-bound father-in-law, who transforms Uma's wife into a goddess, in the process de-sexualizing her identity. The last scene of the film shows Doyamoyee dressed in the Victorian-style blouse, adorned with jewelry, messy hair, and smeared kohl on her eyes, running through the fields, with her head uncovered and the "pallav" trailing behind her. Through the choice of this attire, she breaks out of the shackles put around her through her deification. Though her actions are based on her loss of sense due to extreme emotional trauma, by her sartorial choices Doyamoyee overcomes the dilemma between being a tradition-bound daughter-in-law and a modern Bengali "bhadramohila," supported by the liberal husband, studying English literature in the city.

In the next film, Arati, Ray's female protagonist in *Mahanagar* (1963) breaks the societal shackles and leaves behind the boundaries that were imposed on her by patriarchy, in order to support her family financially. She hits the world outside along with her husband, Subrata, in search of livelihood. Arati's determination to work and earn for her family was a huge leap; for the first time she was leaving her house to work in a man's world.

Breaking free, though, sounds like an easy and fast process, but that is a myth. Empowerment does not happen overnight. There are many steps to be crossed to reach the stage of empowerment and freedom. While signing her job application, Subrata's protective gesture makes Arati uncomfortable. As a husband, Subrata's gesture may look protective, but at the same time it is posing questions on the independent aspect of Arati. Ray depicts this very first step of Arati's independence in an extremely delicate fashion. To the audience, this depiction makes it clear that at many moments in our daily life the independence

Figure 5.3 *Modern Bengali woman in Satyajit Ray's* Mahanagar *(The Big City). [1963]. British Library, EAP127/9/898, https://eap.bl.uk/archive-file/EAP127-9-898*

of women is being questioned under the façade of protection. It also loudly shouts back that just walking out of home to an office and earning money might not be enough for independence.

Ray depicts Arati's office as a space of female camaraderie. A designated space is something that is often denied to women even in their homes. Arati finds the same in the office, and it turns out to be a space where the women may discuss topics which they are otherwise not allowed to. Arati's job profile gives her the chance to go out of the office and to roam in certain parts of the city as a saleswoman. Here Arati is doing her work on her own and the audience suddenly realizes that she is doing it without the protection of Subrata. This Arati is capable of making decisions and can express herself. Finally at the end of the month when Arati draws her first salary, she chooses to escape to the washroom, exclusively her space, to have a silent dialogue with her new self, whom she sees in the mirror. Holding a bunch of currency might not be a very new thing for her, but this bunch of currency is her own. This bunch was earned by her. It represents her first taste of financial independence.

The portrayal of the female bond between Arati and her colleague Edith takes us to a moment where the two women are exchanging confidences. Wearing lipstick might be helpful for business is the tip that Edith shares with Arati, who later gains the confidence to use it. Ray thus takes his audience through different steps towards women's emancipation, but at the same time very delicately handles the hidden gender politics of how and why women need to "look good" for men as it might help in the workplace. While focusing on burning issues of gender identity, we often tend to forget these subtleties of formation of gender identity and other identities on the basis of how we look. Arati is not an exception in this regard. Her requirement to feel fashionable or attractive alters her sartorial taste. Her dress code seems different when she is at home as a wife taking care of the whole family, where she does not have to feel fashionable or to look attractive, but at the same time Arati needs to feel fashionable and attractive when she is a working woman. Thus, as discussed earlier, Arati is also forging identities using her clothing and at the same time carefully negotiating with the issue of societal approval for the same. One may observe very interestingly in the film that although her husband Subrata is lending a helping hand in turning her from a housewife into a working woman, he is still not very comfortable with the fact that his wife is also a working woman and thus needs to be attractive. This in a way highlights the whole issue of women's emancipation in a very complicated fashion. This slow, changing, and complex picture of gender identities takes a few more steps when the audience encounters Arati taking over from Subrata as the earning member of the family, as Subrata becomes jobless and she secures her job with a salary increase.

To delve deeper into these "modern" women that we have been discussing and to have a better understanding of the sartorial taste and acceptance of the female body in modern Bengal, we must go back to the nineteenth century, often referred to as the Bengal Renaissance. As discussed earlier, the nineteenth and twentieth centuries were a time for drastic changes in Bengali society in every sphere, from reform movements to the development and practice of various art forms and literary genres and from politics to philosophy. It was also a time when the sartorial taste of Bengali women was going through a change, though initially it was limited only among the elite women of the "bhadralok" group. This change in the traditional Bengali attire of saree was enjoying an important Western influence called a blouse, adding a touch of modernity to the appearance of the modern Bengali women. Saree was a very traditional attire of Bengali women, as they were trained to wear this from their childhood without any petticoat or blouse. As stated earlier, it was probably Jnanada Nandidni Devi, wife of Satyendranath Tagore, who introduced this style of wearing saree with a blouse in the nineteenth century. She also started the trend to drape saree in a completely different manner. Initially her style of draping the saree came to be known as Brahmika Saree. Gradually the blouse and petticoat became part and parcel of saree.

As we have seen, Arati Majumdar, the protagonist of *Mahanagar*, leaves the conventional domestic territory of a Bengali woman to take a leap and turns into a modern Bengali working woman. This change is also visible in her sartorial identity. One of the remarkable changes that we get to see in Arati's dress code is her shift to a translucent blouse with a clearly visible white bra when she leaves for work. It is interesting to note the acceptability of this identity and how it gains some agency while negotiating with the traditional space of family and home and the modern city, where Arati goes to earn money.

This sartorial image of Arati sets a dialogue with the postcolonial backdrop of the city of Calcutta, narrating its journey of modernization followed by globalization, which is further followed by urbanization. The film asks the question: where is the place of the modern Bengali woman? and tries to investigate it. In the light teasing and jokes cracked by Arati's husband Subrata about Arati, being an attractive person, might be a troublesome employee of any organization, Subrata's traditional understanding that the place of a woman is within the household and thus, her roaming around in the city is not very desirable, remains hidden.

Nineteenth-century Bengal witnessed the rise of nationalism, following the trail of reformists movements that were forming around the women. In these reform movements, to ensure the empowerment of women in Bengal and India, various European educational reformists and women's education advocates such as John Elliot Drinkwater Bethune and David Hare were involved, as they believed that the redemption of the Indian community lies in the treatment of the women in their society. Thus, women became the torch-bearers of Indian modernity as well as the epitome of Indian tradition. This combination of values seems to be quite complex as they are often conflicting, but the Indian woman was hailed as the capable creature who can attain balance even under such complex conditions. We must not forget that most of these reform movements that happened in Bengal were heavily based on Western social ideologies. It seems that in maintaining this balance of modernity and tradition, sartorial appearance helped these women to incarnate in different avatars, of housewife and of working woman, as seen in the case of Arati. In nineteenth-century Bengal, we get to see the women of the Brahmo Samaj, who tried to attain the identity of the modern Indian woman through their sartorial appearance. The *babu(s)* of Bengal, who were a product of the Western education system that was introduced in India in the nineteenth century, also used their sartorial tastes to maintain the balance between the modern and the traditional. In the process they also encouraged the women of their household to decorate themselves in a Western fashion and tried to draw a line between what should be worn inside the household and what should be worn outside. This practice affirms the formation of identities based on the dress code. We must not ignore that while the nineteenth-century Bengali middle-class babu is encouraging Western modernity among the women of his household, at the same time, he also believes that too much exposure to (Western) education and Western culture is not good for the woman, as she might tend to forget the traditional Bengali norms, resulting in disruption to his family life. This seems to be an extremely complex thought process—a complicated blend of orthodox Hinduism, Western modern (liberal) values, and Indian nationalism. Arati's husband Subrata and her father-in-law are the products of this blend of ideologies and thus their masculinity often seems to confront Arati's identity of working as a (modern) Bengali woman. Arati's sartorial choice emerges as the ground of this conflict.

This son/father duo has been confirmed as the *babu(s)* of Bengal from their sartorial identities, as both could be seen wearing *babu* style of clothing such as dhoti with a shirt. Still, there is a sense of conflict between the ideologies of these two *babu(s)* of two generations. They also have a difference of opinion regarding working women. Subrata supports Arati's incarnation as a working woman at the initial stage to compensate for his joblessness and to boast his persona as a supporter of women's empowerment. His father, on the other hand, who was a teacher, has a very clear understanding of women in the society. He believes that the real place of a woman is within the household. She is not supposed to go out in search of money. She is supposed to take care of the household chores and to attend the needs of the children and other members of the family. He believes that it is the male member/s of the family who are solely responsible for earning money and providing for the entire family. Thus, he seems to be extremely upset to realize himself as the father of a jobless son, who is incapable of providing for his family and is thus letting his own wife go out and make money. Arati's new role as a working woman remains unacceptable to him.

Subrata too has been depicted in many junctures dwindling between his bookish faith in women's empowerment and the reality of his attractive wife going out to work as a modern woman. The conversations between husband and wife showcase their anxiety towards the Indian modernity which is knocking on the door. In Arati we may find a modern Bengali woman who aspires to a better living standard by ensuring more financial freedom. Arati appears as a modern Bengali middle-class working woman in an almost see-through blouse that prominently displays her Western bra; this sartorial choice acts as a gendered marker on all the social, national, and political ideologies that we were discussing earlier. This implies a sense of gender to every dream and aspiration that Arati and Subrata cherish as an educated Bengali middle-class family in the process of attaining modernity. Arati's desire for fashionable clothing could be read as an association of the same with success. This paves the way to enter into the world of "power dressing."[11] Arati evolved into power dressing from her thick cotton saree and blouse to an almost see-through blouse with a prominent display of her bra, accompanied by a revealing drape of a fashionable saree. One may also notice a drastic change in her accessories as well. Being respectable and fashionable both must go hand in hand in the sartorial discourse of a Bengali "bhadramahila," as she is the Bengali version of the European *memsahib*. We must not ignore the strong exposure of Western norms of femininity among the Bengali "bhadralok(s)," who thus tried to redesign the feminine identity of the female members of their family. For instance, while commenting on the travelogue by Krishnabhabini Das (1864–1919), Jayati Gupta says:

> From the period that she stepped out of the confines of her home in India and lived in England, her sartorial preference, manners and etiquette were in her own words adapted to the land which was her temporary home. When they returned to Calcutta, Devendranath's family and friends had ostracized them. She continued to wear Western attire, which she finally abandoned when she became a widow in 1909 … She reinvented herself by wearing the traditional, white widow's saree prescribed by Hindu orthodoxy … and returned to the folds of Hindu religion.[12]

These transitory phases of sartorial choices are clearly visible in the character of Bimala in Ray's film *Ghare Baire*. In her narration, Bimala mentions how her husband worked towards "making a memsahib out of me." She styles her fine silk sarees with a brooch and elaborately designed blouses with lace ruffles: "Bimala proudly shows off the frilled and long-sleeved 'jackets' she has designed—delivered by the tailor to her husband—as she preens in front of the mirror."[13] Bimala's clothes mirror the style of Ms. Gilby, her tutor training her to become a *memsahib* with English cultural influences, stepping out of the "andar mahal" in a bright red saree stylized in the Brahmika form of draping saree coupled with a white three-quarters blouse reminiscent of the Victorian style seen in the earlier sections of the film. The last scene focuses on Bimala's transformation from the modern "bhadramahila" to a widow shackled by the traditional rules and laws.

In contrast to these films, later ones showcase a very transformed idea of the "bhadramahila" which is still rooted in the colonial history of Bengal. Ray's films such as *Nayak* (1966) and *Kanchenjunga* (1962) capture changing attitudes to the modern Bengali woman born out of the nineteenth-century Bengal Renaissance. The character of Ms. Aditi Sengupta, in *Nayak*, is a quintessential professional, draping a saree further modernized by the demands of convenience of a working woman. She carries a pen tucked into the borders of her blouse, marking her as a professional journalist. The protagonist, Arindam Mukherjee, refers to Ms. Sengupta as "Ms. Adhunika," meaning modern. The representation of Ms. Sengupta through her sartorial choices and her agency can be connected back to Arati from *Mahanagar*. However, unlike Arati, Ms. Sengupta is unmarried and answerable to no one but herself. This traces the changes in Bengali women's individuality through their interactions with the saree and blouse.

Conclusion

In conclusion, This chapter has delved into the intricate relationship between clothing and identity, particularly through the lens of saree draping styles and blouse designs in Satyajit Ray's films. By highlighting the sartorial choices of Bengali women, Ray not only captures their evolving roles in society but also reflects the larger cultural and colonial influences that shaped these identities. The saree and blouse in his films act as more than mere garments; they are cultural signifiers, a concept that aligns with Roland Barthes' notion of dress as a system of signs. Drawing from Saussure's semiotics, the saree becomes the signifier, while its cultural, historical, and social implications form the signified.

Through the evolution of these sartorial elements, we witness how colonial legacies and nationalist aspirations intertwine, influencing the self-representation of Bengali women. The interplay between traditional draping styles and modern blouse designs, often seen in Ray's depiction of his female characters, speaks to a negotiation between the past and present—between colonial imposition and the assertion of a uniquely Bengali, and often feminist, identity. By reading the saree and blouse as signs in Ray's films, we gain a deeper understanding of how clothing operates not only as a marker of individual identity but also as a reflection of cultural memory and resistance.

Notes

1 Devapriya Sanyal, *Gendered Modernity and Indian Cinema: The Women in Satyajit Ray's Films*, New York: Routledge, 2022, 3.

2 J. H. Broomfield, *Elite Conflict in a Plural Society: Twentieth Century Bengal,* Kolkata: Jadavpur University Press, 2018, 5.

3 Ibid., 7–8.

4 Himani Bannerji, *The Ideological Condition: Selected Essays on History, Race and Gender,* Boston: Brill, 2020.

5 Ibid., 256.

6 Sanyal, *Gendered Modernity and Indian Cinema*, 11.

7 Ibid.

8 Tumpa Mukherjee, *Amritaspeaks,* October 7, 2017. https://amritaspeaks.com/2017/10/07/heres-what-you-never-knew-about-satyajit-rays-mother-suprabha/

9 Shoma A. Chatterji, *Women at the Window: The Material Universe of Rabindranath Tagore Through the Eyes of Satyajit Ray,* Noida: HarperCollins, 2017.

10 Ibid., 70.

11 J. Entwistle, *The Fashioned Body: Fashion, Dress and Modern Social Theory,* Cambridge: Polity Press, 2000.

12 Jayati Gupta, *Travel Culture, Travel Writing and Bengali Women,* New York: Routledge, 2020, 55.

13 Chatterji, *Women at the Window*, 122.

Bibliography

Bannerji, Himani. *The Ideological Condition: Selected Essays on History, Race and Gender.* Boston: Brill, 2020.

Broomfield, J. H. *Elite Conflict in a Plural Society: Twentieth Century Bengal.* Kolkata: Jadavpur University Press, 2018.

Chatterji, Shoma A. *Women at the Window: The Material Universe of Rabindranath Tagore Through the Eyes of Satyajit Ray.* Noida: HarperCollins, 2017.

Entwistle, J. *The Fashioned Body: Fashion, Dress and Modern Social Theory.* Cambridge: Polity Press, 2000.

Gupta, Jayati. *Travel Culture, Travel Writing and Bengali Women.* New York: Routledge, 2020.

Mukherjee, Tumpa. *Amritaspeaks.* October 7, 2017. https://amritaspeaks.com/2017/10/07/heres-what-you-never-knew-about-satyajit-rays-mother-suprabha/.

Sanyal, Devapriya. *Gendered Modernity and Indian Cinema: The Women in Satyajit Ray's Films.* New York: Routledge, 2022.

Part Three

Fashioning Cultural Heritage and Popular Culture: "The Robe of Feathers"

"The Robe of Feathers," a children's fairy tale from Japan, explores the intersection between dress in the human world and dress in the yokai world. I use the Japanese term *yokai* rather than the Chinese *yaoguai* or Korean *yogoe* here, as I am discussing Japanese spirits. The story begins:

> Once there was a fisherman who lived all alone on a tiny island in Japan. He was very poor and very lonely. Early one morning he started toward his boat; there had been a bad storm the night before but now the sun was shining brightly. As he walked along, he saw something hanging on a branch of one of the pine trees along the beach. It was beautiful and shining. He took it down from the branch and found that it was a wonderful robe made of feathers. The feathers were all of different colours, as lovely

> and soft as the rainbow, and they shined and sparkled in the sunlight like jewels. It was the most beautiful thing the fisherman had ever seen in his whole life.[1]

Later in the story, the reader learns that the robe in fact belongs to a yokai, described simply in the English translation as an angel.[23] The fisherman nobly returned the robe back to the angel, and she gifted him with a dance so beautiful that he would treasure its memory for the rest of his life. Most important for our purposes here is the sheer beauty of the clothes of the yokai. The robe is variously described as lovely, soft, like a rainbow, shiny, sparkling like jewels, and significantly, the most beautiful thing the protagonist had ever seen in his life. The fisherman longed to keep the robe for himself, but resisted, knowing that a human being should not steal the clothes of the spirits. The legendary beauty of the angel's robe underscores the desirability of a yokai's garments for a human being, and this children's story may be seen as a metaphor for the contemporary mania for dressing like yokai, whether in a full cosplay or wearing a statement piece, or wearing clothing depicting yokai or brands named after yokai.

The theme of *yogoe* (Korea) or *yaoguai* (China) manifests itself everywhere in East Asian popular culture these days—from fashion to manga, anime, and Pokémon to dance. Each of the essays in this section on Fashioning Cultural Heritage and Popular Culture explores the connection between these uniquely East Asian spirits (*yokai* in Japan, *yaoguai* in China, *yogoe* in Korea) and contemporary fashion cultures in some way. Sun Jingru's Chapter 6 looks at both hanfu and nationalism in China, but also the huli jing (fox yokai), Daji. And at the same time, this chapter is a meaningful way to begin the final section of this book, as it brings the reader back to the introduction and idea of Asia Pacific, most particularly the idea of Asia Pacific leaders making a unified statement by wearing the Tang suit at the 2001 APEC summit. Cringuta Irina Pelea's Chapter 7 explores the variety of yokai featured in kimono, particularly in television productions and manga and anime. And the editor's own Chapter 8 explores yogoe in contemporary Korean fashion, through two case studies: costuming in the K-Drama, *My Girlfriend is a Gumiho,* and clothing worn by K-Pop BTS.

Notes

1 Florence Sakade, ed., "The Robe of Feathers," in *Japanese Children's Favorite Stories,* vol. 2, Boston: Tuttle Publishing, 2005, 21–2.

2 Ibid., 22.

3 Angel is Sakade's translation here.

6

Hanfu as a Role-related Culture: Daji, Femininity, and Everyday Nationalism[1]

SUN JINGRU

Introduction

Hanfu is the traditional dress of the Han Chinese people and began in the period of the Yellow Emperor, 5,000 to 6,000 years ago. Since the Zhou Dynasty (1046–221 BCE), the ancient Hanfu system has gradually taken shape and has developed into four major styles, namely the Yichang style (衣裳制), the Yiku style (衣裤制), the Shenyi style (深衣制), and the Tongcai style (通裁制).[2] Beginning with the Hanfu Movement at the beginning of the twenty-first century, hanfu has been recognized and loved by an increasing number of Chinese people. As Na Yang suggests, "the modern Hanfu is a modern dress system constructed on the basis of the clothing styles worn by ancient Han Chinese on a daily basis, inheriting the typical production techniques, styles, aesthetics and other cultural connotations."[3] In recent years, the term "Sankeng girl" has become an internet buzzword in China,[4] referring to girls who simultaneously like the following three styles of dress: hanfu, lolita, and JK (Joshi Kousei) uniforms. Unlike lolita and JK uniforms, which are two styles of clothing influenced by Japanese subculture, hanfu culture has a stronger local flavor. Although some hanfu enthusiasts do not recognize the confusion between hanfu and cosplay clothing, the term shows the affinity between these two cultures. To a certain extent, hanfu culture is also related to roles.

The cosplay of characters in ancient-style games and ancient-style movies and TV dramas was one of the important motives for the early popularity of hanfu.[5] Unlike consumers' views of general clothing, their understanding and perception of hanfu are largely influenced by movies and TV dramas. iiMedia Research shows that in 2022, movies and TV dramas accounted for the greatest proportion of Chinese people's understanding of hanfu.[6] Hanfu brands are interested in cobranding with costume dramas and anime about Chinese mythological characters, designing distinctive hanfu for the characters, and utilizing popular characters to drive sales of hanfu.[7] As a result, characters have become one of the most important ways for the public to understand hanfu culture. On the other hand, the mythical tradition has increasingly become an inseparable part of the Chinese cultural imagination. Supernatural films (shenguaipian, 神怪片) have always occupied an important position in ancient Chinese costume movies (guzhuangpian, 古装片). In recent years, the adaptation of myths and legends in Chinese cinema has constituted a new wave of these films. The Xianxia genre, which tells stories of gods, fairies, demons, and devils, has emerged as an important category in Chinese televisions and games. These two premodern symbols, ancient costumes and myths, merge in the portrayal of demons in Chinese movies and dramas, and the image of demons has become an important entry point for understanding Chinese hanfu culture.

In this paper, I characterize Daji to explore the relationship between hanfu and nationalism and further explore how fashion intervenes in the process of constructing nationalism. In addition, how can ordinary people draw on the characterization of hanfu to transform nationalism by playing roles?

The Nine-tailed Demon Fox Daji and the Transformation of her Image

The nine-tailed fox is a significant figure in Chinese mythology. In China, the nine-tailed fox is understood to possess both auspicious and demonic qualities. The *Song of Mount Tu*, a masterpiece ballad of the Xia dynasty (2070–1600 BCE), speaks of the nine-tailed white fox as a good luck charm that can bring prosperity to the country. The nine-tailed fox is frequently depicted alongside the Queen Mother of the West in portraits of the Han Dynasty (202 BCE–220 CE), symbolizing the prosperity of her progeny. Additionally, *The Classic of Mountains and Seas* asserts that those who consume the nine-tailed fox can resist the effects of poisonous parasites.[8] On the other hand, the nine-tailed fox is associated with demonic characteristics. Indeed, the most well-known image of the nine-tailed fox in China is that of Daji, who was the favored concubine of King Zhou of the Shang Dynasty (1600–1046 BCE). *Kobiki*, written by Ōe no Masafusa (1041–1111 CE), is regarded as the earliest extant record of the nine-tailed fox in Japan. It mentions that "The Daji of the Shang dynasty is a nine-tailed fox" (殷之妲己为九尾狐), indicating that the idea of Daji as a nine-tailed fox had already spread to Japan by the beginning of the twelfth century.[9] The historical figure known as Daji is depicted as an enabler of the tyrant King Zhou. In *Records of the Grand Historian (shiji,* 史记*)*, it is written that King Zhou of Shang was killed because he favored Daji. In the *Biographies of Exemplary Women (lienvzhuan,* 列女传*)*, the death of Bigan and other events unrelated to Daji are blamed on Daji, which suggests that a woman's beauty can precipitate the downfall of a country.[10] Daji's image, as it is currently known, is primarily derived from the Song Dynasty (960–1276 CE) huaben,[11] *The Story of King Wu Conquering Zhou and Bringing Peace* (武王伐纣平话). This story recounts the tale of a nine-tailed fox that sucked out Su Daji's soul and subsequently possessed her, thereby becoming King Zhou's favored concubine. King Zhou was lured into a state of inebriation and encouraged to engage in frivolous pursuits, while political affairs were set aside. Daji incited him to perpetrate the murder of numerous individuals, including his own ministers, which ultimately resulted in the demise of the imperial dynasty. Eventually, Daji was subdued and annihilated by Jiang Taigong.[12] From this, the image of Daji in the widely circulated Chinese works in the gods and demons (shenmo) genre *Investiture of the Gods* (Fengshen Yanyi, 封神演义) evolved. Thus, the nine-tailed demon fox Daji has become a representative of the Chinese femme fatale.

With the emancipation of women in China, the pervasive prejudice against women that underpinned the "female scourge" theory became more widely recognized. Indeed, Xia Zenmin and Chi Mingxia's research indicates that Daji's numerous transgressions were gradually fabricated. Blaming Daji for King Zhou's malevolent government is a manifestation of the "misogyny" inherent in a patriarchal society.[13] However, the representation of Daji has undergone a significant transformation in recent years. In the *Legend of Deification* (《姜子牙》,2020), Daji is depicted as an innocent human genie, while the aspiration of Nine Tails to become a deity is exploited by Tianzun to reinforce his authority. In *Creation of the Gods I: Kingdom of Storms* (《封神第一部：朝歌风云》,2023), Daji, the nine-tailed demon fox, assumes a more animalistic form. She is merely a tool for King Zhou to realize his ambition. King Zhou had accidentally lifted the seal of the nine-tailed fox, which is why Daji was willing to be a pawn.

In Chinese social media, Daji is also lauded for her physical beauty and seductive abilities rather than being depicted solely as a malevolent character. On China's social media Red (Xiaohongshu), #Daji has received 700 million views.[14] Many posts showcase how to emulate Daji's make-up and hanfu shoots that are styled based on her. This phenomenon is attributed to a shift in Chinese people's perceptions. On the one hand, the "influencer economy" has made beauty a form of capital and a desirable object of pursuit for consumers. In this era, Daji's beauty and seduction are among the most sought-after traits. The "2021 Young User Group Content Consumption Analysis Report" reveals that among China's top five social platforms, namely Tiktok, Kwai, Weibo, bilibili, and Red, individuals born after 2000 pay the most attention to beauty and handsome bloggers in various content areas, accounting for 20.2 percent. In contrast, individuals born after 1995 paid the most attention to the fashion field, accounting for 24.4 percent, followed by beauty and handsome, accounting for 12.6 percent.[15] The appreciation and pursuit of beauty have become a central focus for young people in China. Additionally, Chinese hanfu has emerged as a new fashion trend that is highly sought after by young people. According to iiMedia Research data, China's hanfu market has grown and expanded continuously. It has been projected that China's hanfu market would reach 14.47 billion yuan in 2023, with significant potential for further growth in the future.[16] Some scholars suggest that the popularity of hanfu may be a result of Chinese identity anxiety and resistance to Western cultural colonization.[17] Young Chinese people, growing up in a modernized and Westernized society, may be attempting to reconnect with their prosperous classical Chinese roots by wearing hanfu and establishing a sense of national identity. The concept of "classical China" and the pursuit of beauty converge in Daji, creating a distinct image of Daji that differs from that of the past.

What Should Daji Wear? Hanfu and Everyday Nationalism

The costume worn by Daji in the 2023 Chinese film *Creation of the Gods I: Kingdom of Storms* was the subject of controversy on the Chinese internet. On one side of this controversy, there were questions about whether Daji's costume in the stills was Japanese, as the wide, rectangular sleeves are similar to the furisode (振袖) of a kimono. People criticized the film for replacing Chinese clothing styles with Japanese clothing styles. However, people with the opposing viewpoint asserted that the sleeves of Daji's costume were the guangxiu (广袖) of the hanfu, with the distinction being that the furisode are not sewn under the armpits, while the guangxiu are sewn under the armpits. Thus, Daji is wearing not a Japanese costume but a traditional Chinese costume.[18] Such a controversy may appear somewhat trivial in the context of a supernatural film with strong fantasy overtones. However, the controversy surrounding Daji's costume is rooted in the establishment of hanfu as a tradition. According to Hobsbawm, the creation of tradition is practiced in both unofficial and official contexts.[19] The creation of modern hanfu as a tradition has been unofficially practiced.

Against the backdrop of Asia-Pacific leaders wearing the new Tang suit[20] at the 2001 Asia-Pacific Economic Cooperation (APEC) summit, the question of the traditional costume of the Chinese nation and what can be considered China's national costume has prompted a debate among the Chinese public. The goal of the Hanfu Movement, which was started in 2002 by the Chinese people, was to restore traditional Chinese dress from before the Qing Dynasty (1644–1911 CE), which had been reduced to a mere "lost civilization" by the Han Chinese.[21] The rise of modern hanfu culture can be seen as a form of everyday nationalism from the bottom up. In contrast to traditional theories of nationalism, which often view national consciousness as an imagined community spreading from the elite to the masses and from the center to the periphery, the Hanfu Movement challenges this perspective. In line with Hobsbawm's perspective "from below,"[22] the concept of everyday nationalism posits that "nations are not merely the consequence of structural forces; they are also the practical outcome of ordinary people engaging in the process of nation-building and the creation of a nationalist society."[23]

Clothing serves as a crucial way in which an average person can express their national identity in their daily lives. An essential aspect of the Hanfu Movement is the integration of hanfu into people's daily lives. In 2003, Wang Letian, a worker in Zhengzhou's electric power system, donned a handmade hanfu inspired by the character Li Yong's costume from the TV series *The Prince of Han Dynasty*.[24] He was subsequently featured in Singapore's *Lianhe Zaobao* newspaper, where reporter Zhang Congxing stated: "Hanfu, which had been extinct in the daily lives of Chinese men for more than 300 years, had reappeared on the streets of China."[25] This was a landmark event in the Hanfu Movement. The resurgence of hanfu was met with considerable support. Some hanfu enthusiasts wear the traditional dress to study and work, thereby practicing the concept of hanfu in daily life. The Hanfu Movement originated from the actions of ordinary people and subsequently evolved into a bottom-up cultural revival movement. As Kaufmann postulates, instead of following a carefully thought-out plan that is systematically developed and distributed by elites, nationalist ideas may spread like a virus that incubates along a network until it reaches a tipping point.[26] The majority of the participants in the nascent Hanfu Movement were ordinary individuals who gathered on websites and online forums such as Hanwang, Tianhanwang, and Baidu hanfu tieba. Wang Letian was a member of Hanwang, which was the earliest Hanfu website that gained popularity on the internet. Furthermore, every individual who wears a hanfu is a carrier of hanfu culture. Hanfu examinations on social media and online forums and hanfu photos all serve as nodes of dissemination. When a tipping point was reached, the hanfu became a fashion choice in and of itself.

Importantly, the popularity of hanfu culture should not be equated with the revival of Han culture. Although the Hanfu Movement emerged from the ethnic identity of the Han Chinese people, the subsequent banning of the Hanwang due to the use of extreme ethnic rhetoric led to a gradual shift in hanfu culture from an ethnic to a national identity. The rejection of Qing Dynasty clothing also represents, to a certain extent, a rejection of the weak national image of the semicolonial and semifeudal periods. The leader of a Douban hanfu-related group has presented some hitherto unknown aspects of Chinese history, citing China's historical strength in terms of urbanization rate and economic output.[27] The underlying implication is that hanfu represents a culture that is just as important as Western culture. In a sense, hanfu fashion can be regarded as a form of decolonizing fashion. The hanfu serves as a conduit for Chinese people to reconnect with their ancestral heritage and envision a once-mighty nation. This has led to the official embrace of hanfu culture as part of the national identity. In 2018, the Communist Youth League of China established "Chinese National Costume Day" using the term "huafu" to refer to Chinese clothing. Although the event also aims to include the dress of China's ethnic minorities, the hanfu is the clear subject, and the logo for "Chinese National Costume Day" shows the hanfu's signature feature: cross collars, with the left crossing over the right (jiaoling youren, 交领右衽).

As He Guimei notes, "the failure of the capitalist/socialist ideological confrontation has made the important resources that China, which has already entered the global pattern, can effectively borrow in establishing its subjective identity, mainly the historical and cultural traditions of the pre-modern empire."[28] In this context, hanfu has become part of the Chinese national identity and an important way for ordinary people to engage, perform, and consume nationalism in their daily lives. This has brought the development of hanfu into a new stage. In 2019, the Chinese hanfu market showed considerable growth at a rate of 318.5 percent.[29] As Anthony D. Smith explains, the resonance of popular traditions, values, memories, myths, and symbols—the very things that

Figure 6.1 *Hanfu's signature feature: jiaoling youren.*
Collage featuring royalty-free images from Pixabay and author's hand-drawn schematic.

nationalists "rediscover" and adapt for new political purposes—is a necessary condition for the appeal of nationalism.[30] The process of moving from ethnic identity to national identity can be described as the state discovering hanfu culture and transforming it into a cultural narrative of the nation. However, this narrative was already put forward by the masses, the subject of the Hanfu Movement, in the early days of the movement. The hanfu was reclaimed by the masses as a symbol of nationalism, transforming it into a fashion statement. This practice of everyday nationalism from below demonstrates that the relationship between fashion and nation can also be constructed by non-elites.

Now, let us return to the original question: what should Daji wear? Daji's costume is related not only to the plot needs of the film and the character's styling aesthetics but also to the construction of a symbolic system of national identity. The style of Daji's costume is not fixed. The earliest known image of Daji as a fox spirit is the portrait of "Duke Zhou killing Daji" on a portrait stone in the front room of the Han dynasty tomb in Panjiatong, Feixian County, Shandong Province, China. In this depiction, Su Daji is depicted wearing the robe worn by officials in the Han Dynasty, and her long tail is seen rising upward behind her, thereby identifying her as a fox demon.[31] The image of Daji that is most familiar to the general public today is largely derived from cinematic and televisual adaptations. For example, shenguaipian was one of the most prominent genres in early Chinese cinema. Daji appeared in the Chinese shenguaipian *Fengshen Bang: Jiang Ziya Burns Pipa Spirit in Fire* (《封神榜之姜子牙火烧琵琶精》, 1927) and wore the Peking Opera costume.[32] Daji's costume resembled that of the sculptures of ancient Greek goddesses in the mainland China TV series *The First Myth* (《封神榜》, 1990). The costume style of this television series has recently been criticized for failing to reflect the Chinese style. As the culture of monsters has come to be seen as part of traditional Chinese culture and the function of myth as a central symbol of ethnic identity has become recognized and utilized, Chinese people have begun to emphasize the ethnicity of the costumes in such mythological films and TV dramas. As a kind of traditional national dress, hanfu is distinctive because it had completely disappeared from daily life. The inaugural branded hanfu brick-and-mortar store did not emerge until 2006, during which time modern hanfu were typically crafted by enthusiasts themselves rather than purchased. To ascertain the correct Xingzhi (the form, shape, and rule) of the hanfu, enthusiasts typically referred to archaeological artifacts, ancient portraits, and other trustworthy sources.

As the popularity of hanfu culture grew, some hanfu enthusiasts' strict and meticulous requirements for Xingzhi became a requirement and standard for the costumes of ancient movie and TV drama characters. Accompanying one similar controversy after another is a desire to establish a paradigm about clothing that possesses a Chinese national style. Noting the fallacies of costumes in movies and TV dramas has become a way for ordinary people to participate in and construct everyday nationalism.

Auspicious or Demonic? Hanfu, Cosplay, and Femininity

The relationship between fashion and nationalism is reciprocal. Employing clothing as a vehicle and medium for nationalism is insufficient; rather, it is possible to actively transform the national symbolism of clothing through fashion. The concept of everyday nationalism encompasses not only how ordinary people engage with and interpret nationalism through their everyday behavior but also how they ignore and deflect nationalism through their everyday behavior. When individuals wear hanfu in a role-playing context, the cultural connotations of the role influence the symbolism of the hanfu to a certain extent. Hanfu cosplay represents a means by which ordinary individuals may engage with nationalism in a transformative manner.

In January 2024, at the Yuntai Mountain Ice Festival in China, Daji's cosplay in a straight-hem, cross-collar hanfu style proved so popular that it became a secret weapon for attracting tourists. However, some media outlets labeled her performances as having a low culture, the cosplayer of Daji Deng Wenwen was blamed for her intimate interaction with the tourists, and her faithful performance of the role was seen as giddy. Many netizens defended her, arguing that her performance did not cross the line. Nevertheless, the controversy concluded with apologies from both the cosplayers and the scenic spot, and the Daji cosplay at Yuntai Mountain has been discontinued. This kind of restriction on cosplayers is not uncommon. Although cosplay provides a fantastic world for participants, cosplayers' bodies are still regulated under convention rules. According to Winge, "'conventions' rules intended to make the space safer and family friendly tend to specifically target female Cosplayers to modify their costumes and roleplaying behaviors."[33] The controversy

Figure 6.2 *The Daji Cosplay at Yuntai Mountain.*
Image courtesy of the Shibachongchuan (十八重川) Photography Team.

surrounding Daji cosplay can be understood as an expression of the discipline of the female body that exists in hanfu culture. Some hanfu enthusiasts maintain that when wearing hanfu, one should behave in a more reserved and modest manner in alignment with the traditional norms of etiquette.

This outcome reflects the intricate relationship between femininity and nationalism in China. Women in hanfu can only exist to a certain extent as symbols of traditional cultural images,[34] and such images must be submissive, harmless, and not challenging.

> If beauty in the past emanated from the inside out, and if cosmetics serve as an external disguise for the internal decay of the modern woman, the notion of traditional culture as deployed in these Han Clothing Movement narratives of femininity is then the forceful insertion of an externally defined and highly limiting vision of traditional beauty into the interior of contemporary individuals as their proper essence, to which they must conform or risk being judged in violation of their proper selfhood.[35]

As Carrico notes, the femininity of the Hanfu Movement has a conservative aspect, and women in hanfu can easily be put into the fantasy of obedient traditional women. In ancient China, where hanfu was worn as everyday clothing, women were marginalized under the patriarchal system of Confucian society. Confucius said, "Let lords be lords; ministers be ministers; fathers be fathers; and sons be sons," which shows that women were excluded from the whole political structure of the country and that it was considered dangerous for women to interfere in politics. For this reason, the rebellious nature of Daji's image comes to the fore. By playing the role of Daji, an image that has been demeaned and discredited in traditional culture, female hanfu enthusiasts challenge the constraints imposed on contemporary women by the submissive and dignified image of traditional women in hanfu culture.

Women have always been a force to be reckoned with in the Hanfu Movement. According to iiMedia Research, women constituted the majority of hanfu consumers in 2022.[36] A member of the first generation of hanfu revivalists and practitioners, Fang Zhexuan, who goes by the screen name "Tianya in Xiaolou," is a woman. She has published numerous widely circulated articles lamenting the demise of the national spirit and calling for the revival

Figure 6.3 *Chinese woman in Hanfu.*
Royalty-free images from Pixabay.

of hanfu and Chinese culture to support the backbone of the nation. In 2019, Zhuo Tongzhou organized a flash mob in front of the Sydney Opera House in Australia, where Chinese dress enthusiasts (mostly girls) sang "My Motherland and Me" in hanfu and held up the Chinese national flag. These examples show us that women are a force to be reckoned with in the reproduction of nationalism. They actively incorporate hanfu culture into the discourse of national rejuvenation. Seemingly echoing the lyrics that compare the country to a mother's expression, female hanfu enthusiasts have taken it upon themselves to act as signifiers of national difference, becoming China's national symbols and icons in the world. However, today's female hanfu enthusiasts are not merely passive consumers who can be held hostage by the conservative side of nationalism; they can transform nationalism by playing different role images. Even the discourse surrounding traditional culture can be used by hanfu enthusiasts to emphasize the legitimacy of femininity.

The manner in which Deng Wenwen defends herself after being criticized by the media is worth considering. Deng notes that she was portraying the nine-tailed fox from *The Classic of Mountains and Seas* and modeling her character after Daji from *The Legend of Nezha.*[37] It is evident that the negative connotations associated with the name Daji in the past continue to influence contemporary discourse to a significant degree. Today, two labels surround Daji: one for the revival of traditional culture and the awakening of national consciousness behind the nine-tailed fox and the myth, and the other for the long-standing charge that Daji is a scourge of the nation and a calamity to the people. The divergence between the two contrasting portrayals of the nine-tailed fox, as previously discussed, is illuminated by the controversy in question. The cosplayer aims to challenge the negative connotations associated with the fox-spirit image by highlighting its traditional cultural significance and the national discourse behind her costume and image. Thus, the auspicious and demonic sides of the nine-tailed fox become the center of discourse in this conflict. Many online users have expressed support for the Daji cosplayer by invoking the previously mentioned auspicious aspect of the nine-tailed fox. "She's clearly auspicious," they emphasized. The multifaceted nature of the nine-tailed fox as a symbol affords Daji's image a greater degree of interpretive flexibility. By rearticulating the auspicious side of the nine-tailed fox, people are refuting the female scourge theory while attempting to establish a positive connection between women and the country. Netizens post their own Daji cosplay photographs in the same Chinese costume on social media as a sign of solidarity. At this point, Daji's hanfu cosplay has assumed a formative quality, representing a reinterpretation of the image of women in hanfu. In this instance, the individual's performativity is not unconscious; rather, it actively deviates from the norms of the traditional cultural image of women. The act of portraying iconic historical figures such as Daji and Hua Mulan, as well as a multitude of characters from film and animation, facilitates the demonstration of a vast array of femininity through hanfu. As Butler notes, if gender attributes and actions are performative, there will be no right or wrong gender behavior and no authentic or constant femininity.[38] Hanfu cosplay may seem limited to a single character, but it is precisely through the performative nature of cosplay that the body can transcend the writing of history and cultural repression. The tension between hanfu as a role-related culture and hanfu as a national costume provides more space for the relationship between fashion and the nation.

Conclusion

The process of Hanfu becoming a fashion is also a process of nationalist construction. Unlike many national costumes, hanfu has been revived as a part of modern culture through a bottom-up process. Ordinary people produce and reproduce nationalism in their daily lives by discussing, making, wearing, consuming, and displaying hanfu. The role-related nature of hanfu culture empowers hanfu enthusiasts to transform its symbolism. Female hanfu enthusiasts transform the femininity of traditional culture through the imitation of Daji and deconstruct the negative association between femininity and national discourse in nationalism through conscious manipulation. The connection between hanfu and Daji, while not mainstream, is a deliberate choice to highlight the lesser-known aspects of hanfu culture that have been overshadowed by more prominent elements. The act of cosplaying Daji exemplifies constructive aspect of hanfu cosplayers who alter traditional culture to align with contemporary trends.

However, importantly, although the Hanfu Movement is a bottom-up cultural revival movement, its face in the public sphere is still largely determined by national ideology. Hanfu enthusiasts can only be allowed to manifest themselves as participants in social change if they accept the organization of a nationalist-based state ideology. Female hanfu enthusiasts are supported by the ideologically dominated public sphere only when they serve as symbols of nationalism, and in such a context, real women's issues are obscured.

Although today's hanfu enthusiasts have begun to resist the traditional values that have disciplined women, when they appeal to the legitimacy of youth and beauty, an elaborate hanfu portrait becomes a form of aesthetic labor,[39] and the display of hanfu and standards of beauty on social media may become a new form of control in the patriarchal society of the digital age. As female hanfu enthusiasts reject the traditional image of submissive women through their cosplay and performativity, they unwittingly fall into the shackles of the sophistication and beauty that come with a role. In the case of Daji's celebrity actors, we can also see how the celebrity system establishes a standardized aesthetic of beauty, which, through the transmission of influencers and bloggers, has become a template for people's self-presentation on social media. Importantly, while roles provide female hanfu enthusiasts with the opportunity to redefine femininity and the role of women in nationalism, it is crucial to avoid reducing performativity to a mere programmed and repetitive act of beauty. Instead, it is essential to attempt to truly free oneself from the shackles of history by deconstructing a certain kind of femininity for the definition of a woman, deconstructing a specific form of hanfu for the definition of hanfu, and embracing more possibilities of hanfu as a fashion.

Notes

1 I would like to express my gratitude to Ms. Danqi Lu for her valuable input during the initial brainstorming phase of this chapter.

2 The Yichang style is characterized by the wearing of a top and a skirt underneath. The Yiku style is distinguished by the wearing of a top and pants underneath. The Shenyi style is exemplified by the cutting of the top and skirt separately and then sewing them together, which can be divided into Quju (diagonal body wrapping and diagonal hem) and Zhiju (straight hem). Finally, the Tongcai style is characterized by the cutting of the top and bottom of the dress from a single piece of cloth, with no seams in between.

3 Na Yang, Mengyue Zhang, and Hehua Liu, *Han fu Tong Lun—A General Introduction to Hanfu*, Beijing: China Development Press, 2021.

4 Zhou Jie, "Wearing the Self, Willing to Sink into the 'Sankeng'!" *Xinmin Weekly*, last modified July 15, 2020. https://www.xinminweekly.com.cn/lunbo/2020/07/15/14521.html

5 Zhe Cao, *Hanfu*, Beijing: Zhonghua Book Company, 2022, 21.

6 "Research Report on the Current Status and Consumer Behavior of China's Hanfu Industry, 2022–2023," *iiMedia Research*, last modified February 8, 2024. https://www.iimedia.cn/c400/87077.html

7 Zhaozuo Feng, *The Network Survival of Chinese Traditional Culture in the Post-Subculture Era*, Beijing: Jiuzhou Publishing House, 2022, 152.

8 Changyi Ma, *Illustrated Discussion of the Ancient Edition of* The Classic of Mountains and Seas, Jinan: Shandong Pictorial Publishing House, 2001, 20.

9 Jianguo Li, *Chinese Fox Culture*, Beijing: People's Literature Publishing House, 2002, 150–1.

10 Yihui Li, "A Study on the Image of Daji," *Ming and Qing Dynasties Literature and Documentation* 1: 2017, 297–308.

11 Huaben, a base text on which Chinese storytellers based their folk art, emerging in the Song Dynasty.

12 *Wu Wang Fa Zhou Ping Hua (The Story of King Wu Conquering Zhou and Bringing Peace)*, Nanchang: Yuzhang Book Society, 1981.

13 Zengmin Xia and Mingxia Chi, "The Theoretical Construction of Confucianism and the Gender System in the Han Dynasty: Centered on the Historical Narrative of Mo Xi, Daji, and Bao Si under the 'Female Calamity Historical View,'" *Journal of Huazhong University of Science and Technology (Social Science Edition)* 26 (04): 2012, 94–100. doi: 10.19648/j.cnki.jhustss1980.2012.04.015.

14 Data from Red (xiaohongshu.com), accessed May 21, 2024.

15 "2021 Young User Group Content Consumption Analysis Report," Topklout, last modified September 2021. https://www.topklout.com/static/pdf/web/viewer.html?file=https%3A%2F%2Fimg.topklout.com%2Fwebsite%2Freport%2F6142a16753aa6.pdf%3Fr%3DFri+Mar+29+2024+14%3A39%3A45+GMT%2B0800+%28%E4%B8%AD%E5%9B%BD%E6%A0%87%E5%87%86%E6%97%B6%E9%97%B4%29

16 iiMedia, "Analysis Report on the Status Quo and Consumer Behavior of Chinese Hanfu Industry from 2024 to 2025," iiMedia, last modified November 24, 2023. https://www.iimedia.cn/c400/97076.html.

17 Juanjuan Wu, *Chinese Fashion: From Mao to Now*, Oxford: Berg, 2009, 124.

18 "Comments on 'The First Part of Creation of the Gods': A Discussion on the Alleged Japanese Style Elements," last modified July 30, 2023. https://baijiahao.baidu.com/s?id=1772823610253602044

19 Eric J. Hobsbawm and Terence O. Ranger, eds, *The Invention of Tradition*, Cambridge: Cambridge University Press, 2012, 307.

20 The new Tang suit is a modified version of the Manchu dress of the Qing Dynasty, based on the magua (马褂).

21 *Qing Shilu* (清史录) records that in May of the first year of the Shunzhi reign (1644), Prince Regent Dorgon decreed: "All officials, soldiers, and civilians who submit shall shave their heads and follow the dress code and customs of our dynasty." *Qing Shilu*, vol. 3, Beijing: Zhonghua Book Company, 1985, 57.

22 Hobsbawm and Ranger, *The Invention of Tradition*, 307.

23 Jon E. Fox and Cynthia Miller-Idriss, "Everyday Nationhood," *Ethnicities* 8 (4): 2008, 553. https://doi.org/10.1177/1468796808088925. For further discussion on the everyday nationalism/nationhood, see Michael Skey and Marco Antonsich, eds, *Everyday Nationhood*, London: Palgrave Macmillan UK, 2017. https://doi.org/10.1057/978-1-137-57098-7; Michael Skey, "The National in Everyday Life: A Critical Engagement with Michael Billig's Thesis of Banal Nationalism," *The Sociological Review* 57 (2): May 2009, 331–46. https://doi.org/10.1111/j.1467-954X.2009.01832.x

24 Yanrui Xu, *Yi Han fu zhi ming: Mei Jie Zhong de Wen Hua Yi Xiang – The Development of Hanfu*, Hangzhou: Zhejiang University Press, 2023.

25 "The Essence of Hanfu Appreciation: An Exploration into Cultural Identity and Aesthetics," *NetEase News*, last modified August 17, 2021. https://www.163.com/dy/article/GGR1HIKC0541040Y.html

26 Eric Kaufmann, "Complexity and Nationalism," *Nations and Nationalism* 23 (1): 2017, 6–25. doi: 10.1111/nana.12270.

27 "Little-known Facts about Chinese History," *Douban*, last modified January 15, 2021. https://www.douban.com/group/topic/207269730/?_i=5585708BbWeUVX,5587253BbWeUVX

28 Guimei He, *Da Kai Zhong Guo Shi Ye: Dang Dai Wen Xue Yu Si Xiang Lun Ji – Opening Chinese Horizons: Essays on Contemporary Literature and Thought*, Beijing: Peking University Press, 2020, 139–40.

29 "Research Report on Hanfu Industry, 2022–2023," *iiMedia Research*.

30 Anthony D. Smith, *Ethno-symbolism and Nationalism: A Cultural Approach*, London: Routledge, 2009, 59.

31 Sheng Jiang, "The Fox Spirit Daji and the Study of the Six Heavenly Palaces in Han Dynasty Tombs," *Fudan Journal (Social Sciences Edition)* 60 (04): 2018, 85–99.

32 Ji Hua Cheng, ed., *Zhong Guo Dian Ying Fa Zhan Shi – A History of Chinese Cinema*, Beijing: China Film Press, 1963, 88.

33 Therèsa M. Winge, *Costuming Cosplay: Dressing the Imagination*, London: Bloomsbury Visual Arts, 2019, 177.

34 Masculinity is typically expressed through the wearing of suits, which serve to assert the wearer's status as a world citizen. In contrast, femininity, especially in developing countries, has become emblematic of traditional cultural imagery. See Susan B. Kaiser and Denise Nicole Green, *Fashion and Cultural Studies*, 2nd ed., London: Bloomsbury, 2021, 21. https://doi.org/10.5040/9781350104716.

35 Kevin Carrico, *The Great Han: Race, Nationalism, and Tradition in China Today*, Oakland, CA: University of California Press, 2017, 166.

36 "Research Report on Hanfu Industry, 2022–2023," *iiMedia Research*.

37 Baoqing Huang, "Sincerely Accepted and Has Been Corrected! Yuntai Mountain Scenic Area Apologizes for 'Male and Female Daji'!" *Qianjiang Evening News*, last modified January 19, 2024. https://baijiahao.baidu.com/s?id=1788502443984290745&wfr=spider&for=pc

38 Judith Butler, *Gender Trouble*, London: Routledge, 2002, 180.

39 "Whereas aesthetic capital refers particularly to bodily styles and appearances as outcomes of certain cultural taste patterns, aesthetic labour refers particularly to the practices that are geared towards attaining or shaping specific corporeal dispositions in people." For further discussion on aesthetic labor, see Sylvia Holla and Giselinde Kuipers, "Aesthetic Capital," in *Routledge International Handbook of the Sociology of Art and Culture*, New York: Routledge, 2015, 290–303.

Bibliography

"2021 Young User Group Content Consumption Analysis Report." *Topklout*, 2021. https://www.topklout.com/static/pdf/web/viewer.html?file=https%3A%2F%2Fimg.topklout.com%2Fwebsite%2Freport%2F6142a16753aa6.pdf%3Fr%3DFri+Mar+29+2024+14%3A39%3A45+GMT%2B0800+%28%E4%B8%AD%E5%9B%BD%E6%A0%87%E5%87%86%E6%97%B6%E9%97%B4%29

"Analysis Report on the Status Quo and Consumer Behavior of Chinese Hanfu Industry from 2024 to 2025." iiMedia Research. https://www.iimedia.cn/c400/97076.html

Butler, Judith. *Gender Trouble*. London: Routledge, 2002.

Cao, Zhe. *Hanfu*. Beijing: Zhonghua Book Company, 2022.

Carrico, Kevin. *The Great Han: Race, Nationalism, and Tradition in China Today*. Oakland, CA: University of California Press, 2017.

"Comments on 'The First Part of Creation of the Gods': A Discussion on the Alleged Japanese Style Elements." Last modified July 30, 2023. https://baijiahao.baidu.com/s?id=1772823610253602044.

Feng, Zhaozuo. *The Network Survival of Chinese Traditional Culture in the Post-Subculture Era*. Beijing: Jiuzhou Publishing House, 2022.

Fox, Jon E., and Cynthia Miller-Idriss. "Everyday Nationhood." *Ethnicities* 8 (4): 2008, 553–73. https://doi.org/10.1177/1468796808088925

Guimei, He. *Da Kai Zhong Guo Shi Ye: Dang Dai Wen Xue Yu Si Xiang Lun Ji – Opening Chinese Horizons: Essays on Contemporary Literature and Thought*. Beijing: Peking University Press, 2020.

Holla, Sylvia, and Giselinde Kuipers. "Aesthetic Capital." In *Routledge International Handbook of the Sociology of Art and Culture*. New York: Routledge, 2015, 290–303.

Jiang, Sheng. "The Fox Spirit Daji and the Study of the Six Heavenly Palaces in Han Dynasty Tombs." *Fudan Journal (Social Sciences Edition)* 60 (04): 2018, 85–99.

Kaiser, Susan B., and Denise Nicole Green. *Fashion and Cultural Studies*, 2nd ed. London: Bloomsbury, 2021. https://doi.org/10.5040/9781350104716.

Kaufmann, Eric. "Complexity and Nationalism." *Nations and Nationalism* 23 (1): 2017, 6–25. doi: 10.1111/nana.12270.

Kaufmann, Eric, and Terence O. Ranger, eds. *The Invention of Tradition*. Cambridge: Cambridge University Press, 2012.

Li, Jianguo. *Chinese Fox Culture*. Beijing: People's Literature Publishing House, 2002.

Li, Yihui. "A Study on the Image of Daji." *Ming and Qing Dynasties Literature and Documentation* 1: 2017, 297–308.

"Little-Known Facts about Chinese History." *Douban*, 2021. https://www.douban.com/group/topic/207269730/?_i=5585708BbWeUVX,5587253BbWeUVX

Ma, Changyi. *Illustrated Discussion of the Ancient Edition of* The Classic of Mountains and Seas. Jinan: Shandong Pictorial Publishing House, 2001.

"Research Report on the Current Status and Consumer Behavior of China's Hanfu Industry, 2022–2023." *iiMedia Research*, 2024. https://www.iimedia.cn/c400/87077.html.

Smith, Anthony D. *Ethno-symbolism and Nationalism: A Cultural Approach*. London: Routledge, 2009.

"The Essence of Hanfu Appreciation: An Exploration into Cultural Identity and Aesthetics." *NetEase News*, 2021. https://www.163.com/dy/article/GGR1HIKC0541040Y.html.

Winge, Therèsa M. *Costuming Cosplay: Dressing the Imagination*. London: Bloomsbury Visual Arts, 2019.

Wu, Juanjuan. *Chinese Fashion: From Mao to Now*. Oxford: Berg, 2009.

"Wu Wang Fa Zhou Ping Hua" (The Story of King Wu Conquering Zhou and Bringing Peace). Nanchang: Yuzhang Book Society, 1981.

Xia, Zengmin, and Mingxia Chi. "The Theoretical Construction of Confucianism and the Gender System in the Han Dynasty: Centered on the Historical Narrative of Mo Xi, Daji, and Bao Si under the 'Female Calamity Historical View.'" *Journal of Huazhong University of Science and Technology (Social Science Edition)* 26 (04): 2012, 94–100. doi: 10.19648/j.cnki.jhustss1980.2012.04.015.

Xu, Yanrui. *Yi Han fu zhi ming: Mei Jie Zhong de Wen Hua Yi Xiang – The Development of Hanfu*. Hangzhou: Zhejiang University Press 2023.

Yang, Na, Zhang Mengyue, and Liu Hehua. *Han Fu Tong Lun – A General Introduction to Hanfu*. Beijing: China Development Press, 2021.*Figure 6.2 The Daji Cosplay at Yuntai Mountain.*

7

The Kimono Narratives: Mythical and Legendary Creatures in Japanese Fashion

CRINGUTA IRINA PELEA

Introduction

"Women, they love kimonos with beautiful patterns and porcelain tea cups, as those are truly the only reasons worth living. Admiring their ever-changing nature is the very purpose of being alive. Besides that, what else would one ever need?"[1] exquisitely writes Dazai Osamu in *Skin and Heart* (Hifu to Kokoro, 皮膚と心),[2] a literary work that remains untranslated until this moment.

What represents the kimono (着物), if not the very essence of the Yamato spirit? As a quintessential component of the Japanese spirit (Yamato damashii, 大和魂), the kimono (in literal translation, "a thing to wear") embodies Japan's cultural heritage, national identity, historical struggles, nonlinear evolution, and aesthetic conscience. Recognizable through its "T-shaped style of clothing,"[3] this iconic Japanese robe-like garment is worn wrapped across the front, with wide, floating sleeves sewn together with the modular part of the body to form a wide, flat surface ready to be painted and decorated with various images, designs, patterns, or crests.[4] Although its design, sociocultural and practical functions, and meaning have registered dramatic shifts across generations, what remains constant nowadays is its worldwide increasing popularity and recognition as a Japanese national fashion icon within an increasingly globalized and cosmopolitan media ecosystem.[5]

Much has been written about the kimono, from wide-ranging and ever-changing perspectives (aesthetic, social, cultural heritage, historical evolution, and permutations, textiles, and fashion) and covering a plethora of scholarly fields across different historical eras or reception media spaces (fashion studies, visual arts, clothing history, sociology, anthropology, cultural studies, and communication sciences). Considering the vastness of the already published academic studies concerning this topic, one may even critically question the potential of novelty associated with the kimono, both as a timeless choice of garment and a non-Western clothing style. Nonetheless, the present chapter aims to adopt a different and pioneering approach to the multifarious cross- and interdisciplinary explorations of the kimono and examine the symbiotic relation between the kimono and Japanese mythical and legendary creatures across domestic popular culture genres and media productions.

In order to achieve this general objective, the chapter is structured as follows. The first section provides a brief review of Japanese and English academic literature that traces the historical evolution of the kimono and reviews several decorating techniques and types of fabrics employed throughout the creation and production process. The second section explores the cultural semantics of the most significant Japanese mythical and legendary figures, which are deeply anchored in the national ethnocultural and mythological landscape. In this regard, we will focus on how Japanese popular culture genres and products nest or confiscate and reconfigure the intersectionality of a wide variety of mythical figures and symbols with the kimono narratives. The analysis will take into consideration two aspects. On the one hand, the genres of *taiga dorama* and *jidaigeki* unfold a discourse of autochthonous heritage by employing totemic animals, birds, and other fantastic beings as kimono patterns; on the other hand, manga works and historical anime productions present a noticeable tendency to anthropomorphize mythical figures as independent characters wearing kimonos.

The third section provides a short glimpse into the kimono festivals as forms of street discourse and the artistic performances of the cosplay subcultures that have been heavily influenced by the visual imagery exerted by Japan's national attire. The fourth section concludes this study by inviting the reader to critically reflect on how the latest generative AI tools and immersive technologies frame, represent—or is it misrepresent?—and render kimono-associated cultural heritage.

Literature Review: Japanese Cultural Legacy and National identity

The secular history of the kimono, otherwise acknowledged as a significant fashion item falling within the Japanese-style clothing (wafuku, 和服), together with its extraordinary variety in terms of models, types, pattern designs, materials or dyeing techniques and color choices would seem to render futile any attempt to summarize the essence of this apparel in a necessarily brief literature review. Nonetheless, in this section setting grounds for the analysis to be later developed, we aim first to lay out a brief chronological history of the kimono and second, to examine the social evolution of the dyeing techniques and types of materials employed throughout the creation and production process of this clothing.

Historical records dating back as early as the Heian period (794–1185) describe the first evidence of the kimono under the shape of kosode (小袖, in translation, "small cuffs"), an undergarment exclusively worn by the aristocracy in the beginning, while its transition to being used as a high-class outer garment starts with the Kamakura period (1185–1333).[6] Variations in style, type, color, shape, and length of sleeves communicate the social class, traditional rigid gender binaries, age and wealth differences that permeated the Japanese society of those times: teboso (手細, "a tube-shaped single costume") considered specific to the samurai's formal daily clothing or adorned by ordinary people, characterized by modest tie-dyeing applied on a white-ground, whereas any decorations were absent due to the class-difference restrictions.[7]

It was during the Momoyama period (1568–1603) when the kosode consolidated its image as the kimono, "the traditional Japanese folkloric costume" that is recognized nowadays. The richness of patterns, the complexity of embroideries, and the exquisite variety of handcrafted decorations and ornaments that emerged from the Momoyama until the end of the Edo period (1603–1868) reflected the socioeconomic stability and increasing prosperity of those times.[8]

However, the modernization policies of the Meiji period (1868–1912) were accompanied, on the one hand, by an aggressive industrialization process that altered the production and consumption process of the kimono and, on the other hand, by a fast permeation of Western philosophy and style of clothing (yōfuku, 洋服)[9] that led to the hybridization of clothing styles. Consequently, individuals wore Western fashion items such as scarves and leather shoes, as well as kimono and additional garments.[10] The mixed style can be observed since the beginning of the Shōwa period (1926–89), while after the mid-1950s, wearing a kimono became a relatively rare experience, mainly associated with festive occasions such as the New Year (Oshōgatsu, お正月), ikebana (生け花), the tea ceremony (chadōu, 茶道), or formal life-changing events such as the traditional childhood rite of passage (shichi-go-san, 七五三お祝い)[11] and the coming-of-age celebration at the age of twenty (seijin-no-hi, 成人の日).[12]

Significant variations in styles, types, and accessories not only express and convey cross-generational transformations of Japan's social performances and political and economic circumstances but also mirror at a micro-level the evolution of individual lifestyle and enhance the sense of national and cultural belonging.[13] The formal kimonos such as furisode (振袖, in translation, "long sleeves"), kurotomesode (黒留袖), irotomesode (色留袖), and hōmongi (訪問着) are dressed for rare occasions, and are season, gender, and age-specific, while fitting distinctive social expectations and ceremonial roles.[14] Among the casual kimonos, best known and worn daily are tsumugi (紬), fudan yukata (普段浴衣), and yosoyuki yukata (よそゆき浴衣).[15] Nonetheless, the above-provided enumeration is far from being exhaustive.

Entangled with the complex and multilayered history of the kimono is the evolution of the fabric weaving, dyeing techniques, colors, and types of material employed throughout the production process of this garment. With origins tracing back to the Edo period, the yūzen dyeing technique (yūzen-zome, 友

Figure 7.1 *Kimono for an unmarried woman, anonymous, 1920–40.*
Source: Rijksmuseum of the Netherlands

禅染め) holds the merit for revolutionizing the kosode and marks the transition from the repetitive patterns to free-hand painted "large size images" in many brilliantly rich colors. Although in the beginning, blending plant dyes and "used glutinous rice flour and glutinous rice bran powder"[16] served as a dyeing paste, the later industrialization, modernization, and advancement of the textile industry, combined with the emergence of chemical dyes, increased design variety and made yūzen kimonos more widely available.[17] As a regional variation, kyō-yūzen (京友禅) is associated with the city of Kyōto,[18] which during the Edo period was renowned as "a place of production," "lavish spending," and "a display of beautiful and extravagant clothes."[19] Other influential Japanese decorating techniques that require a high standard of craftsmanship are shibori-zome (絞り染め, "the oldest method of pattern dyeing"),[20] shishū (刺繍, embroidery),[21] and Nishijin-ori (西陣織, Nishijin weaving),[22] all of them encompassing myriad procedures linked either to specific geographical regions, periods, artisan families, or fashion trends.[23]

In the past, "the dress was not entirely a free, personal choice," as it was regulated either by the shogunate or by social conventions.[24] Likewise, the type of fabric reflected the social class and the way of life of its users. For instance, silk kimonos were produced by full-time professional artisans and restricted to the higher social classes and the nobles,[25] whereas the ordinary people would have access only to cotton-made kimonos crafted by amateurs, without any colorful patterns or elaborated embroidered decorations.[26] However, nowadays, as a consequence of the ongoing modernization and industrialization, silk kimonos have lost their status as articles of luxury traded exclusively to nobility and have spanned across generations to permeate other social classes as well.[27] This particular deviation in production and consumption is one of the critical elements that fostered the perpetuation of the kimono not only as Japan's national attire, independent of any attempt of social segmentation or ethnic discrimination, but also as an immutable lifestyle that provides a cultural, aesthetic, and historical articulation of national heritage.

The Kimono Narratives in Japanese Popular Culture

Counting on the virtues of its perceived foreignness and cultural distinctiveness, Japanese mass culture (Nihon taishū bunka, 日本大衆文化) holds a significant merit in raising the popularity of the kimono at an incommensurable global level. The miracle of mass production, through the multifariousness of media genres, transnational networks, and international platforms of distribution, has marked a fundamental shift in the reconfiguration of the kimono into a form of entertainment or, at least, a powerful visual support in conveying national media narratives or domestic street performances.

Nonetheless, as stated in the introduction, in this section we will take distance from the prevailing academic performances surrounding the kimono and propose an innovative and transdisciplinary approach that draws on Japan's popular culture symbiosis between the kimono and Japanese mythical and legendary figures. As we shall demonstrate, intertwining the kimono—both as a national garment and ubiquitous yet pervasive lifestyle—with the imageries and folk narratives of mythological beings transforms the kimono into a popular culture construct predefined by a nexus of core values represented by three categories: historical, sociopolitical, and entertainment. The proposed historical and sociopolitical categories should be interpreted as grounded in Japan's culturally sensitive context that encapsulates the national aesthetic and philosophical conscience; the entertainment value is circumscribed here strictly to "popular culture" as the "culture of the masses."

Domestic Television Series: The Kimono, Japanese Mythology and Legends

From taiga dramas (大河ドラマ) to period films, also known as jidaigeki (時代劇), moving images provide manifold opportunities to dive into the visual and cultural representations of the kimono in association with mythical narrative motifs. In this regard, two mainstream production norms that eventually are prone to lead to different types of interpretation seem to be reinforced. The first one refers to using a repertoire of mythical and legendary creatures as kimono patterns, and the second one underpins the strategy of associating or even portraying the kimono-dressed characters as sharing a significant connection with national mythological and folk narratives.

Briefly defined as a "historical drama series" broadcast by the NHK,[28] taiga dramas offer glimpses of Japanese history, interlaced with artful media constructions of the characters' kimonos; the fabric, color, design varieties, symbolic functions, and changing styles coalescence in a macro-level visual effect. Therefore, the kimono mirrors not only a lifestyle specific to a particular historical period or social class but also the character and personality traits of the wearer. Besides the above-mentioned fabric color, textile type, or style, the patterns symbolizing mythical and legendary creatures are prone to suggest the symbolic transfer of specific attributes (courage, femininity, and perseverance) to the wearer, the passing of seasons, the occurrence of unfortunate events, or dramatic plot shifts.

In productions such as *Princess Atsu* (Atsuhime, 篤姫, 2008), *Burning Flower* (Hanamoyu, 花燃ゆ, 2015), *Here Comes Asa* (Asa ga kita, あさが来た, 2015), and *The Inner Palace* (Ooku, 大奥, 2023), the audience is exposed to a continuous negotiation of both historical and contemporary ideals of femininity and socially constructed gender roles. Adopting quite the opposite stance are taiga dramas like *Yoshitsune* (Yoshitsune, 義経, 2005), *Ryōmaden* (Ryōmaden, 龍馬伝, 2010), *Heart of a Samurai* (Tenchijin, 天地人, 2009), *Taira no kiyomori* (Taira no kiyomori, 平清盛, 2012), *Strategist Kanbei* (Gunshi Kanbei, 軍師官兵衛, 2014) and *Sanada Maru* (Sanada Maru, 真田丸, 2017), which emphasize an idealized construction of the aggressive, patriarchal, and dominating masculinity, primarily associated with the imagery of the samurai and the military and political ruler.

Nonetheless, decorating the characters' kimonos are motifs and patterns of mythical and legendary creatures. As the ultimate symbol of the archetypal physically strong masculinity, the Japanese dragon (ryū, 龍) stands for "the power of gods,"[29] and holds an ambivalent character, reflecting both good and bad natural phenomena. Thanks to its inherent historical, Buddhist, and Shintoist religious roots, intertextual links can be established with a variety of mythical tales and legends. For example, *Yamata No Orochi* (大蛇), the tale of the gigantic eight-headed dragon serpent slayed by Susanoo, is featured in *Kojiki* (古事記, 712) and *Nihon shoki* (日本書紀, 720), while Watatsumi (海神) is "the [dragon] spirit (kami) of [the oceans and] the seas."[30]

Other water creatures that embellish the kimonos in taiga dramas weave their symbolism within the plot line: the carp (koi, 鯉), goldfish (kingyo, 金魚), frog (kaeru, 蛙), shrimp (ebi, 海老), and tortoise (kame, 亀).[31]

Bird patterns often come in sight as well: the crane (tsuru, 鶴・雲鶴・松喰鶴), hawk (taka, 鷹), heron (sagi, 鷺), long-tailed fowl (onaga-dori, 尾長鳥), Mandarin duck (oshidori, 鴛鴦), phoenix (hoūoū, 鳳凰), peacock (kujaku, 孔雀), plover (chidori, 千鳥), sparrow (suzume, 雀), swallow (tsubame, 燕), and wild goose (gan, 雁).[32]

Figure 7.2 *Character in formal Heian period attire from* Hikaru Kimi e *(2024). The luxurious gold outer robe with subtle patterns and multi-layered kimono ensemble illustrates the historical dimension of traditional Japanese dress in taiga dramas depicting Japan's classical literary era.*

Figure 7.3 *The Lady Shogun in an ornate ceremonial kimono ensemble from NHK's* Ooku *(2023). The vibrant red outer robe with gold embroidery featuring auspicious symbols and mythical creatures represents both political authority and the reversal of traditional gender roles in this alternative historical narrative, embodying the "feminist kimono" concept.*

"大奥 PR動画 Long version 4分)", NHKエンタープライズ ファミリー倶楽部, uploaded June 2, 2023, YouTube video, 4 min 5 sec, https://www.youtube.com/watch?v=wNZL4tRha8c&t=3s.

Finally, equally popular are motifs depicting the dragonfly (tonbo, 蜻蛉) and butterfly (chō, 蝶),[33] which suggest not only instances of sacrality and nationalism—Japan's archaic name was Akitsu Shima, the Dragonfly Island,[34]—but also supernatural beliefs deeply anchored in animism and Buddhism: folk tales of human soul reincarnation and transmigration into a butterfly.[35]

In addition to the above-described supernatural and legendary beings as kimono patterns, in other taiga dramas, the heroine's kimono functions as a plot and character development tool when juxtaposed with accounts of Japanese mythology, history, and literature. For instance, the TV production *Dear Radiance* (Hikaru Kimi e, 光る君へ, 2024) follows throughout the mid-Heian period the life journey of Japanese female poet Murasaki Shikibu (紫式部), the author of *The Tale of Genji* (Genji Monogatari, 源氏物語). While the mid-to-late Heian period overlaps with the early manifestations of the kimono and thus renders time-specific depictions of Japanese femininity, aesthetics, and social difficulties, it also coincides with the writing and public distribution of the first Japanese-language novel. Therefore, it is an iconic historical moment in the evolution of Japanese literature.[36]

Albeit plain and unpretentious in terms of chromatic and fabric variations, the kimono of protagonist actress Yoshitaka Yuriko featured as the feminist pioneering activist Itō Noe (伊藤野枝) in the movie *The Wind, the Storm*[37] (Kaze yo, Arashi yo, 風よあらしよ, 2024) disguises an analogy of a famous and first-of-its-kind Japanese feminist manifesto that epitomizes the idea of the Japanese woman being the sun. On a side note, in Japan's genesis myth listed in the *Kojiki*, a fundamental role is played by the Sun Goddess, Amaterasu Ōmikami (天照大御神).[38] The scene of the kimono-dressed heroine reading the first lines of this feminist manifesto encapsulates the metaphor of the ordinary Japanese woman as Amaterasu and her subsequent fall into social disgrace under the umbrella of the patriarchal ideologies that promote male superiority and authority:

> In the beginning, [the] woman was truly the sun. An authentic person. Now, she is the moon, a wan and sickly moon dependent on another, reflecting another's brilliance. The time has come to recapture the sun hidden within us. "Reveal the sun hidden within us, reveal the genius hidden within us!"

> This is the cry we unceasingly cry out to ourselves, the thirst that refuses to be suppressed or quenched, the one instinct that unifies all [women] and sundry instincts and ultimately makes us a complete person . . .[39]

Historical Value: The Empty Shell Kimono

A major issue raised by a great number of Japanese kimono historians, local fabric dyeing artists, and domestic audience is the questionable historical value and low accuracy of the costumes featured in most recent taiga dramas, which fail to follow actual historical records of everyday fashion of past times.[40] One example of Japanese TV production that has blithely ignored historical fashion conventions is *Awaiting Kirin* (Kirin ga kuru, 麒麟がくる, 2020), which builds on the life story of renowned samurai Akechi Mitsuhide (明智光秀) and reworks Japanese classical mythology by integrating "the kirin" (麒麟).

Roughly translated as "the unicorn," the kirin represents one of the Four Miracles Creatures[41] and foresees the leader's birth and arrival. Hence, it links metaphorically with the protagonist's development.[42] It would be hard to associate these much-criticized historical inaccuracies either with the fact that this is the first taiga drama shot at an enhanced resolution of 4K or the first one that benefitted from the contribution of a non-Japanese film composer, John R. Graham.[43] Nevertheless, despite the emphasis on visual attractiveness and high production standards, the historical value and relevance of the costumes remain relatively low.

Based on the assertion that in some televised productions the historical significance of the clothing is at risk of being depleted, we compared the kimono with "an empty shell": it might meet the visual requirements of the form, but it lacks the substance. Taking the above-mentioned taiga drama as an example, at least four obstacles are expected to contribute to depleting the historical value of the kimonos featured on the screen. First, the nature of the handmade fabrics prepared a hundred years ago is highly difficult to replicate in modern times. Whereas handmade textiles represented the norm in the past, nowadays, synthetic fibers (cotton-synthetic mixes and synthetic-blend fabrics as well) have become more prevalent in the fashion scene, taking over the market.

Second, the radical transition from natural dyes extracted from plants or high-quality minerals to high-performance chemical dyes wreaked havoc with the production process of the kimono. One of the major effects of this sudden shift to chemical dyes was disrupting the traditional established dyeing methods and accelerating the kimono's mass manufacturing. Historically speaking, the yellow pigment was extracted from gardenia seeds, commonly known as cape jasmine (kuchi nashi, 梔), and for the red, safflower (benibana, 紅花) from the Iga Ueno city of the Yamagata Prefecture was used as raw material.[44] Nowadays, for reasons of optimizing the production costs and thanks to the technical innovations that have led to an explosion of chemical pigments, the actors' kimonos are most likely colored with chemical and synthetic dyes. For these reasons, it would have been historically unlikely for the main character of *Awaiting Kirin* (2020) to wear lime green, a color otherwise impossible to achieve during that period by using natural dyes.

Third, specific taboo colors reserved for high-rank officials and prepared after secret recipes have become nowadays impossible to reproduce:[45] dark purple (kokimurasaki, 濃紫) was assigned to the nobles, dark yellowish red (kōrozen, 黄櫨染) to the emperor, and yellow-green tinged with grey (kikujin, 麹塵) for the emperor as the informal dress code, and for the crown prince.[46] Fourth, the sewing and dyeing techniques are also significantly different in present times: the aggressive industrialization has impacted not only the West but also the Japanese traditional kimono industry, which has shifted from handmade and artisanal manufacturing in small family workshops with a historical reputation to the mass industrialized kimono production system.[47]

Sociopolitical Value: The Feminist Kimono

In an attempt to encompass the sociopolitical value exerted by the kimono as a Japanese popular culture construct, we propose the concept of the "feminist kimono" that perceives "gender" and "feminist ideologies" as deeply embedded in the media portrayal of the kimono-dressed feminine characters. Without overly generalizing and pretending it describes the entire Japanese media ecosystem, what gave rise to this concept is noticing the intertwining of feminist emancipation narratives and hybrid-style kimonos. For instance, the movie *The Inner Palace* (2010) takes as its subject the reverse harem imagery where, throughout an alternative Edo period, the Lady Shogun, dressed in lavish, rich, and brightly colored kimonos adorned with cranes and dragon motifs, rules in a utopian matriarchal society as the quintessential figure of political power that exerts authoritarian control over the men bodies.

In *The Tempest* (Tenpesuto, テンペスト, 2011), the heroine disguises herself as a eunuch to become a government official, while in *Yae's Sakura* (Yae no Sakura, 八重の桜, 2013), the protagonist Nijima Yae is an expert in gunnery and stands as the archetype of the feminist leader promoting women's social liberation, emancipation, and education rights, topics that throughout the late Edo period would have been considered dangerously radical. Likewise, in *Naotora: The Lady Warlord* (Onna Jōshu Naotora, おんな城主 直虎, 2017), the female lead exhibits a gender-fluid clothing style that subsumes the cultural and symbolic capital of the tiger (tora, 虎), a legendary animal gifted with supernatural forces. Therefore, the "cross-dressing" and "gender-bender" themes crystalize, encapsulate, and disguise real-life transgressions against Japanese gender social expectations and toward nonconforming and fluid sexual identities. It is precisely the kimono's hybridization that accounts for the visual codes signifying the Japanese women's exclusion from political life—a gender discrimination issue that has not changed nor registered outstanding progress throughout the history of Japan.[48]

Albeit lacking to some extent historical clothing accuracy—a fact that has amplified conversations surrounding the performative value of such productions—what we have coined as "the feminist kimono" functions as a tool of gender justice within Japanese popular culture and conveys to create an alternative and empowering space for the feminine (and feminist!) audience. On the one hand, the masculinized visual imagery of the heroines functions as a rich repository that empowers Japanese women who adopt a "masculinized" femininity or those taking distance from social expectations in terms of clothing and dressing style. Therefore, the feminist kimono converts into a counter-cultural practice that allows the audience to resist gender norms through the adaptation and subversion of the classic kimono. On the other hand, amid national, long-lasting gender inequality and discrimination against sexual minorities,[49] the counter-cultural fashion practice of the fluid kimono converts into a semiotic system of resistance for the LGBTQIA+ communities, particularly those living in Japan.

Entertainment Value: The Sensationalized Kimono

Moving forward to the final established category, the critical factor that predetermines the visually pleasant and exciting aesthetic experience for the audience when admiring the exquisite and ephemeral kimonos of Princess Atsu in the taiga drama of the same name is the sensationalized character of her costumes.

The visual spectacle of lavishly embellished kimonos, adorned with rich floral and other picturesque patterns, provides not only a sense of luxury associated with the character's high social status but also reasserts her performative femininity without diminishing her aura as a leader with considerable political influence. Symbolizing kindness, loyalty, honor, and also resilience,[50] the sparrow (suzume, 雀) that frequently decorates the kimonos of Princess Atsu is also a central metaphor of Japanese folk stories and legends such as *The Tongue-Cut Sparrow* (Shita Kiri Suzume, 舌切り雀).

However, the details of the protagonist's silk kimonos go beyond acting as a frivolous embellishment and convert into signifiers of Japanese socially and culturally constructed ideals of femininity and sensuality during the Edo period. The complex and delicate nature of the intricate decorations—the sparrows and the embroidered bamboo suggesting resilience and perseverance—ties the heroine's distinctive personality traits and character development to the course of the narrative and adds depth and complexity to the plot's progression. Hence, we coined the expression "the sensationalized kimono" to encapsulate, on the one hand, the visual luxurious experience of the audience and, on the other hand, the Japanese media narrative and sartorial conventions of what might be, in fact, a timeless representation of Japanese femininity.

Manga and Anime Productions: The Fantastic Kimono

The kimono exhibits a complex cross- and multimedia genre adaptability that allows an in-depth investigation of how Japanese postmodern identity,

Figure 7.4 *Anthropomorphized yokai in kimonos from* Kamisama Kiss *(2012). The kitsune character Tomoe (center) wears a refined white and purple kimono that reflects his supernatural status and dignified personality, while other characters display varied kimono styles with traditional patterns.*

Kamisama Kiss, *season 1, episode 1, "Nanami Becomes a God," directed by Akitaro Daichi, aired October 1, 2012, Tokyo TV.*

historically rooted traditional culture, fashion evolution, and consumerism intertwine within the domestic popular culture ecosystem. In addition to the above-referred genre of taiga drama that weaves mythological narratives around the kimono and the people wearing it, manga (Japanese comics, 漫画) and anime (Japanese animation, アニメ) adopt a different approach from the cinematic canon and move toward mythical creatures wearing the kimono. In light of the existing intertextual imbrications between manga and anime—in terms of visual conventions, storytelling techniques, plot development, and characters' archetypes—we will refer hereinafter to both genres simultaneously.

Mythical and legendary creatures such as yūrei (幽霊, ghosts), yōkai (妖怪, supernatural beings) that encompass kitsune (狐, fox spirits), kaibyō (怪猫, supernatural cats), ayakashi (妖, water spirits), yuki onna (雪女, snow woman), and finally, oni (鬼, demons) are dressed in colorful kimonos and generate countless narrative possibilities in jidaigeki and isekai anime and manga series. By definition, "jidaigeki" (時代劇) refers to "period" productions, usually set

Figure 7.5 *Nezuko Kamado from* Kimetsu no Yaiba *(2019). The half-demon character wears a distinctive pink kimono with geometric patterns, exemplifying the "fantastic kimono" concept where supernatural beings in anime are anthropomorphized through traditional Japanese attire while embodying kawaii aesthetics. The Demon Slayer, season 3, episode 11, "A Connected Bond: Daybreak and First Light," directed by Haruo Sotozaki, aired June 18, 2023, Fuji TV.*

before Japan's modern era (1868),[51] with "jidai" (時代) being translated as "period" and "geki" (劇) as "theater play." "Isekai" (異世界) is roughly the equivalent of an "alternative and fantastic world" and represents a significant media genre within Japanese popular culture.

Within these popular culture genres, the kimono-dressed bodies become analogical for a wide range of new cultural meanings predetermined by two significant tendencies: anthropomorphism, which subsumes idealization and sexualization, and incorporation of the Japanese popular culture philosophy anchored in aesthetic values such as the kawaii (可愛い, cuteness) and chibi (チビ, smallish) trends.

The fantastic characters play boldly with repositories of meanings that alternate from submissive, passive, and domestic femininity to erotic and sensual instances of cross-dressing, gender bender, and romantic interspecies relationships between supernatural heroes and human heroines. Depictions of relationships between human and superhuman characters can be encountered in the jidaigeki and isekai anime series *Kamisama Kiss* (Kamisama

Hajimemashita, 神様はじめました, 2012), *Repeat! Kokkuri-san* (Gugure! Kokkuri-san, 繰繰れ！コックリさん, 2014), and *Kakuriyo: Bed and Breakfast for Spirits* (Kakuriyo no Yadomeshi, かくりよの宿飯, 2018). As such, the portrayal of interspecies love relationships and mentor–mentee or master–servant dynamic negotiations often intertwines with the larger narrative that underpins socio-philosophical themes of human power, limits of knowledge, and subjective identities on micro and macro levels.

A first representative example that simultaneously encompasses the above-stated tendencies is Nezuko (禰豆子), the half-demon and half-human character of *The Demon Slayer* (Kimetsu no Yaiba, 鬼滅の刃, 2019) and the sister of protagonist Tanjirō Kamado. Standing for the recognition of the heroine's humanity and humanism is the sister–brother relationship that touches upon psychological and emotional levels. Her beauty, grounded in Japanese anime aesthetic traditions—immense and captivating eyes that suggest youthfulness and purity, complemented by the ephemeral bodily behavior and the sakura pinkish kimono—evokes the image of idealized femininity. As a whole, Nezuko's physical appearance, coupled with her cuteness and childlike demeanor, may evoke a sense of sensuality and eroticism.

The second relevant example is Tomoe (巴衛). The hero of the anime series *Kamisama Kiss* (2012) is a fox yōkai who excels in expressing a wide variety of feelings, from anger of being abandoned by his former master, fear of being betrayed by his love interest, the human Nanami, to finally, love crystalized through marriage. His whitish and refined kimono and seemingly cold demeanor perpetuate the traditional Japanese manly ideal, with qualities like unfading loyalty, honor, overprotectiveness, self-control, emotional restraint, and upholding other desirable moral values.

Another instance of anthropomorphic and dominant masculinity is the supernatural figure of Ōdanna (大旦那), the human-lover ogre (邪鬼), in *Kakuriyo: Bed and Breakfast for Spirits* (2018). By ascribing to his identity sexual attractiveness as a primary value, Ōdanna challenges and defies the Western-specific perception of "the common demon" as it has been stipulated according to the Judeo-Christian eschatology and intimately linked to the imagery of the malevolent "(d)evil."[52] The ever-present devil-like horns and the hideous mask Ōdanna occasionally wears come in stark contrast with the attractiveness of his face and the kimono elegance that exudes a sense of manliness. This particular combination of visual signifiers that oscillate between extremes of grotesqueness and beauty and isekai clothing can imply the character's dual nature, fluid personality, or inhabiting a dual world.

We shall continue by making a series of observations pertaining to the proposed conceptual framework of kimono values ascribed to the historical, sociopolitical, and entertainment categories.

Circumscribed to this alternative, fantastic world—isekai—the kimonos of mythical creatures have no pretense of historical accuracy, as this is not a value the producers or the viewers are seeking or one that might affect the commercial viability and success of the production. Far from being historically grounded, the kimonos such as the ones featured in *Nura: Rise of the Yokai Clan* (Nurarihyon no Mago, ぬらりひょんの孫, 2010) are fantastic by nature and do not attempt whatsoever to meet accuracy requirements. For instance, the kimono of young Nurarihyon, the yōkai powerful leader of the Nura clan, sensually reveals the upper part of his chest to the extent that it represents a flirtatious, sexualized, and trans-human form of desirable masculinity. Likewise, as a yuki onna spirit associated with winter and snowstorm imagery, Tsurara Oikawa (及川氷麗) of the same series is equally sensual through her cuteness and purity suggested by her ever-white kimono. However, in the case of both supernatural characters and many others as well, there is a striking and huge difference between their Japanese folklore and mythology-rooted representation and the one displayed in isekai productions. The merciless, ruthless, and hideous yuki onna portrayed in the classic *Myth of the Snow Woman*[53] inspires fear and terror, whereas the anime version elevates emotions of aliveness and adoration within the audience while also inspiring affective attachment that is prone to translate into fan-specific performance productivity (fanfictions or cosplay display).

As a whole, the clothing emphasizes entertainment and sociopolitical values: the visually appealing construction of the vestimentary code is tightly linked not only with the characters' on-screen representation by suggesting personality traits and identity but also pertains to immaterial issues and societal concerns specific to contemporary Japan. For instance, Nezuko's portrayal hints at the problematic over-sexualization of female children within Japanese media and popular culture, while Tomoe struggles with chronic, severe depression and long-lasting self-esteem issues.

Albeit anchored in fantastic narratives, the "fairly realistic" approach in tackling Japan-specific concerns such as suicide, depression, loneliness, or hikikomori casts these manga and anime productions in a more valuable light. Moreover, as featured in the above-mentioned (and not only!) isekai works, the fantastic kimono endeavors to complete the characters' biographical representation and addresses multilayered and stringent issues that remain insufficiently addressed in the public sphere. Anthropomorphizing the behavior of such supernatural characters thus serves as a vital instrument that facilitates public conversation and debate surrounding delicate psycho-social issues, otherwise silenced in real-life contexts, particularly for cultural reasons of shame (haji, 恥) and others' judgment.

Street Performances and Cosplay Subcultures: The Subjective Kimono

The genres of taiga drama, jidaigeki, and isekai manga and anime inspire the audience to adopt an active and performative role, reflecting the consumption process of these genres and the massification of kimono manufacturing. From this perspective, at least three different phenomena can be noticed: first, the matsuri (祭り)—the street festival performances; second, the cosplay countercultures and subcultures; and third, the hybrid fashion items that mimic the original kimono in style, accessories, design, patterns, colors, and textiles.

Besides the already-introduced official ritualized ceremonies that require dressing the kimono—the tea ceremony, the traditional childhood rite of passage, the coming-of-age or the marriage religious ceremony—several street festivals, also referred to as "matsuri," bring the cultural fashion heritage brand into the streets.

One of the major festivals in Kyoto, Japan, is the *Festival of Ages* (時代祭), held each year on October 22. The large parade traveling from the Imperial

Palace to the Heian Shrine is also the occasion for a massive exhibition of accurate costumes representing a wide array of periods throughout Japan's history and dressing and acting as famous historical characters during the festival.[54] A more kimono-centered approach lies at the core foundation of the *Tōkamachi Kimono Festival* (十日町着物祭り), held annually on May 3 in Tōkamachi city, widely renowned for its secular and "unique history as a kimono and textile production" center.[55] Finally, a more relaxed atmosphere and a yukata-wearing opportunity can be encountered at the fireworks festivals, referred to as *Hanabi* (花火大会) and particularly at the Sumidagawa Fireworks Festival (隅田川花火大会), which are held throughout the entire country each July.

As the second relevant phenomenon that needs further highlighting, cosplay (コスプレ) represents the art and street subculture—and we might add "counterculture"—of "costume playing," where fans perform and act as fictional popular culture characters in self-made costumes.[56] Besides the much-appraised escapism reflecting the underground philosophy of cosplay performers, we will bring a new dimension into the discussion: "the subjective kimono." Fans dressed as heroes and heroines from the jidaigeki and isekai anime imprint the kimono with their own handmade work and view of the costumes, fantastic characters, and narrative lines. They become actively engaged in the production process of the kimono, join networks with individuals with whom they share the same interest, adopt different roles, and perform fictional identities according to their desires and personal expression. By arousing great interest in the manufacturing process, the kimono becomes fan-driven. Therefore, the cosplay street performances, parades, and related exhibitions convert into an aestheticized and sociopsychological celebration of the subjective self and the inner persona of the fan.

Central to the modernization of the kimono and engagement with globalization, technological advancement in fashion, and deeper penetration of foreign influences as well, are the third phenomenon. The hybrid kimono expresses the shift from the Japanese traditional and austere conception of the national attire to the transnational perspective that has diluted the costume's aesthetics. The kimono dress (着物ドレス), the yukata dress (浴衣ドレス), or jinbei ladies (甚平レディース) represent modernized and hybrid versions of the kimono that encapsulate Japan's tension between deeply stratified tradition and the fast-speed and aggressive innovation. Reinterpreting garments, patterns, and colors or shortening the dress length mirrors the practice of mixing Western and Japanese fashion styles.

Above all and most importantly, all these three phenomena reveal the many facets of the changing practices in wearing the kimono and the dynamics of the socio-aesthetic values surrounding it in contemporary times.

Conclusions: The Future of the Kimono

The overall aim of this chapter was to provide a first-of-its-kind analysis of how Japanese popular culture reconfigures the symbiosis between the kimono as the national attire and a vast repertoire of mythical and legendary creatures as part of the national cultural heritage. Two fundamental components laid the ground for the "modernization" of the kimono and rewriting folk and mythology-rooted heritage narratives within Japan's media and public ecosystem. The first component is the scientific developments and technological advances in production techniques and distribution processes, and the second is the social media networks, streaming platforms, and overall the AI-powered communication that launched, propagated, and encouraged new kimono trends. What joins the network system is the cosplay subculture as well, given that the communication between the members is, in most cases, transferred within the World Wide Web. Such consumer and fan-driven kimono trends might register profound divergences from the traditional kimono consumption patterns. Nonetheless, historical details concerning types of fabrics, dyeing techniques, pigment preparation, or the nature of additional garments have had to be omitted due to space constraints.

This study also introduced and presented a framework for analyzing the values associated with the kimono within Japanese popular culture genres. In this regard, we suggested three main categories corresponding to the values affiliated with Japanese folk clothing: historical, sociopolitical, and entertainment. Throughout the subsequent analysis of multifarious media genres, from taiga dramas, jidaigeki, and isekai manga and anime to street fashion and cosplay subcultures, each category generated a corresponding dimension that stemmed from the kimono representation: the empty shell, feminist, fantastic, and subjective. The blurred boundaries between the media genres (manga and anime connect with cosplay) might lead to the occasional overlapping between the proposed categories and dimensions. As such, a character's kimono can simultaneously be feminist and fantastic.

We will conclude by inviting the reader to an in-depth reflection on the evolution of the kimono in the foreseeable future under the progressive influence and permeation of generative AI models in the fashion industry. Aspects such as AI-generated designs and AI-initiated (kimono) trends require further analysis. In this futuristic, yet not-that-distant context, human-produced clothing and human-inspired patterns are prone to become symbolically more valuable. Would further labels be necessary to distinguish human-made versus AI-generated kimonos? Who should claim the intellectual property and authorship of AI kimono designs that, in fact, employ a pre-existing database built on the artistic creativity of a massive number of human designers? Would this pioneering technology throw even more into despair the struggling sector of Japanese professional and small-scale artisans that invest decades into acquiring kimono manufacturing knowledge and skills? Is there any risk of cultural appropriation, colonization, and Westernization of the kimono when employing this tech-grounded approach? These questions can be nonetheless extended to other folk costumes and the entire fashion industry.

While an AI-powered design process and kimono virtual try-ons might be equally attractive for the producer and the consumer, we should consider that a mindful, culturally appropriate, and ethical usage of generative AI in this field is stringently needed.

Note

The translations from Japanese to English presented in this chapter are the author's original work, unless stated otherwise, and were specifically prepared for the purpose of this study.

Notes

1 The original quote is as follow: 「女が、お茶碗や、きれいな柄の着物を愛するのは、それだけが、ほんとうの生き甲斐だからでございます。刻々の動きが、それがそのまま生きていることの目的なのです。他に、何が要りましょう。」

2 Osamu Dazai, 皮膚と心 – Skin and Heart, Tokyo, Japan: Shinchosha, 1974.

3 Sophia Luu and Ellen Mckinney, "Kimono: Elucidating Meanings of Japanese Textile Artifacts for a Museum Audience," *Anais Do Museu Paulista: História e Cultura Material* 29: 2021. https://doi.org/10.1590/1982-02672021v29e9

4 "Woman's Kimono," Philadelphia Museum of Art – Education Section, n.d. https://legacyweb.philamuseum.org/doc_downloads/education/object_resources/89297.pdf

5 Terry Satsuki Milhaupt, *Kimono: A Modern History*, London: Reaktion Books, 2016, 26.

6 Makoto Mori, "History and Techniques of the Kimono," *Shibusa: Extracting Beauty*, March 1, 2012, 117–34. https://doi.org/10.5920/shibusa.08

7 Ibid.

8 Ibid.

9 Kenichi Ohno, "Meiji Japan: Progressive Learning of Western Technology," in *How Nations Learn: Technological Learning, Industrial Policy, and Catch-Up*, Arkebe Oqubay and Kenichi Ohno, eds, Oxford: Oxford University Press, 2019, 85–106.

10 Anne Van Asche, "Japanese Kimono Fashion of the Early Twentieth Century," Digital Commons @ University of Nebraska – Lincoln: Textile Society of America Symposium Proceedings, 2000. https://digitalcommons.unl.edu/cgi/viewcontent.cgi?article=1800&context=tsaconf

11 Stephanie Assmann, "Between Tradition and Innovation: The Reinvention of the Kimono in Japanese Consumer Culture," *Fashion Theory* 12 (3): September 2008, 359–76. https://doi.org/10.2752/175174108x332332

12 Van Asche, "Japanese Kimono Fashion of the Early Twentieth Century."

13 Takami Kuwayama, "The Making of Women's Kimono as Japan's National Dress: The Dynamics of Gaze from Within and Without," EAAA Meeting, October 7, 2019. https://www.academia.edu/40521457/The_Making_of_Women_s_Kimono_as_Japan_s_National_Dress_The_Dynamics_of_Gaze_from_Within_and_Without_2019_EAAA_Meeting_

14 Akemi Morita, 森田空美のはじめてきものきほん事典, Tokyo, Japan: Sekaibunkasha, 2018.

15 Ibid.

16 Jiayi Zhang, "Analysis of the Japanese Printing and Dyeing Techniques: Yuzen Dyeing," *BCP Social Sciences & Humanities* 19: August 30, 2022, 142–7. https://doi.org/10.54691/bcpssh.v19i.1596

17 Yuko Fukatsu-Fukuoka, "The Evolution of Yuzen-Dyeing Techniques and Designs after the Meiji Restoration," Digital Commons @ University of Nebraska – Lincoln: Textile Society of America Symposium Proceedings, 2004. https://digitalcommons.unl.edu/cgi/viewcontent.cgi?article=1474&context=tsaconf.

18 Mori, "History and Techniques of the Kimono."

19 Giorgio Riello, "Fashion in the Four Parts of the World: Time, Space and Early Modern Global Change," in *Dressing Global Bodies*, Beverly Lemire and Giorgio Riello, eds, London, UK: Routledge, 2019, 133–59.

20 Sasaki Chigako, "Weaving, Dyeing and Kimono," Japan SPOTLIGHT | Japan Economic Foundation, n.d. https://www.jef.or.jp/journal/pdf/gallery_0409.pdf

21 "Japanese Fabrics Have Their Global Reputation Wrapped Up," *Niponica* 11: 2013. https://web-japan.org/niponica/pdf/niponica11/no11_en.pdf

22 Chigako, "Weaving, Dyeing and Kimono."

23 Sheila Cliffe, *The Social Life of Kimono: Japanese Fashion Past and Present*, London, UK: Bloomsbury Visual Arts, 2020.

24 Monika Bincsik, *Kimono Style: Edo Traditions to Modern Design. The John C. Weber Collection*, New York: Metropolitan Museum of Art, 2022.

25 Anna Jackson, *Kimono: Kyoto to Catwalk*, London, UK: Victoria and Albert Museum Publishing, 2020.

26 Riello, "Fashion in the Four Parts of the World."

27 Zhang, "Analysis of the Japanese Printing and Dyeing Techniques: Yuzen Dyeing."

28 Philip Seaton, "Taiga Dramas and Tourism: Historical Contents as Sustainable Tourist Resources," *Japan Forum* 27 (1): December 15, 2014, 82–103. https://doi.org/10.1080/09555803.2014.962568

29 "動物の着物の柄，" わかる着物の柄, May 5, 2019. https://www.kimono-gara.com/syurui/doubutsu/

30 David Adams Leeming, *The Oxford Companion to World Mythology*, New York: Oxford University Press, 2009.

31 Ibid.

32 Ibid.

33 Hideto Hoshina, "The Mythology of Insect-Loving Japan," *Insects* 13 (3): February 26, 2022, 234. https://doi.org/10.3390/insects13030234

34 Ibid.

35 *The Dream of Akinosuke* (Akinosuke no Yume, あきのすけの夢) is a relevant example.

36 Royall Tyler, "The Structure of Genji's Career: Myth, Politics, and Pride," in *Murasaki Shikibu's* The Tale of Genji*: Philosophical Perspectives*, James McMullen, ed., New York: Oxford University Press, 2019, 36–67.

37 A TV series released in 2022 and a movie released in 2024 are available at time of writing.

38 Russell Kirkland, "The Sun and the Throne: The Origins of the Royal Descent Myth in Ancient Japan," *Numen – International Review for the History of Religions* 44 (2): 1997, 109–52.

39 Raichō Hiratsuka, *In the Beginning, Woman Was the Sun: The Autobiography of a Japanese Feminist*, New York: Columbia University Press, 2010.

40 Denshi Fukuda, "カラフルな大河「麒麟がくる」　実際はどんな色だったのか京都「有名染師」に聞いた（全文）," *Daily Shincho*, February 15, 2020. https://www.dailyshincho.jp/article/2020/02160802/?all=1

41 The other miraculous beings are the phoenix, the turtle, and the dragon.

42 Marta Michalska-Kurczyńska, "Dragons, Gods, Demons – Ojime – Symbolic Content Hidden in Miniature Form," *Art of the Orient* 2 (1): 2013, 117–30. https://doi.org/10.15804/aoto201306

43 IMDb, "John R. Graham – Composer, Music Department, Soundtrack," n.d. https://www.imdb.com/name/nm0334138/

44 Sachio Yoshioka and Denshi Fukuda, "紫〜染織史家・吉岡幸雄＋染師・福田伝士：ドキュメンタリー，"　いつか・住もう・京都・２　, 2013. http://cherubinpriel.blog.fc2.com/blog-entry-91.html

45 Sachio Yoshioka, "失われた「いにしへの色」に挑み続けた染織史家・吉岡幸雄ー初の回顧展で現代によみがえった色に触れる," Tsumugu: Japan Art & Culture, April 5, 2021. https://tsumugu.yomiuri.co.jp/feature/%E5%A4%B1%E3%82%8F%E3%82%8C%E3%81%9F%E3%81%84%E3%81%AB%E3%81%97%E3%81%B8%E3%81%AE%E8%89%B2%E5%90%89%E5%B2%A1%E5%B9%B8%E9%9B%84/

46 Ibid.

47 Ibid.

48 Alisa Gaunder, "Women and Political Inequality in Japan: Gender Imbalanced Democracy," *Social Science Japan Journal* 26 (2): February 24, 2023, 247–50. https://doi.org/10.1093/ssjj/jyad001

49 Amnesty International, "Human Rights Law and Discrimination against LGBT in Japan," 2021. https://www.amnesty.org/en/wp-content/uploads/2021/05/ASA2259552017ENGLISH.pdf

50 "Symbolism in Japanese Art: Plants and Birds," *Reader Collection*, n.d.. http://readercollection.com/x4%20Symbolism.pdf

51 Ian Akbar, "The 'National Style' of Japanese Film by the 1930s (1930年代における日本映画の'　国民スタイル')," *SSRN Electronic Journal*, September 25, 2016, 1–11. https://doi.org/10.2139/ssrn.2859869

52 Fernando Gabriel Pagnoni Berns, Subashish Bhattacharjee, and Ananya Saha, *Japanese Horror Culture: Critical Essays on Film, Literature, Anime, Video Games*, Lanham, MD: Lexington Books, 2021, 141.

53 F. Hadland Davis, *Myths and Legends of Japan*, La Vergne, USA: Neeland Media LLC, 2020.

54 "Jidai Matsuri," Traditional Kyoto, n.d.. https://traditionalkyoto.com/culture/jidai-matsuri/

55 "The Tokamachi Kimono Festival: 十日町市観光協会," 十日町市観光協会 | My trip TOKAMACHI, March 10, 2024. https://www.tokamachishikankou.jp/en/event/kimonomatsuri/

56 Garry Crawford, "What Is Cosplay?" in *Cosplay and the Art of Play: Exploring Sub-Culture Through Art*, David Hancock and Garry Crawford, eds, Cham, Switzerland: Palgrave Macmillan, 2019, 1–21.

Bibliography

"動物の着物の柄." わかる着物の柄, May 5, 2019. https://www.kimono-gara.com/syurui/doubutsu/.

Akbar, Ian. "The 'National Style' of Japanese Film by the 1930s (1930年代における日本映画の'国民スタイル')." *SSRN Electronic Journal*, September 25, 2016, 1–11. https://doi.org/10.2139/ssrn.2859869.

Asche, Anne Van. "Japanese Kimono Fashion of the Early Twentieth Century." Digital Commons @ University of Nebraska – Lincoln: Textile Society of America Symposium Proceedings, 2000.

Assmann, Stephanie. "Between Tradition and Innovation: The Reinvention of the Kimono in Japanese Consumer Culture." *Fashion Theory* 12 (3): September 2008, 359–76. https://doi.org/10.2752/175174108x332332.

Berns, Fernando Gabriel Pagnoni, Subashish Bhattacharjee, and Ananya Saha, *Japanese Horror Culture: Critical Essays on Film, Literature, Anime, Video Games*, Lanham, MD: Lexington Books, 2021.

Bincsik, Monika. *Kimono Style: Edo Traditions to Modern Design. The John C. Weber Collection*. New York: Metropolitan Museum of Art, 2022.

Chigako, Sasaki. "Weaving, Dyeing and Kimono." Japan Spotlight – Japan Economic Foundation, n.d.

Cliffe, Sheila. *The Social Life of Kimono: Japanese Fashion Past and Present*. London: Bloomsbury Visual Arts, 2020.

Crawford, Garry. "What Is Cosplay?" In *Cosplay and the Art of Play Exploring Sub-Culture Through Art*, David Hancock and Garry Crawford, eds. Cham, Switzerland: Palgrave Macmillan, 2019, 1–21.

Davis, F. Hadland. *Myths and Legends of Japan*. La Vergne, USA: Neeland Media LLC, 2020.

Dazai, Osamu. 皮膚と心 – *Skin and Heart*. Tokyo, Japan: Shinchosha, 1974.

Fukatsu-Fukuoka, Yuko. "The Evolution of Yuzen-Dyeing Techniques and Designs after the Meiji Restoration." Digital Commons @ University of Nebraska – Lincoln: Textile Society of America Symposium Proceedings, 2004.

Fukuda, Denshi. "カラフルな大河「麒麟がくる」　実際はどんな色だったのか京都「有名染師」に聞いた（全文）" *Daily Shincho*, February 15, 2020.

Gaunder, Alisa. "Women and Political Inequality in Japan: Gender Imbalanced Democracy." *Social Science Japan Journal* 26 (2): February 24, 2023, 247–50. https://doi.org/10.1093/ssjj/jyad001

Hiratsuka, Raichō. *In the Beginning, Woman was the Sun: The Autobiography of a Japanese Feminist*. New York: Columbia University Press, 2010.

Hoshina, Hideto. "The Mythology of Insect-Loving Japan." *Insects* 13 (3): February 26, 2022, 234. https://doi.org/10.3390/insects13030234

"Human Rights Law and Discrimination against LGBT in Japan." Amnesty International, 2021. https://www.amnesty.org/en/wp-content/uploads/2021/05/ASA2259552017ENGLISH.pdf.

Jackson, Anna. *Kimono: Kyoto to Catwalk*. London: Victoria and Albert Museum Publishing, 2020.

"Japanese Fabrics Have Their Global Reputation Wrapped Up." *Niponica* 11: 2013.

"Jidai Matsuri." Traditional Kyoto, n.d. https://traditionalkyoto.com/culture/jidai-matsuri/.

"John R. Graham – Composer, Music Department, Soundtrack." IMDb, n.d. https://www.imdb.com/name/nm0334138/

Kirkland, Russell. "The Sun and the Throne. The Origins of the Royal Descent Myth in Ancient Japan." *Numen – International Review for the History of Religions* 44 (2): 1997, 109–52.

Kuwayama, Takami. "The Making of Women's Kimono as Japan's National Dress: The Dynamics of Gaze from Within and Without." EAAA Meeting, October 7, 2019.

Leeming, David Adams. *The Oxford Companion to World Mythology*. New York: Oxford University Press, 2009.

Luu, Sophia, and Ellen McKinney. "Kimono: Elucidating Meanings of Japanese Textile Artifacts for a Museum Audience." *Anais do Museu Paulista: História e Cultura Material* 29: 2021. https://doi.org/10.1590/1982-02672021v29e9.

Michalska-Kurczyńska, Marta. "Dragons, Gods, Demons – Ojime – Symbolic Content Hidden in Miniature Form." *Art of the Orient* 2 (1): 2013, 117–30. https://doi.org/10.15804/aoto201306

Milhaupt, Terry Satsuki. *Kimono: A Modern History*. London: Reaktion Books, 2016.

Mori, Makoto. "History and Techniques of the Kimono." *Shibusa: Extracting Beauty*, March 1, 2012, 117–34. https://doi.org/10.5920/shibusa.08

Morita, Akemi. 森田空美のはじめてきものきほん事典. Tokyo, Japan: Sekaibunkasha, 2018.

Ohno, Kenichi. "Meiji Japan: Progressive Learning of Western Technology." In *How Nations Learn: Technological Learning, Industrial Policy, and Catch-Up*, Arkebe Oqubay and Kenichi Ohno, eds. Oxford: Oxford University Press, 2019, 85–106.

Riello, Giorgio. "Fashion in the Four Parts of the World: Time, Space and Early Modern Global Change." In *Dressing Global Bodies*, Beverly Lemire and Giorgio Riello, eds. London: Routledge, 2019, 133–59.

Seaton, Philip. "Taiga Dramas and Tourism: Historical Contents as Sustainable Tourist Resources." *Japan Forum* 27 (1): December 15, 2014, 82–103. https://doi.org/10.1080/09555803.2014.962568

"Symbolism in Japanese Art: Plants and Birds." Reader Collection, n.d. http://readercollection.com/x4%20Symbolism.pdf.

"The Tokamachi Kimono Festival: 十日町市観光協会." 十日町市観光協会 | My trip Tokamachi, March 10, 2024.

Tyler, Royall. "The Structure of Genji's Career: Myth, Politics, and Pride." In *Murasaki Shikibu's* The Tale of Genji*: Philosophical Perspectives*, James McMullen, ed. New York: Oxford University Press, 2019, 36–67.

"Woman's Kimono." Philadelphia Museum of Art – Education Section, n.d. https://legacyweb.philamuseum.org/doc_downloads/education/object_resources/89297.pdf

Yoshioka, Sachio. "失われた「いにしへの色」に挑み続けた染織史家・吉岡幸雄ー初の回顧展で現代によみがえった色に触れる." Tsumugu: Japan Art & Culture, April 5, 2021.

Yoshioka, Sachio, and Denshi Fukuda. "紫〜染織史家・吉岡幸雄＋染師・福田伝士: ドキュメンタリー." いつか・住もう・京都・ 2, 2013.

Zhang, Jiayi. "Analysis of the Japanese Printing and Dyeing Techniques: Yuzen Dyeing." *BCP Social Sciences & Humanities* 19: August 30, 2022, 142–7. https://doi.org/10.54691/bcpssh.v19i.1596

8

Fashioning Yogoe Through K-Drama and K-Pop

AMANDA SIKARSKIE[1]

Nailing down the terminology for yogoe is difficult in Korean, perhaps more so than in Chinese or Japanese. Some useful Korean yogoe words are: *goemul* (monster), *gwisin* (ghost), *wonhon* (vengeful spirit), and *yuryeong* (spooky). The following are particularly Korean yogoe, though some do have analogues in China, Japan, or Southeast Asia: haechi, or haetae, is the horned lion that is the symbolic protector of Seoul (though this is a more recent association). Bulgasari, somewhat similar to Baku, the dream-eating Malayan tapir that one encounters in folk beliefs in Japan, China, and Southeast Asia, feasts upon nightmares (and sports a long nose). This Korean dream-eater is also known as Bukesa (不可殺) in Mandarin, meaning "can't be killed." Chollima is also a symbol of Korea, particularly North Korea. It is related to the Japanese word "Senrima," or "thousand mile horse," as well as cheonma, which may be translated as a pegasus, or immortal flying horse. According to Nicholas J. Saunders, author of *Animal Spirits*, in Greco-Roman mythology, it was not just coral (as described later in this chapter in BTS's appropriation of Medusa), but also Pegasus that sprang from the blood of the decapitated Gorgon Medusa.[2]

The dokkaebi is a goblin wielding a magical club. The dokkaebi can be utilized as a protective emblem, as depicted on the packaging for products such as children's facemasks. Supporters of the South Korean national football team, the Red Devils or *Bulgeun Agma*, wear shirts printed with a dokkaebi

Figure 8.1 *South Korea v China, FIFA World Cup Asian 2nd Qualifier, Shenzhen, China. November 21: Son Heung-min #7 of South Korea celebrates after scoring his team's first goal with a penalty during the 2026 FIFA World Cup Qualifier second round Group C match between China and South Korea at Shenzhen Universiade Sports Centre on November 21, 2023 in Shenzhen, Guangdong Province of China.* *Photo by VCG/VCG via Getty Images*

image. Meanwhile, the South Korean national footballers themselves do not wear a dokkaebi on their jerseys, but instead a white tiger. "Sonny" Son Heungmin, who plays for Tottenham Hotspur in the English Premier League, wears the white tiger upon his jersey.

The mythical White Tiger is a national symbol of Korea. *Soohorang*, the name given to the white tiger mascot of the 2018 Pyongchang Winter Olympiad, stands for the protection of all athletes. Soohorang may be compared to Bing Dwendwen, the mascot of the 2022 Beijing Olympiad, but while Bing Dwendwen represents an actual animal, the giant panda, Soohorang represents a mythical creature.

Two fantastical creatures depicted in embroidery on *hyungbae*, or rank badges (*buzi*, in Mandarin), are the *girin* and *hopyo*.

The girin (or *qilin*, in Mandarin) is somewhat analogous to the Western chimera. The hopyo, or tiger-leopard, on the other hand, has no such equivalent,

Figure 8.2 *Hyungbae (rank badge) of a Girin, late nineteenth century. Los Angeles County Museum of Art.*

and in fact has been misinterpreted as simply a leopard or a tiger, a real animal, in Western museum collections. The hopyo hyungbae depicted in Figure 8.3, for example, is described as depicting a pair of tigers in the Los Angeles County Museum of Art online collections catalog.[3] But as historian of Korean dress Minjee Kim noted in her lecture "Hanbok: Gender, Class, and Modernity," animals with the body and head of a tiger but the spots of a leopard are actually hopyo, or tiger-leopards, which are semi-fantastical animals in Korean iconography.[4] Interestingly, quadrupeds, both mythical and actual, only

Figure 8.3 *Hyungbae (rank badge) of two Hopyo, late nineteenth century. Los Angeles County Museum of Art.*

appeared on the hyungbae of high-ranking military officials; the hyungbae of civil servants depicted birds such as peacocks and pheasants, and often clouds, as civil servants existed between heaven and earth to serve the Heavens.

Another type of yogoe that bears mentioning, not for its dress but for its cultural impact, is the agwi. Agwi may be understood as a starving ghost, the spirit of a person who died in hunger and is doomed to walk as a specter with an insatiable appetite. Poverty was rampant at the end of the Joseon Period, a time of economic devastation and systematic corruption. Kimberly Chung describes the agwi first seen by the main character in Yi Hyoseok's "City and Specter" (1928), middle-class flaneur horrified by the ghastly human byproducts of the capitalist system that had made possible their own success:

> The main character describes an encounter with a specter that he at first mistakes for a goblin (dokkaebi). Attempting to face his fear, the protagonist returns to the site of his ghost sighting, and it is revealed that what he thought was a specter was in fact a mother and a child, a "pair of beggars." Upon meeting these colonial "ghosts," the protagonist instead discovers true horror in the mother's condition." [5]

In Yi Hyoseok's Joseon Korea, the poor were "alive, but as good as dead."[6] The dress of the agwi, as one might imagine, has not been influential on the costuming of contemporary K-Drama, as it consisted customarily of tattered rags. But otherwise, agwi wore the same sort of hanbok that were typical for everyday wage laborers in the late Joseon. It seems fitting that Karl Marx described capital—produced by the continuous expenditure of wage labor—as a vampire, which itself is a kind of monster or yogoe, writing: "Capital is dead labor; which, vampire-like, lived only by sucking on living labor, and lives the more, the more labor it sucks."[7] One difficulty in writing on yogoe in English is working with translations of primary sources. For example, in English, Im Bang's story "An Encounter with a Hobgoblin," translated by James S. Gale, makes reference to a titular "hobgoblin"[8] Hobgoblin is of course an English word, with no direct Asian equivalent. In fact, it is about as specific as the very non-specific umbrella term "yogoe." A close reading of the text suggests that the titular hobgoblin may actually be a gumiho.

The gumiho, or nine-tailed fox, is perhaps the most iconic of all Korean yogoe. The fox spirit (*jiuweihu*, literally "nine-tailed fox") is mentioned in the classical Chinese travelogue, *The Classic of Mountains and Seas*, the earliest parts of which date to the Han Dynasty.[9] (See the introduction to this book for a description and extended commentary on *The Classic*.) Translator Anne Birrell describes the fox as depicted in *The Classic* as

> . . . bushy-tailed, or more frequently nine-tailed. In the text this fabled creature is not bound to the mythical figure of Queen Mother of the West, for whom it became a divine guardian animal in the later tradition. Kuo[10] notes that in its manifestation in the text it is an omen of great peace. In later folklore, but not in this text, the fox had the function of a trickster.[11]

The nine-tailed fox makes its introduction in Book 9, which described regions beyond the borders of China to the East: "Greenmound country [*Qingqiu guo*] lies to its north. The foxes there have four paws but nine tails. One author says this country lies north of Dawnsunny Valley."[12] Geographically speaking, it is unclear from the text whether *Qingqiu guo* refers to Korea or to an area far to the northeast of Classical China, but within the bounds of the modern Chinese state, such as Anshan. But this ancient account does provide evidence that nine-tailed fox tales originated from the northeast of China's Central Plain. Birrell's notes on *Qingqiu guo* are sparse:

> (*Ch'ing – ch'iu kuo*): The term "mound" usually denotes the burial place of a great god. Green is the colour motif of spring, water, and fertility. The height of Green Mound was used by the god Youth Dozen as a standard and starting-point from which he measured the earth, in one of the world-measuring myths of the text.[13]

In Sun Jiankun and Chen Siyu's, *Fantastic Creatures of the Mountains and Seas: A Classic*, a book that illustrates and explicates the monsters featured in *The Classic*, Sun describes Qingqiu shan (Qingqiu mountain) as 300 *li*[14] east of Jishan and notes that images of nine-tailed foxes appeared in Chinese ceramics of the Western Zhou (1045–771 BCE) period.[15]

Nine-tailed Foxes in Korean Horror Cinema

In their introduction to *Korean Horror Cinema*, Alison Peirse and Daniel Martin note that "Classic Korean horror is a cinema of folklore and ghosts, of *gumiho* and *wonhon* [a vengeful spirit]."[16] This phenomenon can be seen in Korean films such as *The Thousand Year Old Fox* (*Cheonnyeonho*, 1969), which is set in the Kingdom of Silla during the Three Kingdoms Period (57 BCE–668 CE), and *The Fox with Nine Tails* (*Gumiho*, 1994) and *The Fox Family* (*Gumiho gajok*, 2006), both set in the contemporary period in Seoul or its environs. In their essay "Creepy Liver-eating Fox Ladies: The Thousand Year Old Fox and Korea's Gumiho," Alison Peirse and James Byrne note a distinct difference from the fox spirits of Japan (which inspired the fashion brand Maison Kitsune) and China amongst Korean fox tales.

> While the Japanese kitsune or Chinese huli jing are often benevolent and wise, the Korean fox is almost always cunning and evil. For each hundred years that the fox lives it receives another tail, and when it becomes nine-tailed, in its thousandth year of existence, it becomes a gumiho. With this, the opportunity arises for it to become human, often on the condition that it eats a human organ. In these situations it frequently poses as a beautiful young woman in order to seduce unwitting young men.[17]

From the following passage of "The Fox Empress of China," a traditional folktale, one can infer that articles of human clothing are critically important to the gumiho, serving to disguise or obscure those parts of their body that persist in their fox form:

> It was arranged that the boy should examine the empress . . . Pretending to measure her pulse, he quickly whipped off her gloves. Just as he had expected, her hands were the hands of a fox. He immediately drew his sword and stabbed the empress. With a shriek of "Kya!", the empress transformed into a fox and died.[18][19]

The hanbok is the traditional dress of Korea for both men and women. Minjee Kim notes that while the hanbok was in use for centuries, it did undergo many changes over time, and was not static, as Western scholarship on traditional dress often suggests. "Riding the Korean Wave sweeping the world, the traditional Korean costumes have become increasingly visible in global media. In 2021, hanbok— - the generic term referring to traditional style Korean clothing— - was registered in the Oxford English Dictionary."[20]

Similarly, in the film *The Thousand Year Old Fox* (1968), a human woman, Yeo-hwa, has been possessed by a fox spirit. She (the gumiho) intends to murder the Queen of Silla, and shows up at the palace wearing a white hanbok[21] and veil.[22] The palace guards demand that she remove her veil to reveal her face, and the changes in Yeo-hwa's features brought about by the fox possession blow the gumiho's cover. (She then goes on a murderous rampage.)[23] In the 1994 film *The Fox with Nine Tales,* this situation is somewhat reversed; again, a human male removes the female gumiho's clothing—this time in a sort of parody of the rape trope in horror cinema—but in addition to exposing the fox, the act of undressing the gumiho also seals the human man's bloody fate at the hands of the foxy femme fatale.[24] One of the appeals of fox spirits in contemporary culture is that they can effectively "flip the script," reversing traditional power dynamics as seen in both Western horror cinema tropes and in Confucian patriarchal cultural norms.

"My Girlfriend is a Gumiho"

The popular K-Drama *My Girlfriend is a Gumiho* starred Shin Min-ah[25] as Park Seonju, the titular gumiho or nine-tailed fox, dating a human being.

In the drama, the gumiho girlfriend had been sealed inside a painting for 500 years, dreaming of escaping and disguising herself as a human. Like other female-presenting fox yogoe, she represents the stereotypical femme fatale archetype. Accessories are important in the series, or more specifically, the gumiho's fox bead, which holds and channels her qi, or life force. The bead is made from goblin fire, and significantly, she gifts her precious bead to her boyfriend Daewoong when he is in mortal peril.

In his essay "Uniformity and Nonconformity: The Packaging of Korean Girl Groups," Roald Maliangkay describes the fashion worn by female Korean idols as "controlled rebellion within uniformity."[26] That is, K-fashion, especially for female idols, typically creates only the illusion of rebellion, while ultimately conforming to the traditional values of a still predominantly Confucist society. Maliangkay writes:

> Simon Frith has argued that music is worn as a badge informing others of the wearer's values and opinions and that this may result in the formation of subcultures (North and Hargreaves 1999, 76). The argument that leading styles in Korean popular culture represent subcultures seems, however, untenable. Kim Yeran posits that earlier acts such as Fin.K.L. and Baby V.O.X. were intended for female subcultures, but if Dick Hebdige's concept of subculture as a "form of resistance in which experienced contradictions and objections to the ruling ideology are obliquely represented in style" is

Figure 8.4 *Shin Min-A attends the SBS TV drama 'My Girlfriend is a Gumiho' press conference at SBS Building, Seoul, South Korea, August 4, 2010.*
Photo: Choi Soo-Young/Multi-Bits via Getty Images.

> applied, it is doubtful that the term applies (Hebdige 1979, 133; Lee 2007, 65; Kim 2011, 338).[27]

Rather than contradict or object to the ruling ideology, K-fashion is largely intended to uphold the ruling ideology, as idols and actors represent the wholesomeness of Korean culture to the rest of the world. According to Marx and Engels,

> The ideas of the ruling class are in every epoch the ruling ideas, i.e. the class which is the ruling material force of society is at the same time its ruling intellectual force. The class which has the means of material production at its disposal, has control at the same time over the means of mental

> production, so that generally speaking, the ideas of those who lack the means of mental production are subject to it. The ruling ideas are nothing more than the ideal expression of the dominant material relationships grasped as ideas; hence of the relationships which make the one class the ruling class, therefore the ideas of its dominance.[28]

This dominance of the ruling taste and ideology is not the normative mode, however, in the case of the costume of characters playing yogoe roles in K-Drama, such as that of the gumiho, or nine-tailed fox.

Across the sixteen episodes of the series, Park Seonju, the titular gumiho, wears typically modest Korean "girlfriend" fashion, with plenty of creams and ivories and pale blues and pinks, crew necklines, and midi skirts. Figure 8.5 shows the distribution of colors worn by the title character in *My Girlfriend is a Gumiho*.

In fact, the gumiho's color sense in dress is quite typical of traditional Korean dress. Samuel Songhoon Lee, author of *Hanbok: Timeless Fashion Tradition*, writes:

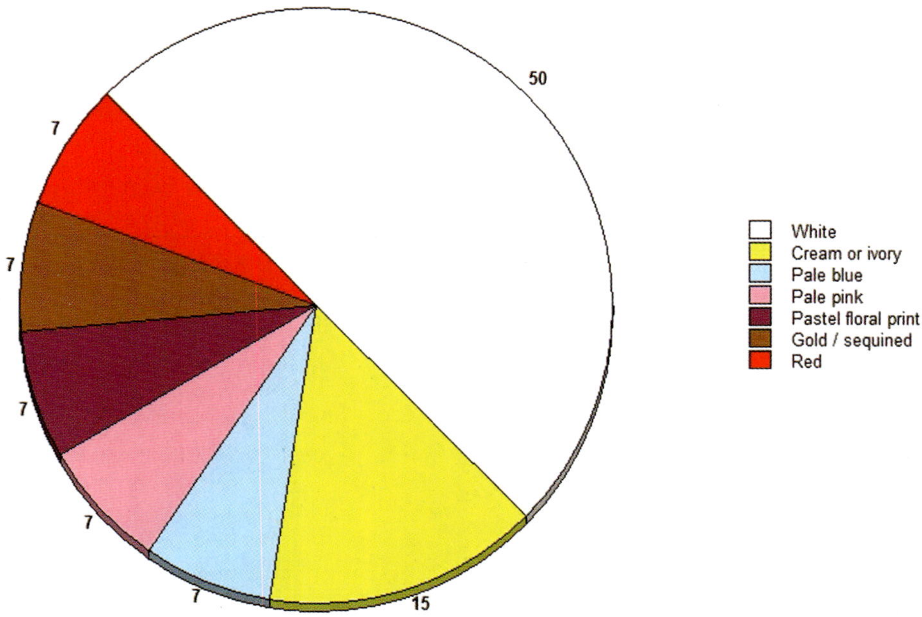

Figure 8.5 *Distribution by percentage of colors worn by the protagonist in* My Girlfriend is a Gumiho. *Created by Amanda Sikarskie.*

> Koreans have traditionally held a preference for the color white. They were long known as the "white-clad people" for frequently wearing white-colored clothes. . . . . The Korean preference for white clothes was so excessive that the government often issued special orders to ban white clothes, but the people responded by dyeing their clothes the lightest shade of blue, ivory or gray. [These colours reflect perfectly the protagonist's wardrobe in *My Girlfriend is a Gumiho*.] The frequent bans suggest that Koreans continued to wear white despite government orders.[29]

A ban on white clothing was instituted by the Japanese colonial government in Korea in the 1920s. This followed a previous ban, which was largely ignored, on wearing white in the wintertime, which had been issued by the Korean government at the advice of the Japanese Resident General.[30]

Another seemingly modest—and very typically Korean—dress of the gumiho, but one that is made provocative by her innate foxiness, is the dress worn in the promotional image on the series landing page on Amazon Prime Video. The "foxy" dress is light blue, strapless, with a cinched-in black waist separating bodice from skirt. The overall effect is quite similar to that of the dress emoji in the iPhone keyboard. The skirt is similar in volume to the white Travilla New Look-style dress worn by Marilyn Monroe in *The Seven Year Itch* (dir. Billy Wilder, 1955) that famously blows up from the breeze from a subway grate, exposing her legs provocatively.

In the title screen for *My Girlfriend is a Gumiho*, a similarly provocative exposure occurs as several of her foxtails have popped out, lifting up her dress at the back. The viewer cannot see any exposed skin as we view her (and her tails) in profile, but it is clear from the look on the face of her human boyfriend, who stands directly behind her, that he can see her bottom. In the example of *My Girlfriend is a Gumiho*, the yogoe attempts to dress in a normative and modest manner in keeping with the typical Korean woman, but her inherent otherness prevents her from succeeding in this. Instead, her writhing, fluffy tails, which may pop out at any inopportune time, transform her into the femme fatale, à la Marilyn Monroe.

Marilyn Monroe herself wrote the foreword to Peter Noble and Yvonne Saxon's classic, *Glamour*.[31] In their introduction to the book, Noble and Saxon

Figure 8.6 *Actress Marilyn Monroe tries to hold down her dress as breeze from a subway grate blows it upward during filming of* The Seven Year Itch *motion picture in Manhattan.*

Photo: Getty Images.

defined "glamour" variously as "delusive charm," "enchantment," "a form of fascination," and "witchery."[32] Interestingly, in contemporary vampire literary parlance, "to glamour" is a verb essentially meaning to hypnotize or bewitch their unsuspecting human prey. Needless to say, all this enchantment and witchery is quite at home in the world of the gumiho. Strikingly, they also wrote that, in order to become glamorous, "You have no need to be a raving beauty. Your features need not be particularly regular; in fact you can easily get away with a face which is definitely *not* pretty."[33] This statement likely reflects Monroe's own feelings regarding her own childhood, in which she, as Norma Jean, felt something of an ugly duckling. But it also resonates with the yogoe woman, who may naturally have irregular or non-normative features when in human form—to say nothing of the tails. So it seems uncoincidental that this K-Drama reenacted the famous dress scene from *The Seven Year Itch*. It is actually quite a savvy reference to Hollywood fashion history, in keeping with the character's powers of bewitchment and liminal existence between woman and fox.

My Roommate is a Gumiho

A related series to *My Girlfriend is a Gumiho, My Roommate is a Gumiho*, is in production at time of writing.[34] The following copy is iQIYI's media release regarding the project, as published in the *Business Monitor*:

> Global on-demand video streaming service iQIYI International announced today the coming release of its first Korean Original, My Roommate is a Gumiho . . . In the romantic horror comedy drama, Jang Ki Yong stars as the titular Gumiho – a nine-tailed fox spirit – who has spent the last 999 years trying to attain human form. Just as he is about to succeed, he bumps into a college student, played by Hyeri, who accidentally swallows his gumiho pearl without which he cannot become human. To find out how to extract the pearl from her body, she has no choice but to live in fear with him as her roommate for three months, a situation which brings about unexpected consequences.[35]

Interestingly, this new series reverses the expected gender roles, with the male as the gumiho; though, significantly, it still makes the female protagonist's body the site of the gumiho pearl. But in an early Chinese travelogue (and de facto text on yaoguai), *The Classic of Mountains and Seas,* Guo Pu described huli jing (gumiho) as able to transform into a woman, or a man:

> When a fox is fifty years old, it can transform itself into a woman. When it is one hundred years old, it becomes a beautiful woman or shaman; some become men and have sex with women. They even know events from more than one thousand li away and are good at witchcraft, causing people to be beguiled and lose their senses. When they are a thousand years old, they can commune with the heavens and become heavenly foxes.[36]

As Colette Balmain explains, the blurring of gender boundaries is inherent in the gumiho's existence, as the nine tails represent phalluses while the fox jewel or pearl represents the womb.[37] This new *Roommate* series, by placing the gumiho's pearl within the body of the human female love interest, may be effectively unqueering the male gumiho, by emphasizing only his phallic features as a fox spirit. But, as a gumiho, the male retains a certain softness. This is in keeping with the soft masculinity which has dominated in K-Drama and K-Pop, as well as the Korean cosmetics industry, for over a decade.

The gumiho femme fatale represents a subcultural style; according to Dick Hebdige:

> Style in subculture is, then, pregnant with significance. Its transformations go "against nature," interrupting the process of "normalization." As such, they are gestures, movements towards a speech which offends the "silent majority," which challenges the principle of unity and cohesion, which contradicts the myth of consensus. Our task becomes, like Barthes', to discern the hidden messages inscribed in code on the glossy surfaces of style, to trace them out as "maps of meaning" which obscurely re-present the very contradictions they are designed to resolve or conceal.[38]

As this particular yogoe—the gumiho—is traditionally understood as demonic and having the potential for evil (at least in the Korean tradition; Chinese and Japanese foxes may be good or bad), and represents the femme fatale archetype, the dress of a yogoe in human form may adopt the hyper-sexual or vulgar or pull from various subcultures, such as goth or punk. When yogoe costume is more wholesome, it is generally worn for the purpose of deception, that the yaoguai wishes to fool humans into thinking that it is just a normal (albeit otherworldly beautiful) human woman.

In the conclusion to her essay "Meta-Hallyu TV: Global Publicity, Social Media, and the Citizen Celebrity," Michelle Cho writes:

> The critical capacity of Korean TV dramas' metatextuality suggests that the Internet's decentralization and diffusion of reception sites create the conditions for unpredictable appropriations and creative resignification of Hallyu commodities. Read in this light, Korean TV dramas' current obsession with metatextuality suggests that media consumption remains a dynamic and contested arena for the construction of models of public participation and social relations, rather than a monolithic apparatus for shaping consumer behavior.[39]

The inherent subversiveness of the gumiho archetype already represents a dynamic and contested fashion image, rather than a monolithic, culturally conforming one.

The Monster in the Flowering Arboretum: Yogoe Fashion in K-Pop

Seventy-eight rpm records of Korean folk songs such as "Arirang" and "Doraji" ("The Bellflower Song") were quite popular in early twentieth-century Japan and constituted the first Hallyu, or Korean wave.[40] In 1955, the Cuban-inspired mambo craze hit South Korea, via the United States, and these folk songs were re-recorded as mambos. For example, "The Doraji Mambo" (1955) featured lyrics taken from the original folk ballad such as "Flowers white, growing by the mountain stream," but with a refrain of "hey mambo" added to the end of each line.

Such mash-ups of Korean folk music and popular song styles of the Americas represent the genesis of K-Pop. The combination of yogoe folktales with (mostly Western) high fashion brands has a similar sort of feel, that the world is perhaps witnessing the origin of what will become a new form in fashion.

Similar to Korean popular music in the 1950s, in their book *K-Pop Idols* (2019), Dal Yong Jin and Hark-Joon Lee argue that while K-Pop became an increasingly global phenomenon in the 2010s, it did so while largely preserving its local character:

> K-pop started its regional penetration in East Asia in the late 1990s; therefore, its global presence has been relatively new, mainly since the early 2010s. Right before and after Psy's "Gangnam Style" became a global sensation in 2012, K-pop has experienced substantial global popularity . . . Local popular music created from a small East Asian country has witnessed tremendous growth, as several K-pop musicians, whether solo artists or idol groups, have appeared in many parts of the world, including North America, Europe, Latin America, and even Africa. Global youth, from the US to Chile, chant for K-pop and local [from the Korean perspective] musicians. The

> recent flows of K-pop around the world in the 2010s suggest that K-pop exists as a local-based type of music in the global markets, including the Western markets. In other words, it seems to be increasingly becoming a unique local culture, distancing itself farther from Western Culture and representing more of Korea's youth culture.[41]

In terms of K-idol elements such as choreography, musicality, gender presentation—including the soft masculinity of male artists—and temperament, this seems to be a sound assessment. For example, in his essay "Uniformity and Nonconformity," Roald Maliangkay noted that "The stars do indeed remain courteous and unassuming in public life. It is this trait that allows fans to feel a connection with their idols, and it is this aspect that distinguishes Korean idols from most Western ones."[42] But in the realm of dress and fashion, much of the K-Pop look remains reliant on Western luxury brands. These Western brands are worn, however, in a distinctly Korean context. Therefore, Western motifs—such as the Medusa head, symbol of the House of Versace, by supergroup BTS—take on a certain Koreanness when appropriated by K-idols and consumed in the K-Pop context. In the second and final major section of this chapter, I argue that Korean folk beliefs, including those surrounding yogoe, are layered upon Western folkloric symbols, such as Medusa, creating a new hybridized visual culture of fantastical creatures and spirits. Further, I explore the hidden (from the perspective of a cultural outsider) meaning of monsters in other works by BTS.

Folk Customs and Gangnam Style

In a livestream in February 2022, Suga, RM, and Jimin cracked and ate walnuts, as Suga worried about Jimin's health luck, as he had suffered both appendicitis and COVID-19 in 2021. As explained in Toae Hong Sok-Mo, *Record of the Seasonal Customs of Korea [Tongguk Sesigi]*, "'Cracking blains' is the name for the custom of early-morning chewing of raw chestnuts, walnuts, gingko nuts, pine nuts, or turnip root while inwardly wishing that 'one year, twelve months, be without accidents, be peaceful, and no carbuncle develop' . . . Today it is customary to do this on the first full moon day."[43] Another example is the wearing of blue and red threads by V and Jungkook of BTS,[44] referencing the Korean folktale "Blue Thread, Red Thread."[45] The story itself is somewhat disturbing and violent; in it, a grown man charges upon an elderly woman—a matchmaker—using blue threads and red threads to match couples. He asks whom he is destined to marry, and she answers that he will marry a young girl who lives on the other side of the mountain. Angered that he has to wait so long to marry, he throws a rock at the girl's head to kill her, freeing him up for some other (hopefully older) destined mate. It is not until years later that he eventually marries, and his bride indicates that she wears such heavy make-up to cover the scar of having been hit in the face with a rock as a girl. The man had indeed disfigured his future wife. Though admittedly unromantic, the tale does present a fatalistic worldview in which one's life partner is destined by the Heavens and one has no agency to change this fate. I bring up these anecdotes to show that the members of BTS—particularly Suga, their frequent lyricist and producer—pay attention to traditional customs, beliefs, and ritual practices. As we will see in this chapter, this is seen both in the group's songwriting and in their dress.

We will return to the idea of Western and Korean folkloric iconography in the dress of BTS shortly, but first, it bears pointing out that Korean music videos are rife with local cultural references that are largely opaque to global audiences who have not studied Korean culture in some fashion. Take, for example, perhaps the most famous Korean song, Psy's "Gangnam Style" (2012). Gangnam itself refers to a well-heeled area of Seoul, and the MV for the song is replete with references to the leisure culture of Seoul's elites, including horse ownership (hence the horse dance.)[46] Another example of this is the cultural reference to *gwibulnori*, a fire-spinning dance for the seasonal burning of fields after harvest, in the choreography for UNIQ's "EOEO."

Daechwita

Similarly, the music video for "Daechwita," a song by AgustD (the solo project moniker of Suga from the massively popular K-Pop group BTS), extensively depicts the hanbok, the traditional Korean costume, and features extensive cultural and historical references. *Daechwita* refers to the traditional military music of the Joseon period (1392–1910) and is sampled in the rap song. In the music video, Suga, who has claimed in livestreams to be descended from the yangban,[47] or Korean aristocracy, travels back to the past and commits regicide against a Joseon king, also played by himself. The transition of the king's hairstyle, from a groomed topknot to a cascading almost-ponytail, reflects his descent into madness.[48] His present-day self wears a *satgat*, or hat, usually worn to keep the face out of the sun, but in the MV represents the wearer's desire to remain anonymous as he passes through town on the way to the king's palace.[49] The gun that modern-day Suga uses to assassinate the king at the end of the video is from the turn of the last century, a transitional period from the Joseon to the modern world. All of these songs and videos—"Gangnam Style," EOEO," and "Daechwita"—rely on the viewer's knowledge of Korean culture or, in the absence of such knowledge, compel the viewer to want to learn. In the BTS song "Like," Suga's rap mentions a *dokkaebi gamtu*, or goblin helmet. Dokkaebi are a uniquely Korean yogoe, briefly introduced in the previous chapter. Their clubs have magic properties, and their helmets, as mentioned in the song, grant the power of invisibility, much like the Cloak of Invisibility, one of the Deathly Hallows in the Harry Potter universe.

Medusa: Appropriating a Western Monster

K-Pop artists occasionally employ the visual language of Western monsters and demons, such as the repeated use of the Medusa motif by global K-Pop sensations BTS. As I was organizing my notes for this book, I debated the notion of whether or not Greco-Roman mythical creatures had a home in a book on Korean yogoe. Ultimately, I decided that these Korean appropriations of Medusa and the like were interesting and important 1) because there is a certain Korean-ness to their usage, and 2) because they are a visual and material record of the globalizing world of the early twenty-first century. In "Receptions and Cross-Cultural Transfers: On Greco-Roman Antiquity in East Asia – An Introduction," Almut-Barbara Renger and Xin Fan also grappled with the notion of reception studies between West and East in a globalized society. They write:

> Since the 1970s, the rapid process of globalization has fundamentally transformed the collective consciousness of human communities across the entire world. Yet that is not to suggest that people today have embraced a homogeneous global identity. . . . . When we speak of East and West, or Far East and Far West, we do so with skepticism, fully cognizant of the many complexities and diversities that characterize particular cultures. Following Martin Heidegger and Jacques Derrida, we would retain these terms [Far West and Far East] only "'under erasure,"' deleting them in a way that allows them to remain legible. With these caveats, terms referring to the East and West are used throughout the book for the sake of expository convenience and economy. The primary issue, rather, is to pose significant questions in the context of globalization, concerning the movement and transmission of knowledge between Greek and Roman antiquity and modern East Asia – how such knowledge has circulated within China, Japan, Korea, and Taiwan."[50]

Early readings of Greco-Roman cultural texts in East Asia focused upon Greek values of rationality and reason, to the exclusion of Greek myth, mysticism, and religion. The following commentary explains a Chinese (Neo-) Confucianist reading of Plantonic text by scholar Guo Binhe (1900–87):

> It seems, for example, that Guo [Binhe] intentionally chose not to translate Pausanius' comment on how the noble love is heavenly because it is the love of the heavenly goddess, and how all other loves are the offspring of the common goddess. Omissions like this have the effect of diminishing any mysterious or religious aspect of the Platonic text. More important, the linkage between love (eros), good/noble (kalon), virtue (aretē), and heavenly goddess (tēs ouranias) was modified to that between virtue (de), propriety and righteousness (liyi), good (shan), moral cultivation (xiushen), and love (ai). Liyi was introduced here as a universal regulating principle and a commendable goal for love. Guo specified the purpose of translating Plato's works as showing the fundamental significance of reason and moderation for Plato in order to dispel misunderstandings of Plato as a supporter of naturalism, among others. Far from simply transmitting the Platonic thoughts, however, translation became a site where arguments were integrated and embedded.[51]

Contemporary Korean appropriations of Greek culture take interest in that which most early modern Asian scholars did not: Greek mysticism.

Returning to the Xueheng translations listed above, such a discursive practice is not so dissimilar to the contemporary practice of hashtagging. Na Youngjoo and Kim Jisu found that Korean brands and influencers on Instagram favored some of the following English-language hashtags: #SFW (Seoul Fashion Week), #classic, #essential, #Cool, #naughty, and #feellikeflying.[52] As with the Neo-Platonic and Neo-Confucianist ideals, these hashtags tell the reader something about the values of Korean fashion brands and consumers. #naughty and #feellikeflying, in particular, reflect the youthful and emotional insouciance cultivated by both K-fashion and K-Pop. Rather than for its rationality, K-Pop appropriates Classical Greece for its mystical wildness, or "loves of the common goddess." BTS wore T-shirts and jewelry from the Medusa collection by Versace at the "Dark and Wild" showcase in Seoul in August 2014.

A statue of Perseus triumphantly holding the severed head of Medusa appears in the music video for "Blood, Sweat and Tears," courtesy of the Uffizi

Figure 8.7 *V and Suga of K-Pop band BTS attend the BTS first album "Dark and Wild" showcase at the Samsung Card Hall, Seoul, South Korea, August 19, 2014.*
Photos: by Han Myung-Gu/WireImage

Figure 8.8 *Jungkook of K-Pop band BTS attends the BTS first album "Dark and Wild" showcase at the Samsung Card Hall, Seoul, South Korea, August 19, 2014.*
Photos: by Han Myung-Gu/WireImage

Gallery, Florence. The song itself quotes *Demian*, a novel by German author Herman Hesse, which had Medusa depicted on the book's cover. In their introduction to iconic designer Donatella Versace's book, *Versace*, Maria Luisa Frisa and Stefano Tonchi write: "Versace, a name so powerful and illustrious that it became synonymous with a way of being. Its symbols, the Medusa and the Greek Key, appropriated almost unconsciously from familiar, dignified antiquity, were transformed into icons, driving the beat in the global, cutting edge rhythm of fashion."[53]

But what does Medusa mean here, exactly? Is Medusa still the murderous Gorgon of Greek mythology? In the 2021 Amazon Prime commercial, Medusa is cast as simply misunderstood and desirous for companionship: "The whole turning people to stone thing is a bit of a buzzkill, really," she narrates, and buys sunglasses using Amazon Prime to socialize with newfound friends at a bar, only using her murderous powers when the bartender flirts with her and her new friends. "As if," she narrates, and she pulls down her shades to turn him to stone. But corporate behemoth Amazon is not the only entity to suggest that Medusa has been misunderstood. In "Venusdepression" (1977), feminist artist Ulrike Rosenbach argued for a reevaluation of Medusa. Reflecting on a painting of Medusa by baroque artist Caravaggio in the Uffizi Gallery, she wrote: "The Medusa became a strong image of protection to me: quite different than it was meant by the patriarchal mythology. Also it seemed a mother-earth image as well and I got very fascinated by the idea of using this shield.[54]" In this reading, Medusa is not an adversary to be vanquished, but a protector, a shield to raise against the vagaries of contemporary life. It is in this spirit that one should read BTS's (and Versace's) appropriation of Medusa.

To the East Asian viewer, Medusa may also conjure images of the classical deity Yu'er (literally "Fish"). According to Sun Jiankun in *Fantastic Creatures of the Mountains and Seas: A Classic*, "Like the Guanyin Boddhisattva, Yu'er had the magical power to change its body into any desired form and must be considered neither male nor female."[55] This androgyny is certainly in keeping with the soft masculinity performed by male artists in the K-Pop industry. Sun continues:

> What distinguished this deity were two fearsome snakes that intertwined around her, though some have insisted that she is holding them in her hands. Yu'er delighted in water amusements and emitted a brilliant light whenever she came and went. Yu'er exhibited virtually all human physical features, all but the snakes, which never left her. The reptiles likely connected their host to the human and divine worlds.[56]

Her physical appearance seems quite similar to that of Medusa, and Western images of Medusa may well read as Yu'er in China and Korea.

Flowering Arboretum

Seeking out protection against the happenings of daily life is a recurring theme with BTS, such as in the song "Fly to My Room." In a fictionalized story about Min Yoongi (Suga) and Park Jimin visiting the Flowering Arboretum in Jimin's hometown of Busan, South Korea, published in the accompanying notes to the BTS album *Love Yourself: Tear,* the explanation for the frightening episode witnessed by Jimin may be contact with a yogoe.[57] Is there a yogoe in the Flowering Arboretum? Is the traumatic event that the fictional version of Jimin witnessed related to a yogoe attack? It may be that the attack is related to Medusa, or a Medusa-like creature. This would be in keeping with BTS's previous use of Medusa, as well as the fact that Suga blindfolds Jimin to protect him in the "Blood, Sweat and Tears" video. And in Greco-Roman mythology, coral was made from Medusa's blood, which ran into the sea and hardened after she was decapitated.

Few plant yogoe or yaoguai exist, and as translator of *The Classic* Anne Birrell notes, "Botanical interest in the *Classic* is functionalist in approach. Rather than a complete survey, selected trees and plants are mentioned that are useful to humans, such as varieties of bamboo and mulberry, and plants having medicinal properties."[58] But one documented by Michael Dylan Foster is the yokai ninmenju (or jinmenju), a tree that shares some parallels with the Medusa's mythology, and significantly, hails from the Middle East from the time of Alexander the Great (the 300s BCE). The ninmenju spread across Asia via the armies of Alexander, as well as through Silk Road trade, propagating across China, and eventually Korea and Japan, and is a strong candidate for the mystery yaoguai in the Flowering Arboretum in Busan. According to Foster, "In one of his many encyclopedic compendia of yokai, Mizuki Shigeru describes a tree in Aomori Prefecture that, according to legend, would bleed when cut. He suggests that this strange plant might be a version of the ninmenju (alternatively jinmenju), a tree with human heads instead of flowers."[59] Foster explains that the ninmenju, curiously, was not considered a plant yokai, but rather a spirit from a foreign land. This compares to the portrayals of peoples of foreign lands in the Chinese text *The Classic of Mountains and Seas* (see the introduction to this section of the book).

Foster continues:

> If we continue back in time and along the Silk Road, we find different versions of the great Persian epic poem *Shahnama* (Book of Kings) by Firdawsi (d. 1020), with illustrations of a man conversing with a tree bearing human heads. The man, it turns out, is Alexander the Great (Sikandar or Iskandar),

> and the illustrations portray his legendary encounter with a talking tree, sometimes called the Wakwak Tree, that prophesied his death. By tracing this complex lineage, we can see images and ideas moving across space, time, and cultures. Here a picture of Alexander the Great becomes associated with foreign lands, and enters Japan [and Korea] (through China).[60]

This hypothesis that ninmenju is the murderous creature in the Flowering Arboretum is based on much more evidence than the mere fact that it is one of the few plant yokai in East Asian demonology. In his story, "The Mysterious Hoi Tree," translated by James S. Gale, Yi Ryuk wrote of a supernatural tree that housed the spirits of a company of archers outside a prince's residence:

> Prince Pasong's house was situated just inside of the great East Gate, and before it was a large Hoi tree. On a certain night the Prince's son-in-law was passing by the roadway that led in front of the archers' pavilion. There he saw a great company of bowmen, more than he could number, all shooting together at the target . . . When the son-in-law reached the gate he looked back and saw the man walk under the Hoi tree and disappear. He then learned, too, that all the crowd of archers were spirits and not men, and that the tall one who had befriended him was a spirit too, and that he had come forth from their particular Hoi tree.[61]

This Korean story of human ghosts or spirits residing within a tree shares similarities with the Japanese stories of ninmenju.

The comparisons between ninmenju and Medusa, a monstrous symbol known to have been appropriated by BTS in the past, are not insignificant. Like Medusa, ninmenju has origins in the Greek world (Alexander hailed from Macedon, north of Greece, was educated in the classical Greek tradition, and sought to spread Hellenism across the near East and Asia). Medusa is surrounded by a litany of small faces—those of the snakes in her hair—and similarly, ninmenju is surrounded by faces in its canopy of leaves. (There are multiple references to leaves as hair, or hair turning to leaves, in Greek mythology, from the victor's crown of a laurel wreath, to the transformation of Daphne into a tree, her hair becoming leaves and twigs.) Like Medusa, ninmenju also has associations with blood: ninmenju would bleed when cut and Medusa's blood would turn to coral. Bringing us full circle, the key that Suga finds at the end of the "Daechwita" video is made from coral.

Another plant with mythological connections is local to Busan, Korea: *Adonis multiflora*. The Adonis is a ranunculus in the buttercup family that was discovered in Gijang-gun, Busan.[62] In Greek mythology, Adonis, a beautiful male, was the human lover of goddesses Aphrodite and Persephone and gods Apollo and Dionysus (the latter of which is also the title of a BTS song). In the myth, Adonis tragically died when he was gored by a boar, and when Aphrodite drizzled some of his blood on the ground, the anemone, another plant in the ranunculus family, came into being.[63]

Whalien 52

Gorae, Korean for whale, serves as a powerful symbol, in both visual and written texts, for BTS. BTS designed a purple whale for their logo for the 2022 *BTS Island: In the Seom* video game that the group co-created.[64] Much like the turtle from Chinese and Indian subcontinental mythology,[65] the whale carries BTS Island on its back. Jin (Kim Seokjin) wore a Thom Browne whale sweater[66] in a V Live livestream on November 22, 2021 and again in episode 81 of their reality show, *Run BTS!*, on VR games. Jin's team name for the episode was "Team Kim Seokjin: *Gorae* Edition," and the team speculated that they won the VR racing game against the maknae (younger members) team with the help of the spirit of the whale sweater.[67]

Most significantly, the 2015 BTS song "Whalien 52," written by the BTS rap line, RM, Suga, and J-Hope, was inspired by the so-called 52-hertz whale, otherwise known as "the loneliest whale in the world," because, at 52 hertz, its songs could not be heard by its own kind (which usually communicate at frequencies between 10 and 40 hertz), and yet it continued to sing alone. Whale song is complex: "The half-hour song of the humpback whale contains a million information-carrying changes of frequency. It is the single most elaborate vocal display in the natural world."[68] Whales also spurred yokai legends, particularly in Japan.

The yokai *bakekujira*, literally "ghost whales," are described as animated

Figure 8.9 *Whale jacket: Thom Browne. A model (jacket detail) walks the runway during the Thom Browne Menswear Spring/Summer 2019 show, Paris Fashion Week, Paris, France, June 23, 2018.*

Photo: by Peter White/Getty Images

whale skeletons which sail near the surface of the sea, rising as they did in life when they needed air to breathe. They are followed by a host of eerie birds and strange fish, and appear on rainy nights near coastal whaling villages. In olden days, when whales were still plentiful in the Sea of Japan, a whale sighting was a blessing for the residents of the poor fishing villages. A village could reap huge amounts of wealth from the meat and oil in a single whale. Such a bounty did not come without a price, however. Many fishermen claimed that the souls of these whales lived on as bakekujira, seeking revenge against the humans who took their lives. Those who witnessed a bakekujira were infected with its horrible curse, which they brought back to their villages when they returned home. The whale's curse brought famine, plague, fires, and other kinds of disasters.[69]

Figure 8.10 *Whale bag: Thom Browne A model (bag detail) walks the runway during the Thom Browne Menswear Spring/Summer 2019 show, Paris Fashion Week, Paris, France, June 23, 2018.*
Photo: by Peter White/Getty Images

In *Animal Spirits*, Nicholas Saunders described ritual practices to lift the curse of the bakekujira, as well as minister to living whales: "In Japan, every year a ceremony intended to lift the curse placed on humankind for killing so many whales takes place at the Koganji Temple. The temple is dedicated to dead whales and faces the sea so that living whales can pay homage to their ancestors."[70] In an episode of *Run BTS!*, V (Kim Taehyung) was showing off his fluency in Japanese, noting that ghost (yuryeong) is yuurei in Japanese. One would translate bakekujira, or ghost whale, into Korean as *yuryeong gorae*.

The 52-hertz whale heard by marine biologists in the 1980s is precisely the sort of creature that in traditional East Asia would have been described as a yokai, or yogoe. Defining the term, Michael Dylan Foster wrote:

> In Japan, as elsewhere, inexplicable occurrences and supernatural creatures have been part of the cultural imagination for as long as history has been recorded. Broadly speaking, these diverse mysterious phenomena and 'weird' things have come to be called yokai. In a sense, *yokai* is nothing more than a convenient label to indicate a whole range of otherwise ineffable experiences that might, in English, be translated with the words *spirits, goblins, phantoms, spectres, sprites, shape-shifters, demons, fantastic beings, numinous occurrences, the supernatural,* and perhaps most commonly today, *monsters.*[71]

In traditional East Asia, yokai were invented to explain unusual natural phenomena, much as myth was used in the Greco-Roman world. Why do humans understand how to harness and use fire? Because Prometheus taught us. Why is there a whale singing at 52 hertz? Because it's a yokai. But, for BTS at least, this Whalien 52 is not the demonic bakekujira (or yuryeong gorae) of Japanese folklore, but rather, a kind and gentle—albeit lonely—being that stands in for the tortoise that the goddess Nü Gua used to prop up the celestial plane.[72]

Hallyu: The Korean Wave

In his essay "Hallyu versus Hallyu-hwa: Cultural Phenomenon versus Institutional Campaign," JungBong Choi outlined what he calls the "hypothetical flow of action" of the Hallyu, or Korean Wave, phenomenon. This model describes the pathway towards increased engagement with Korean culture for global fans of K-Pop. Within the eighth step in Choi's model, "picking up cultural idioms and local, traditional customs,"[73] one can easily ascribe phenomena such as folkloric beliefs and superstitions, in particular awareness of yogoe culture and iconography. It seems that just as groups such as BTS have been incorporating Western influences through art and fashion, so too do global K-Pop fans assimilate folkloric culture from Korea. K-Dramas, such as *My Girlfriend is a Gumiho*, introduce global fans to traditional Korean culture through yogoe and other spirits, while K-op groups both embrace Western influences but also serve as ambassadors for Korean traditional culture through their use of traditional music (*gugak*), folk dance elements, and hanbok-inspired costumes.

Notes

1 The author's name may be written in Korean as 송만만 (Song Manman).

2 Nicholas J. Saunders, *Animal Spirits*, Boston: Little, Brown, and Company, 1995, 152.

3 "Rank Badge (Hyungbae) of the Upper Military Rank with Two Tigers," Los Angeles County Museum of Art, https://collections.lacma.org/node/199668

4 Minjee Kim, "Hanbok: Gender, Class, and Modernity," *The Korea Society*, July 21, 2002.

5 Kimberly Chung, "Colonial Horrors: The Starving Ghost in Colonial Korean Mass Culture," *Acta Koreana* 17 (1): 2014, 85. *ProQuest*, https://cmich.idm.oclc.org/login?url=https://www.proquest.com/scholarly-journals/colonial-horrors-starving-ghost-korean-mass/docview/1543474485/se-2 doi:https://doi.org/10.18399/acta.2014.17.1.004.

6 bid.

7 Karl Marx.

8 Im Bang, "An Encounter with a Hobgoblin," in *Asian Ghost Short Stories*, Luo Hui, ed., London: Flame Tree Publishing, 2022, 128.

9 Books 1--9 of *The Classic* date to circa 6 BCE, during the reign of Han Emperor Ai. See: *The Classic of Mountains and Seas*, trans. Anne Birrell, London: Penguin Classics, 1999, 131.

10 Kuo Pu (276–324 CE) was the first known commentator on *The Classic of Mountains and Seas.*

11 Anne Birrell, "Notes of Chinese Names and Terms," *The Classic of Mountains and Seas*, trans. Anne Birrell, London: Penguin Classics, 1999, 221–2.

12 Birrell, *The Classic of Mountains and Seas*, 128.

13 Birrell, *The Classic of Mountains and Seas*, 227.

14 The *li*, or "Chinese mile," is about one-third of an English mile, so the distance would be about 100 miles east of Jishan. 100 miles east of modern-day Jishan County would be somewhere north of Zhengzhou, Henan Province, in China's Central Plain. So this account places the nine-tailed fox much closer to the heart of China than Birrell's translation of *The Classic.*

15 Sun Jiankun and Chen Siyu, *Fantastic Creatures of the Mountains and Seas: A Classic*, trans. Howard Goldblatt, New York: Arcade Publishing, 2021, 14.

16 Alison Peirse and Daniel Martin, "Introduction," *Korean Horror Cinema*, Edinburgh; Edinburgh University Press, 2013, 6.

17 Alison Peirse and James Byrne, "Creepy Liver-eating Fox Ladies: The Thousand Year Old Fox and Korea's Gumiho," *Korean Horror Cinema*, 35.

18 "The Fox Empress of China," Korean folktale transcribed in North Kyongsang Province, August 1923.

19 Donatella Versace, Maria L. Frisa, and Stefano Tonchi, eds, *Versace*, 2016, 397–8.

20 Minjee Kim "Hanbok: A New Lexicon of World Fashion: Women's Hanbok," *The Korea Society*, February 17, 2022.

21 While white is the color of mourning and funerals throughout much of East Asia, the meaning of white dress is much more complicated in Korea, as we will see later in this chapter. See: *Hanbok: Timeless Fashion Tradition*, 69.

22 Minjee Kim notes that the basic elements of the hanbok, or Korean traditional dress—*jeogori*—the short upper garment, and *chima*—the long skirt, do derive from the Three Kingdoms period in which the film is set.

23 Peirse and Byrne, 37.

24 Ibid., 40.

25 Perhaps better known for her role in the K-Drama *Our Blues*, 2022.

26 Roald Maliangkay, "Uniformity and Nonconformity: The Packaging of Korean Girl Groups," in *Hallyu 2.0: The Korean Wave in the Age of Social Media*, Sangjoon Lee and Abe Mark Nornes, eds, Ann Arbor: University of Michigan Press, 2015, 97.

27 Ibid.

28 Karl Marx and Friedrich Engels, *The German Ideology*, Lawrence & Wishart, 1970.

29 Samuel Songhoon Lee, *Hanbok: Timeless Fashion Tradition*, Seoul: Seoul Selection, 2013, 32–3.

30 Hyung Gu Lynn, "Fashioning Modernity: Changing Meanings of Clothing in Colonial Korea," *Journal of International and Area Studies* 11 (3): 2004, 75–93.

31 Marilyn Monroe, "Foreword," in Peter Noble and Yvonne Saxon, *Glamour: Film Fashion & Beauty*, London: Burke, n.d.

32 Ibid., 4.

33 Ibid.

34 As of October 2021.

35 "iQIYI International to Release the First Korean Original 'My Roommate is a Gumiho,'" *Business Mirror*, Makati City, December 4, 2020.

36 Guo Pu, cited in Huntingdon, *Alien Kind: Foxes and Late Imperial Chinese Narrative*, vol. 222, Cambridge, MA: Harvard University Asia Center, 2003, 1.

37 Colette Balmain, "East Asian Gothic: A Definition," *Palgrave Commun* 3 (31): 2017. https://doi-org.cmich.idm.oclc.org/10.1057/s41599-017-0038-8

38 Dick Hebdige, *Subculture: The Meaning of Style*, London: Routledge, 1991. https://search-ebscohost-com.proxy1.cl.msu.edu/login.aspx?direct=true&AuthType=ip,uid,cookie&db=e000xna&AN=504005&site=eds-live

39 Michelle Cho, "Meta-Hallyu TV: Global Publicity, Social Media, and the Citizen Celebrity," in Lee and Nornes, *Hallyu 2.0*, 169.

40 E. Taylor Atkins, *Primitive Selves: Koreana in the Japanese Colonial Gaze, 1910–1945*, Berkeley: University of California Press, 2010, 147.

41 Dal Yong Jin and Hark-Joon Lee, *K-Pop Idols: Popular Culture and the Emergence of the Korean Music Industry*, Lanham, MD: Lexington Books, 2019, 2–3.

42 Maliangkay, "Uniformity and Nonconformity: The Packaging of Korean Girl Groups," 98.

43 Toae Hong Sok-Mo, *Record of the Seasonal Customs of Korea [Tongguk Sesigi]*, trans. Werner Sasse, Honolulu: University of Hawaii Press, 2022, 29.

44 Jungkook (blue) and V (red) wore the threads looped on their belts on stage at the 5th Muster in Seoul concert, June 2019.

45 Park Myungsook, "Blue Thread, Red Thread," *Encyclopedia of Korean Folk Culture*. https://folkency.nfm.go.kr/en/topic/detail/5990

46 Brian Hu, "RIP Gangnam Style," in Lee and Nornes, *Hallyu 2.0*, 230–1.

47 <FOOTNOTE MISSING>

48 Bae Woo-da. https://origin.koreaboo.com/lists/hidden-meanings-in-agust-ds-daechwita-koreans-know/

49 "The Korean Hat Makes the Man." https://m.youtube.com/watch?v=R08JOoIjheo

50 Almut-Barbara Renger and Xin Fan, "Receptions and Cross-Cultural Transfers: On Greco-Roman Antiquity in East Asia – An Introduction," in Almut-Barbara Renger and Xin Fan, eds, *Receptions of Greek and Roman Antiquity in East Asia*, Brill, 2019, 1–2.

51 Liu Jinyu, "Translating and Rewriting Western Classics in China (1920s–1930s): The Case of the Xueheng Journal," in Renger and Fan, *Receptions of Greek and Roman Antiquity in East Asia*, 103.

52 Na Youngjoo and Kim Jisu, "Sensibility and Response Keywords of Users According to Posting Types of Fashion Instagram: Focused on Koreans' Fashion Brands," *International Journal of Clothing Science and Technology*, 32 (1): 2020, 23–36. *ProQuest*, https://cmich.idm.oclc.org/login?url=https://www.proquest.com/scholarly-journals/sensibility-response-keywords-users-according/docview/2534282685/se-2, doi:https://doi.org/10.1108/IJCST-03-2018-0032.

53 Maria Luisa Frisa and Stefano Tonchi, "Introduction," in *Versace*, Donatella Versace, Maria L. Frisa, and Stefano Tonchi, eds, 2016, 13.

54 Ulrike Rosenbach, "Venusdepression," in *Theories and Documents of Contemporary Art*, 2nd ed., Kristen Stiles and Peter Selz, eds, Berkeley: University of California Press, 2012, 886.

55 Sun Jiankun and Chen Siyu, *Fantastic Creatures of the Mountains and Seas: A Classic*, trans. Howard Goldblatt, New York: Arcade Publishing, 2021, 174.

56 Ibid.

57 The BTS album liner notes from *Love Yourself: Tear* containing the Flowering Arboretum narrative cannot be included here for copyright reasons. Readers can consult the album package directly. Readers can also see the arboretum in the *Save ME* album's lyrics book.

58 Birrell, "Introduction," xxxii.

59 Michael Dylan Foster, *The Book of Yokai*, Berkeley: University of California Press, 2015, 151.

60 Ibid.

61 Yi Ryuk, "Faithful Mo," in *Asian Ghost Stories*, Luo Hui, ed., London: Flame Tree Press, 2022, 414.

62 Dong Chan Son, Yoon-Young Kim, Beom Kyun Park, Bong Sik Lee, and Kae Sun Chang, "An Updated Checklist of Adonis (Ranunculaceae) from Korea, with a New Locality Record for Adonis Multiflora," *Journal of Asia-Pacific Biodiversity*, 11 (3): 2018, 462–7.

63 Ovid, *Metamorphoses* X, 519–741.

64 Introduction, *BTS Island: In the Seom*, 2022. https://bts-island.com/en/game/introducion

65 Saunders, *Animal Spirits*, 37.

66 For a replica of the sweater, see: Blue Whale Sweater – BTS, *Fashion Chingu*. https://www.fashionchingu.com/kpop-fashion/kpop-sweaters/blue-whale-sweater-jin-bts/

67 Run BTS!, ep. 81, "VR Games."

68 Saunders, *Animal Spirits*, 132.

69 Bakekujira, *Yokai.com*, https://yokai.com/bakekujira/

70 Saunders, *Animal Spirits*, 132.

71 Foster, *The Book of Yokai*, 14.

72 Saunders, *Animal Spirits*, 37.

73 Adapted from: JungBong Choi, "Hallyu versus Hallyu-hwa: Cultural Phenomenon versus Institutional Campaign," in Lee and Nornes, *Hallyu 2.0*, 36.

Bibliography

Atkins, E. Taylor. *Primitive Selves: Koreana in the Japanese Colonial Gaze, 1910–1945*, Berkeley: University of California Press, 2010.

Balmain, Colette. "East Asian Gothic: A Definition." *Palgrave Commun* 3 (31): 2017. https://doi-org.cmich.idm.oclc.org/10.1057/s41599-017-0038-8

Cho, Michelle. "Meta-Hallyu TV: Global Publicity, Social Media, and the Citizen Celebrity." In *Hallyu 2.0: The Korean Wave in the Age of Social Media*, Sangjoon Lee and Abe Mark Nornes, eds. Ann Arbor: University of Michigan Press, 2015.

Choi JungBong. "Hallyu versus Hallyu-hwa: Cultural Phenomenon versus Institutional Campaign." In *Hallyu 2.0: The Korean Wave in the Age of Social Media*, Sangjoon Lee and Abe Mark Nornes, eds. Ann Arbor: University of Michigan Press, 2015.

Chung, Kimberly. "Colonial Horrors: The Starving Ghost in Colonial Korean Mass Culture." *Acta Koreana* 17 (1): 2014. *ProQuest*, https://cmich.idm.oclc.org/login?url=https://www.proquest.com/scholarly-journals/colonial-horrors-starving-ghost-korean-mass/docview/1543474485/se-2, doi:https://doi.org/10.18399/acta.2014.17.1.004.

Foreman, Liza. "Versace, Versace, Versace." *The Daily Beast*, September 20, 2013. https://www.thedailybeast.com/versace-versace-versace

Foster, Michael Dylan. *The Book of Yokai*. Berkeley: University of California Press, 2015.

Frisa, Maria Luisa. "Contemporary *Wunderkammer*." In *Versace*, Donatella Versace, Maria Luisa Frisa, and Stefano Tonchi, eds. New York: Rizzoli, 2016.

Frisa, Maria Luisa and Stefano Tonchi. "Introduction." In *Versace*, Donatella Versace, Maria Luisa Frisa, and Stefano Tonchi, eds. New York: Rizzoli, 2016.

Golvers, Noël. "Reading Classical Latin Authors in the Jesuit Mission in China: Seventeenth to Eighteenth Centuries." In *Receptions of Greek and Roman Antiquity in East Asia*, Almut-Barbara Renger and Xin Fan, eds. Brill, 2019.

Guo Pu, cited in Huntingdon. *Alien Kind: Foxes and Late Imperial Chinese Narrative*, vol. 222. Cambridge, MA: Harvard University Asia Center, 2003.

Hebdige, Dick. *Subculture: The Meaning of Style*. London: Routledge, 1991.

Hu, Brian. "RIP Gangnam Style." In *Hallyu 2.0: The Korean Wave in the Age of Social Media*, Sangjoon Lee and Abe Mark Nornes, eds. Ann Arbor: University of Michigan Press, 2015.

Im, Bang. "An Encounter with a Hobgoblin." In *Asian Ghost Short Stories,* Luo Hui, ed. London: Flame Tree Publishing, 2022, 128–9.

"iQIYI International to Release the First Korean Original 'My Roommate is a Gumiho.'" *Business Mirror.* Makati City, December 4, 2020.

Jin, Dal Yong, and Hark-Joon Lee. *K-Pop Idols: Popular Culture and the Emergence of the Korean Music Industry.* Lanham, MD: Lexington Books, 2019.

Kang, Jimin. "Why a Giant Fictional Penguin Could be the Cure for Millennial Burnout." *Guardian*, December 3, 2020.

Kim, Minjee. "Hanbok: A New Lexicon of World Fashion: Women's Hanbok." *The Korea Society*, February 17, 2022.

Kim, Minjee. "Hanbok: Gender, Class, and Modernity." *The Korea Society*, July 21, 2022.

Lee, Samuel Songhoon. *Hanbok: Timeless Fashion Tradition*, Seoul: Seoul Selection, 2013.

Liu, Jinyu. "Translating and Rewriting Western Classics in China (1920s–1930s): The Case of the Xueheng Journal." In *Receptions of Greek and Roman Antiquity in East Asia*, Almut-Barbara Renger and Xin Fan, eds. Brill, 2019.

Luo, Hui. *Asian Ghost Short Stories.* London: Flame Tree Publishing, 2022.

Lynn, Hyung Gu. "Fashioning Modernity: Changing Meanings of Clothing in Colonial Korea." *Journal of International and Area Studies* 11 (3): 2004, 75–93.

Maliangkay, Roald. "Uniformity and Nonconformity: The Packaging of Korean Girl Groups." In Sangjoon Lee and Abe Mark Nornes, eds. Ann Arbor: University of Michigan Press, 2015.

Marx, Karl, and Friedrich Engels. *The German Ideology*. Lawrence & Wishart, 1970.

Monroe, Marilyn. "Foreword." In Peter Noble and Yvonne Saxon, *Glamour: Film Fashion & Beauty*. London: Burke, n.d.

Na, Youngjoo, and Kim Jisu. "Sensibility and Response Keywords of Users According to Posting Types of Fashion Instagram: Focused on Koreans' Fashion Brands." *International Journal of Clothing Science and Technology* 32 (1): 2020. *ProQuest*, https://cmich.idm.oclc.org/login?url=https://www.proquest.com/scholarly-journals/sensibility-response-keywords-users-according/docview/2534282685/se-2, doi:https://doi.org/10.1108/IJCST-03-2018-0032.

Park, Hyunhee. *Soju: A Global History.* Cambridge University Press, 2021.

Park, Myungsook. "Blue Thread, Red Thread." *Encyclopedia of Korean Folk Culture.* https://folkency.nfm.go.kr/en/topic/detail/5990

Peirse, Alison, and James Byrne. "Creepy Liver-eating Fox Ladies: The Thousand Year Old Fox and Korea's Gumiho." *Korean Horror Cinema.* Edinburgh: Edinburgh University Press, 2013.

Peirse, Alison, and Daniel Martin. "Introduction." *Korean Horror Cinema.* Edinburgh: Edinburgh University Press, 2013.

Renger, Almut-Barbara and Xin Fan, "Receptions and Cross-Cultural Transfers: On Greco-Roman Antiquity in East Asia – An Introduction." In *Receptions of Greek and Roman Antiquity in East Asia*, Almut-Barbara Renger and Xin Fan, eds. Brill, 2019.

Rosenbach, Ulrike. "Venusdepression." In *Theories and Documents of Contemporary Art*, 2nd ed., Kristen Stiles and Peter Selz, eds. Berkeley: University of California Press, 2012.

Saunders, Nicholas J. *Animal Spirits.* Boston: Little, Brown, and Company, 1995.

Sikarskie, Amanda, ed. *Storytelling in Luxury Fashion.* London: Routledge, 2020.

Son, Dong Chan, Yoon-Young Kim, Beom Kyun Park, Bong Sik Lee, and Kae Sun Chang. "An Updated Checklist of Adonis (Ranunculaceae) from Korea, with a New Locality Record for Adonis Multiflora." *Journal of Asia-Pacific Biodiversity* 11 (3): 2018, 462–7.

Songhoon Lee, Samuel. *Hanbok: Timeless Fashion Tradition.* Seoul: Seoul Selection, 2013.

Sun, Jiankun, and Chen Siyu. *Fantastic Creatures of the Mountains and Seas: A Classic.* Trans. Howard Goldblatt. New York: Arcade Publishing, 2021.

The Classic of Mountains and Seas. Trans. Anne Birrell. London: Penguin Classics, 1999.

"The Fox Empress of China," Korean folktale transcribed in north Kyongsang Province, August 1923.

Toae, Hong Sok-Mo. *Record of the Seasonal Customs of Korea [Tongguk Sesigi].* Trans. Werner Sasse. Honolulu: University of Hawaii Press, 2022.

Tonchi, Stefano. "Image-making." In *Versace*, Donatella Versace, Maria L. Frisa, and Stefano Tonchi, eds. New York: Rizzoli, 2016.

Versace, Donatella, Maria Luisa Frisa, and Stefano Tonchi, eds. *Versace*. New York: Rizzoli, 2016.

Werness, Hope B. *Continuum Encyclopedia of Animals in Art*. New York: Continuum, 2004.

Yi, Ryuk. "Faithful Mo." In *Asian Ghost Short Stories*, Luo Hui, ed. London: Flame Tree Publishing, 2022, 412–13.

Afterword

Media, Aesthetics, Sustainability, and Popular Culture: A Penguin Tale

In his 1995 treatise *Animal Spirits*, penguins are among the few animals that Nicholas Saunders omits, presumably because as natives of the Antarctic, they did not figure in the myths and legends of many, if any, traditional cultures.[1] And Hope B. Werness's *Continuum Encyclopedia of Animals in Art* goes directly from an entry on the pelican to an entry on Persia.[2] Still, images of penguins have been ubiquitous in South Korea in the 2010s and 2020s—so much so that even though Antarctica, where the emperor penguin is endemic, is far from the Korean Peninsula and the traditional sphere of Korean culture, one could argue that the emperor penguin has become a yogoe, or spirit of cultural patrimony, in that country.

Two television penguins took Korea by storm in the past two decades: Pororo and Pengsoo. Both were marketed to children, but while the fans of *Pororo the Little Penguin* (which first aired in 2003) have largely remained young children, Pengsoo is popular with both preschoolers and people in their 20s, 30s, and 40s.

In its origin narrative (Pengsoo is genderless), the approximately 7ft tall Pengsoo—about twice the height of the average emperor penguin—was

Figure 9.1 *Key of Shinee attends the Kolon Sports "Antartika Penguin Campaign" event at Common Ground, Seoul, South Korea, November 24, 2015.*
Photo: ilgan Sports/Multi-Bits via Getty Images

bullied by the other penguins (much like Rudolph the Red-nosed Reindeer), and thus left Antarctica for South Korea in the hope of becoming an idol trainee. The Joseon Period (1392–1910) has also been having a moment in contemporary Korean internet and popular culture through the term #helljoseon:

> In 2015, the term "Hell Joseon" – an allusion to Korea's Joseon dynasty (1392–1897), during which society was structured in a feudal, class-based system – began making rounds on the internet, buoyed by millennials jaded by high unemployment, tough working conditions and growing inequality. No matter how hard one worked, it didn't seem to be enough; the youth unemployment rate was at an all-time high, job competition was stiff, and for those who were employed, long hours and competitive workplace

> environments made their days a "living hell". "Hell Joseon" was tweeted more than 5,000 times by social media users in May that year alone. The terms "destroyed nation", "the hellish peninsula" and "doggish country" followed closely on its tail.[3]

"Hell Joseon" is a term used by young Koreans to refer to the current age.

Interestingly, the words for emperor penguin, 황제 펭귄, or *hwangje penggwin*, are a direct translation of the English regnal term (and penguin). King is *wang* (왕, 王) in Korean (and Chinese) and *hwangje* (황제, 皇帝) is emperor. The trendy emperor penguin therefore seems an appropriate mascot and parting thought for this book on fashioning the Asian century.

Notes

1 Nicholas J. Saunders, *Animal Spirits*, London: Macmillan, 1995.

2 Hope B. Werness, *Continuum Encyclopedia of Animals in Art*, New York: Continuum, 2004, 323–4.

3 Jimin Kang, "Why a giant fictional penguin could be the cure for millennial burnout," *Guardian*, December 3, 2020, last modified September 8, 2021.

Index

[Names are stated traditionally—Surname Given Name—except in the case of a Western name, such as "Adam Smith." People with Western given names are listed Surname, Given Name.]